Berkshire Region Waterfall Guide

Cool Cascades of
the Berkshire &
Taconic Mountains

Russell Dunn

BLACK·DOME

Published by

Black Dome Press Corp.
1011 Route 296, Hensonville, New York 12439
www.blackdomepress.com
Tel: (518) 734–6357

First Edition Paperback 2008

ISBN-13: 978-1-883789-60-2
ISBN-10: 1-883789-60-5

Library of Congress Cataloging-in-Publication Data:

Dunn, Russell.

  Berkshire region waterfall guide : cool cascades of the Berkshire & Taconic
Mountains / by Russell Dunn. — 1st ed.

     p. cm.

  Includes bibliographical references and index.

  ISBN 978-1-883789-60-2 (pbk.)

  1. Hiking—Massachusetts—Berkshire Hills—Guidebooks. 2. Trails—
Massachusetts—Berkshire Hills—Guidebooks. 3. Trails—Massachusetts—
Taconic Range—Guidebooks. 4. Waterfalls—Massachusetts—Guidebooks.
5. Berkshire Hills (Mass.)—Guidebooks. 6. Taconic Trail System (Mass.)—
Guidebooks. I. Title.

  GV199.42.M4D86 2008

  551.48′409744—dc22

                                        2008015500

**Outdoor recreational activities are by their very nature potentially
hazardous and contain risk. See "Caution: Safety Tips," page xiv.**

Maps created with DeLorme Topo USA® 7.0, copyright 2007 DeLorme
(www.delorme.com)

Cover photograph: *Campbell Falls*, photo by Christy Butler,
                 www.berkshirephotos.com

Design: Toelke Associates

Printed in the USA

10   9   8   7   6   5   4   3   2   1

Critical Praise for Russell Dunn's Guidebooks

Adirondack Waterfall Guide

Many of the falls are well known, but this is an especially good guide to cataracts that hikers might otherwise miss. **Adirondack Life**

If you love waterfalls, you'll love the guidebook written by Russell Dunn. [It is] a ... readable and easy-to-use guide to a whole lot of waterfalls in the eastern Adirondacks that you'll want to see if you haven't. **Adirondack Explorer**

This book is indeed a joy to read. Dunn easily draws us into his world with graceful, inspired writing, and provides the kind of insights that may prompt us to keep a copy permanently in our cars. **Trailwalker**

It is the experience *of discovering the unexpected that I treasure most about Adirondack waterfalls, and the fact that there are still such places to 'discover' in New York State in the twenty-first century is no small thing.* **Bill Ingersoll**

Catskill Region Waterfall Guide

Dunn's directions are easy to follow, and he offers some nifty history on each of the cataracts. If that's not enough to make you jump in the car, the dramatic photos should cinch it. **Hudson Valley**

A must-own tool. ... This book fills a real need and is a key to a treasure house of beauty. Altogether the book is a winner. **Arthur G. Adams**

This book is highly recommended for its unique combination of appealing writing, strong research, intriguing destinations, and interesting history. **Kaatskill Life**

Hudson Valley Waterfall Guide

Will very likely open eyes to a world of the outdoors that would have passed us by otherwise. **Times Union**

Those who pick up this extraordinary waterfall guide by Russell Dunn will find countless paths to these and other inspirational places in the Valley. **Ned Sullivan, president, Scenic Hudson**

Trails with Tales (co-written with Barbara Delaney)

Even if you don't plan on taking the hikes, the book offers Dunn's always-entertaining descriptions of each destination's significance, making it a prime candidate for any history lover's bookshelf.
Hudson Valley

To find such a wide and eclectic variety between the covers of one book, and also within an easy drive of home, is a wonderful gift.
Karl Beard, National Park Service

As a reference tool, it is excellent. … the historical insight gives local hikers a broader understanding and appreciation of the land under their feet. **Times Herald-Record**

This is a refreshing twist on the traditional guidebook.
Adirondac

Mohawk Region Waterfall Guide

This is the latest in a series of waterfall guides written by Russell Dunn that I recommend to anyone interested in gems which are often overlooked by the public. … Dunn writes in a lucid style with plenty of historical data and anecdotes which make the guide interesting as just plain reading. **The Long Path North News**

Like its predecessors, the guide is well-organized and thoroughly researched. In addition to his field work, he calls on a large, varied selection of books, magazines and newspapers. … Whether you read his books or hear him speak, Dunn will leave you smarter and more appreciative than before of local places, streams, waterfalls and land-scapes. **Schenectady Daily Gazette**

Following his successful guides to waterfalls in the Adirondacks, Catskills, and Hudson Valley, Russell Dunn continues with a plethora of falls to explore in the Mohawk region. Again, he does so in a liter-ate, fact-filled fashion with anecdotes and historical data to draw one to these sites. **Adirondac**

To Gary Zusman,

a man of many talents—

and a good friend.

Sanderson Brook falls, 1998.

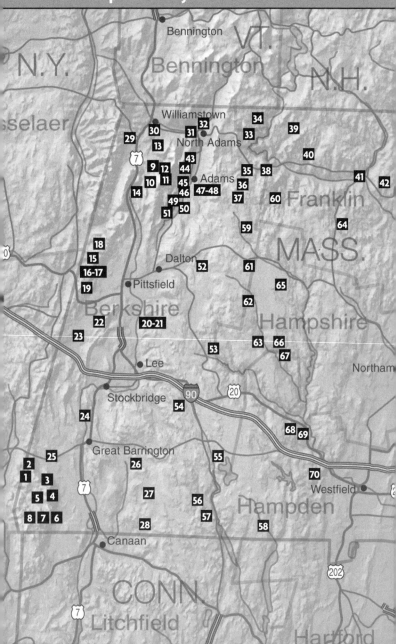

Table of

Contents

Acknowledgments

When a book is published, it is the author who inevitably gets the accolades (as well as the slings and arrows that come just as inevitably), but it's important to realize that the author is merely the front man, the tip of the iceberg beneath which lies an expansive team of professionals (the publisher, editor, graphic artist, and proofreaders) who have worked just as diligently to bring the book to fruition. May these acknowledgments in some small way give recognition to those individuals who would otherwise remain inconspicuously in the background.

I am indebted to the many early explorers and writers and their modern-day counterparts who have ventured out with pen, easel, or camera in hand to capture the wonders of waterfalls. Their words and images give this book its historical depth and relevance.

Many thanks go to my wife, Barbara Delaney, who is the book's cartographer and who continues to serve as my hiking companion of good cheer. She is also my computer consultant and ready to lend a hand when I run into problems (as I always do).

There are times when I wonder what I would do without the generous help of Bob Drew, whose knowledge of geography is encyclopedic, exceeded only by the number of postcards in his collection, which now totals over 200,000. All of the postcard reproductions used in this book are from my private collection, with the exception of Umpachene Falls, Stevens Glen, Fall at Otis Reservoir, and Falls on Buck River, which were contributed by Jim Moore. Jim is an explorer, naturalist, and kindred spirit who has been enormously helpful to me through many consultations.

I am also highly indebted to Christy Butler of Jan & Christy Butler (www.berkshirephotos.com) for many consultations and for his wonderful photograph of Campbell Falls that graces the front cover of this book. Chris has the rare ability to capture on film the magic of waterfalls. The contemporary photographs inside the book were taken by me.

I thank the New York State Library in Albany and the Berkshire Library in Pittsfield, whose staffs have been courteous and helpful.

This book would lack its distinctive and captivating look were it not for Ron Toelke and Barbara Kempler-Toelke of Toelke Associates, who always come up with just the right physical layout and graphics. It is probably because of their efforts that this book first caught your eye.

Special thanks go to my editor, Steve Hoare, whose ability to fine-tune a diligently conceived piece of writing, polishing it so that it shines like gold, is something that is incredibly difficult to do, but which Steve makes look effortless. Copyeditors Matina Billias and Natalie Mortensen added invaluable editorial assistance.

And last, but not least, I am eternally grateful to Deborah Allen, my energetic, industrious, able-to-multitask publisher, whose faith in my writing ability has spurred me on to write more and more books, and who by now is probably wondering if there is ever going to be an end to it (there isn't!)

Fall near gristmill circa 1910.

Caution: Safety Tips

Nature is inherently wild and unpredictable, so play it safe and don't be reckless. Outdoor recreational activities are by their very nature potentially hazardous and contain risk. All participants in such activities must assume the responsibility for their own actions and safety. No book can replace good judgment. The outdoors is forever changing. The author and publisher cannot be held responsible for inaccuracies, errors, or omissions, or for any changes in the details of this publication, or for the consequences of any reliance on the information contained herein, or for the safety of people in the outdoors.

Remember that the destination is not the waterfall or the mountain summit. The destination is home; get back there safely.

Safety Tips Specifically for Waterfalls

1. Always stay well back from the top of a waterfall. Some waterfalls have gracefully curved lips at the top, which means that if you start to slip forward, there is nothing to stop you from continuing over the brink and tumbling to the bottom. Think of how the pitcher plant traps unwary insects and you will have a clear picture of how this mechanism works. The fact that the bedrock near the top of a waterfall is often wet or slimy further increases the likelihood of losing traction and inadvertently riding the waterfall down to a most unpleasant outcome.

2. Never jump or dive off ledges above a waterfall, no matter how inviting the pool of water below looks. You may lose your footing as you make the leap and end up landing on the rocks instead of in the water, or you may collide with unseen objects such as boulders and submerged logs below the waterline. Remember that conditions can change overnight. You cannot rely on the fact that the pool may have been clear of objects or debris the last time you visited the falls.

3. Never swim in a pool of water at the top of a cascade. There's always the possibility that the force of the stream may flush you out of the pool and eject you over the top of the fall. Keep in mind

that rocks are usually worn smooth at the waterfall's summit, which means that there will be nothing to grab hold of to save yourself if you get caught up in the current.

4. Never throw rocks over the top of a waterfall. You never know if someone might be below, even if you just looked over the top.

5. Never try to climb up the face or the sides of a waterfall. Waterfalls are often formed out of sedimentary rocks like shale and slate, which don't provide reliable supports for footholds and handholds. Waterfalls also send up sprays of water that can keep the surrounding rocks damp and slippery.

6. If you decide to cool off in a swimming hole at the base of a waterfall, be sure to enter the water slowly and carefully to avoid injuring yourself on obstructions such as submerged tree limbs and boulders.

7. Enjoy waterfalls by viewing them from the base, whenever possible. This provides the best views, the greatest safety, and the most optimum photo shoot.

8. Never drink water from streams, brooks, and waterfalls, no matter how clean the water may look. Giardiasis is often the result of drinking untreated water.

9. If you are visiting a waterfall in the winter, be on the lookout for blocks of ice above you that could break off and come tumbling down.

10. If you follow a creek upstream to a waterfall, you cannot get lost as long as you follow the creek back downstream to your starting point.

11. Avoid cornering any wild animal as you approach a waterfall in a gorge. The animal's only path of retreat may be right through where you are standing!

General Hiking Safety Tips

1. Always hike with two or more companions. That way, if someone is hurt, one person can stay with the victim while the other goes for help.

2. Make it a practice to always take along a day pack complete with emergency supplies, compass, whistle, flashlight, dry matches,

raingear, high-energy food, extra clothes, duct tape, lots of water (at least twenty-four ounces per person), insect repellent, emergency medical kit, and sun block.

3. Your skin is the largest organ in your body. To protect it, wear sunblock whenever you're exposed to sunlight for extended periods of time, especially in the summer, and insect repellents when you know that you are going into an area where there are mosquitoes or blackflies. Remember that you can get burned even on a cloudy day. Wearing a hat with a wide brim is always helpful to keep out the sun. Wear long pants and a long-sleeved shirt to further protect yourself from both the sun and biting insects.

   One substitute for repellents is to take a lead from horses and bring along a "swisher"—a leafy branch that you can wave in front of and around yourself to keep the air free of biting insects.

4. Wear ankle-high boots—always! Boots provide traction, gripping power, and ankle support that sneakers and shoes do not.

5. Be aware of the risk of hypothermia, and stay dry. Keep in mind that the temperature doesn't have to be near freezing for you to become too cold. If you become accidentally immersed in water in the spring, fall, or winter, return to your car immediately unless the air temperature is above 70 degrees. Also be cognizant of the dangers of overheating (hyperthermia) and always drink plenty of water when the weather is hot and muggy. Stay in the shade whenever possible, and use the stream near a waterfall to cool off in if you begin to overheat.

6. To be on the safe side, stay out of the woods during hunting season. If you do venture into the woods while hunters are about, wear an orange-colored vest and make periodic loud noises to draw attention to the fact that you are a human, and not a wild animal.

7. Always stand back from the base of a tall waterfall. Someone at the top might unthinkingly toss a rock over the edge.

8. Stay on trails whenever possible to avoid the chance of becoming disoriented and lost, and to avoid causing damage to the environment (particularly where there might be rare plants and mosses off-trail). Do not consider bushwhacking through the woods unless you are an experienced hiker, you have a compass with you and you know how to use it, you are prepared to spend sev-

eral days in the woods if necessary, and you are with a group of similarly prepared hikers.

Always know where you are. Guidebooks, topographic maps, and compasses are essential if you venture out into the wilderness. A GPS unit is also worth bringing along. Nothing, however, is a substitute for good judgment and basic common sense.

9. Be flexible and adaptive to a wilderness environment that can change abruptly. Trails described in this book can become altered by blowdown, beaver dams flooding the adjacent land, or even forest fires.

10. Always let someone know where you are going, when you will return, and what to do if you have not shown up by the designated time.

11. Avoid any creature that is acting erratically. If any animal should advance towards you and cannot be deterred, assume that it is either rabid or predatory.

12. If you encounter a problem, do not panic. Unless it is critical that you react immediately and decisively, it is best to stop for a moment and think through what your options are. This is particularly true if you suddenly find yourself lost or disoriented.

13. Leave early in the morning if your hike requires covering a lot of ground. Plan accordingly and allow for plenty of time if the hike is in the winter, when footing may not be easy and nighttime arrives hours earlier than it does in the summer.

Follow these tips and you will maximize your chances for having an enjoyable and safe time visiting waterfalls.

Special Precautions for Children and Pets

This subject takes us back to the underlying premise that waterfalls must always be respected and viewed as wild, unbridled natural wonders. Waterfalls can kill.

No one really knows for sure just how many people have died at Niagara Falls over the last three centuries, for many deaths have occurred without witnesses. We do know, however, that by the end of the nineteenth century, Niagara Falls had not only become the honeymoon capital of the world, but its suicide capital as well (this dubious honor was only brought to an end when the Golden Gate Bridge in San Francisco, California, was erected). Cataracts such as T-Lake Falls in the Adirondacks, Bash Bish Falls in the Taconics, Kaaterskill Falls in the Catskills, Hamilton Falls in southern Vermont, and Canajoharie Falls in the Mohawk Valley, all have a sizable number of casualties and deaths associated with them—generally because youths engage in horseplay, do reckless stunts, get too close to the top of the waterfall, or choose to tempt fate by rock climbing where they shouldn't.

When approaching the top of a large waterfall, keep young children carefully supervised and dogs leashed at all times.

The Wild and Wonderful World of Waterfalls

Welcome to the wild and wonderful world of the waterfalls of the Berkshire and Taconic Mountains of western Massachusetts and eastern New York. It is a world of grand gorges and tumbling torrents, of cascades and cataracts that are not only awesome, but kaleidoscopic, for waterfalls are endlessly recreating themselves, changing according to the seasons and weather: tumultuous and commanding during spring's snowmelt; rocky and moss-covered during the idle, dog days of summer; multi-colored and peacock-splendid throughout autumn's vivid transformation of colors; and austere and silent during winter's deep freeze, when water is transformed into cones of ice and solid blocks of blues and whites.

Who, young or old, hasn't been transfixed by a large, thundering waterfall—to see death dancing on the rocks, writhing between sky and streambed, and to ultimately acknowledge one's own, puny insignificance against the wild turbulence of such monumental power?

Waterfalls are remarkable constructs of nature. But why do they exist? Isn't it just as likely that water should glide down uniformly carved, inclined streambeds, rolling down from the highlands to the flatness of the oceans? Why should there be sudden breaks in the smooth continuity of rivers and streams, where the world suddenly turns vertical and the water momentarily becomes airborne?

It is because the Earth is imperfect in its construction that waterfalls exist. If Earth's surface was perfectly spherical, there would be no upthrust of land, only a world-girdling ocean. There would be no land, and thus, no waterfalls. If there were no winds to carry clouds inland to the mountains, then water as it evaporated would rise above the oceans and rain straight back down onto the seas. No water would be carried inland to produce rivers and lakes, and ultimately waterfalls. If the bedrock of the earth was uniform and unvarying, then all particles of rock would be removed at a constant, unchanging rate by the erosive action of running water. We would have inclined gullies, but not the sudden drops and plunges that form waterfalls.

Waterfalls exist, then, because we live in an imperfect world, a fact that is worthy of contemplation when you look at your next large waterfall and marvel not only at its existence, but at yours as well, since without the imperfect transmission of DNA, you and those you love would not have evolved to our present level of consciousness to appreciate the world around us and its waterfalls.

Despite differences in size, shape, composition, and location, all waterfalls have one thing in common: they function as enormous conveyer belts, slowly and persistently dismantling mountains and hills, one grain, one nugget, or one boulder at a time. This process is so gradual as to be virtually imperceptible during an individual human's lifespan, but it is an inevitability when looked at from the standpoint of geological intervals of time.

Waterfalls are the products of rivers and streams, whose essence is movement. They are not stationary and imperturbable like the mountains from which they initially arise. The water that tumbles over a fall is incessantly in motion, returning to the sea only to be lifted into the atmosphere as evaporation and blown inland again to begin the cycle anew, ad infinitum.

The Berkshires and Taconics, like all mountain ranges, possess numerous streams, and many of these streams have produced waterfalls. No attempt has been made in this book to be encyclopedic, however. Many waterfalls are inaccessible because they are located on private lands, or they are so remote that getting to them involves extensive bushwhacks that go beyond the scope of this book. And some waterfalls may remain unknown to guidebook writers and the general public, remaining obscure and frequented only by a handful of locals and hunters who wish to keep the identity of their favorite glen or waterfall a secret.

Fortunately, the Berkshires and Taconics are not only blessed with numerous waterfalls, but many of them are contained in state forests or located in parks preserved by land conservancies or civic-minded organizations and individuals, and so can be enjoyed by us all for centuries to come.

Pettibone Falls near Cheshire Reservoir circa 1900.

Waterfall Terminology

There are three words in the common vernacular that are used to indicate waterfalls: 1) waterfall (or simply "fall"); 2) cascade; and 3) cataract. As a general rule, "waterfall" is the generic term, encompassing the other two. As to how high a waterfall must be to be considered a true waterfall, or how vertically inclined the streambed must be in order to satisfy waterfall taxonomists, these fine points are best left to those who enjoy arguing over the precise number of angels who can dance on the head of a pin. In the end, what constitutes a waterfall is subjective and relative to one's own values and perceptions.

Although the word "cascade" is sometimes used interchangeably with "waterfall," "cascade" usually describes a waterfall that is in continuous contact with the bedrock, or one where the stream is descending smoothly in a series of small falls or drops. Keep in mind, however, that there is no universal agreement regarding these matters. Bruce and Doreen Bolnick, authors of Waterfalls of the White Mountains,[1] quote the Oxford English Dictionary, which states that "cascades are smaller waterfalls, often in a series, and need not have steep drops or strong currents." In 200 Waterfalls in Central & Western New York, Rich and Sue Freeman contend that a cascade "follows a sloped descent across a rock face with many breaks, leaps, and segments."[2] Cascading streams with many drops and rock-created riffs can be a perfect example of this phenomenon. Gary Letcher, author of Waterfalls of the Mid-Atlantic States, writes that a cascade is "a waterfall with multiple steps from ledge to ledge."[3] Kate B. Watson and Greg Parsons, authors of New England Waterfalls, assert that cascades are "a series of small drops, too many to count, that fall at a low rate of descent."[4] Height can also be a factor when considering what constitutes a cascade. According to Scott A. Ensminger and Douglas K. Bassett, authors of A Waterfall Guide to Letchworth State Park, "a cascade must have a minimum drop of 5 vertical feet."[5]

The word "cataract" suggests something quite different, denoting a larger or more powerful waterfall.[6] What's more, as Ensminger and Bassett point out, a cataract is typically "confined to a narrow channel."[7] Campbell Falls, straddling the border between Massachusetts and Connecticut, serves as a good example of this type of waterfall.

But waterfalls aren't just merely falls, cascades, or cataracts. They can assume a variety of shapes and configurations. They can plunge, meaning that they take off from the top and don't touch rock until they have fallen some distance. There are not many of this type in Massachusetts. Waterfalls can be fan-shaped, narrow at the top and widening as the stream descends. They can be shaped like a punch bowl, so that a narrow, defined stream comes down into a pool of water, creating the effect of a ladle and bowl. Waterfalls can be segmented, where the stream divides into two or more channels, or even parallel, with two waterfalls falling side-by-side. If a stream contains a number of waterfalls that are separated by some distance, they are considered serial; if they are congruent with one another, then they become one continuous waterfall, or

Waterfalls have often been industrialized. Postcard circa 1900.

multi-tiered. Some waterfalls look as though they are contained in a trough; these are called chutes. Others are formed on smooth inclines of bedrock and are sloped gently enough so that swimmers can glide down them. These are called slides or waterslides. A waterfall is considered classical when its height approximately equals its width. It is ribbon-like when its height is considerably greater than its width, and curtain-like when its height is less than its width.[8] As if these labels weren't sufficient, many smaller waterfalls are seasonal, meaning that they must wait for spring's sudden release of snowmelt or for torrential periods of prolonged rain in order to become animated.

Some waterfalls are encased in deep, precipitous gorges and can only be viewed with great difficulty. Others are next to open spaces or near roads, and can be accessed without any effort. There are even waterfalls that have formed underground, at the bottom of a dome or where the cave drops suddenly from one level to another, forming a pit. Clay Perry, in New England's Buried Treasure, states that there are five waterfalls in Eldon's Cave on Tom Ball Mountain.[9] This is the exception, and not the rule. In general, while Massachusetts may contain its fair share of caves, typically formed in limestone or marble, few are waterfall-bearing.

Helpful Tools for Finding Waterfalls

Not to be self-serving, but there is no substitute for a waterfall guidebook if your main objective is to find a specific waterfall. With a guidebook in hand, you will succeed in your quest every time. My wife, Barbara Delaney, and I have undertaken many hikes to remote gorges and promising streams looking for waterfalls, only to come up empty-handed in the end. Using a guidebook ensures that you will not be similarly disappointed. Still, even with a guidebook, there are additional tools that are helpful to have in reserve:

Delorme Atlas & Gazetteer. When you travel with a Delorme Atlas & Gazetteer (in this case, the Massachusetts edition), you have at your disposal a collection of easy-to-read, broad-base topographical maps that show large areas of land with all highways and byways identified. A Gazetteer ensures that you will know where you are and how to get to where you want to go. This is particularly helpful if you are plotting out how to navigate from one waterfall to the next, especially over mixed terrain with hills and valleys.

All of the waterfalls in this book, except for the ones listed as "historic" (not accessible), are identified by a Delorme coordinate, meaning that you can readily locate the approximate area on the Atlas where the waterfall is located. The coordinates for a given waterfall are easy to follow. The designation "p. 22, F12," for instance, instructs you to turn to page 22, scan down vertically to the letter F, and then cross the page horizontally until you come to column 12. The square formed by F12 gives you the approximate area where the waterfall is located.

Compass. It's always a good idea to carry a compass at all times when you're hiking in the woods. Should you become momentarily disoriented (a more positive-sounding term than "lost"), it's comforting to at least be able to determine which way is north, and from that you can reckon the direction in which you're heading. Having a compass handy in the car also can prove beneficial if you find yourself momentarily unsure of where you are. For instance, the Delorme Atlas & Gazetteer may be able to tell you what road you're on, but it can't tell you in which direction you're going. That means that if you're inadvertently traveling west on Rt. 2 when you should be going east, the compass will set you straight before you have gone too far out of your way.

Topographical (Topo) Maps. Nothing is handier than a topo map if want to know the physical layout of the territory being crossed. A topo map will show you all the major land features including mountains, cliffs, valleys, gorges, sinkholes, lakes, rivers, and so on—all in 3-D (once, of course, you have accustomed yourself to reading contour lines).

Some waterfalls, if well known, are identified by name on the topo map; some are indicated as blue slashes across streams (which are color-coded blue on topo maps). In some cases a particularly large waterfall will be revealed by highly compressed topo lines that cross the stream. In other cases, compressed lines on both sides of a stream will indicate a gorge, which are often waterfall-bearing.

GPS (global positioning system). More and more, we are taking technology with us into the wilderness in the form of the latest gear or such high-tech devices as cell phones and global positioning systems. A GPS is helpful if you know the coordinates of your destination and want to get there via the shortest route possible, or if you want to be sure that you can return unerringly to your starting point. They are also helpful if you want to know changes in elevation. However, one should never forsake one's own good judgment or more conventional orienting tools like a compass and a topo map and rely entirely on a GPS. Batteries can fail, or the unit can become damaged, leaving you suddenly helpless.

GPS Designed Specifically for Automobile Travel. If your goal is to remove all uncertainty from the process of getting to the trailhead, then this piece of technology will be your best friend. All you need to do is program in your destination, and the unit will guide you unerringly, street by street, from where you start to where you want to be, accompanied by a pleasant voice that talks you through it, step by step, until you reach your destination.

This may be a presage of things to come, when the guidebook of tomorrow might be a small, hand-held electronic unit with an amiable, knowledgeable voice providing crucial information as you go from one point to the next along the trail, even making sure that you return safely to your car or, if you are injured, ensuring that you are rescued.

Antique Waterfall Postcards

Although some of the illustrations in this book may appear to be from old photographs, in actuality most are reproductions of antique postcards, many of which date back to the beginning of the twentieth century. Their inclusion has three purposes in mind: 1) to give the book a distinctive visual look; 2) to complement the historical flavor of the book; and 3) to allow readers the opportunity to compare today's waterfalls with how they looked in the past, up to 100 years ago.

Photographing Waterfalls

There is a trick to taking good pictures of waterfalls. Despite what intuition may tell you, a clear, bright, sunny day is not the best set of conditions for taking waterfall photographs. Bright sunlight produces sharp contrast between the gleaming white of the waterfall and the darker rocks and deepening shadows cast by bushes and overhanging trees surrounding the fall. If you try to compensate, so that the waterfall is correctly exposed, then the rocks will end up noticeably underexposed; and if you correctly set the exposure for the rocks and surrounding flora, then the waterfall will inevitably come out overexposed. It is a no-win situation.

The optimum time for taking waterfall photographs is when the sky is cloudy and bright, even hazy, but not light enough that pronounced shadows are noticeable. Under these conditions, just point the camera and shoot, and the picture is almost certain to come out properly exposed.

Composition, of course, is important. The best waterfall pictures are usually taken from below and at some distance from the base of the falls. But this is a general rule only. In some instances it is nearly impossible to get down to the base of a waterfall; in other cases one may opt for a less standard, more creative view. Sometimes, shots taken from the side can show the waterfall to its best advantage, while shots taken from the top generally offer little but views of the valley or gorge below.

Listening to Waterfalls

Sound plays an important part in the waterfall experience. Like the howling of wind through tall trees, waterfalls are the voice of nature animated and given life. In the spring, waterfalls reach their full power and majesty, pounding and bellowing like wild beasts as they attempt to break free from the stony bedrock shackling them to the Earth. Undoubtedly those favorite Victorian adjectives, "sublime" and "awesome," will come to mind as you stand in their presence, humbled by their sheer might and towering magnificence.

If you prefer the gentle, babbling sounds of falling water, then summer is the time to visit waterfalls. With the arrival of July and August, streams turn into languid rivulets and waterfalls become entities more of moss and rock than of water. Summer provides an opportunity to stretch out comfortably on a rock slab next to the falls, lie back, and contemplate the mysteries of the universe as you listen to the lulling sound of falling water.

In winter, the world turns ashen, into subtle shades of white and gray, and a much different sound emerges from waterfalls—if any sound is heard at all. Many falls lose their apparent fluidity and become entombed in ice. If you listen closely enough, however, you may still hear the faint sound of water flowing beneath the ice, gurgling as though rushing down a drain.

Whatever the season or time of year, listen, and waterfalls will speak to you.

Mileage

You should find that the mileage indicators given to the trailheads are reasonably accurate, and that the use of clearly identified intersections from which to start will eliminate any ambiguity about whether or not you're taking the right route. The mileages stated should be accurate to within +/- 0.1 mile, but please bear in mind that there can be differences in readings between individual odometers.

Mileage indicators given along hiking trails are less exact and frequently estimated, and therefore they may not be as accurate as the distances measured by odometer. That said, care was taken to ensure that they still be accurate enough to tell you where you are along the trail and how to reach your destination. Hiking mileages given are one-way unless otherwise specified

All distances are given in feet, yards, or miles, even though most of the rest of the world has converted or is ineluctably moving towards conversion to the metric system. For visitors to the U.S.A., the following conversions may be helpful: 1 foot = 0.3048 meter; 1 yard = 0.9144 meter; and 1 mile = 1609 meters (or 1.6 kilometers).

In the book's endnotes, several nineteenth-century writers give distances in terms of rods. The conversion is: 1 rod = 16.5 feet.

Accessing Waterfalls: Degree of Difficulty

The degree of difficulty encountered in any hike is inherently subjective, since individuals vary greatly in terms of ability, age, and conditioning. Presumably the average ninety-year-old will have more difficulty negotiating an "easy" 0.2-mile trek than the average twenty-five-year-old; a super-fit triathlete probably won't even break into a sweat climbing up a steep ravine, while the proverbial couch potato will be winded within 100 feet. What is easy for one may be difficulty for another. Even so, general guidelines can be helpful when applied to the "average" hiker; these are summarized below:

Easy—a short distance, generally less than 0.5 mile; no real effort is required to complete the hike.

Easy to Moderate—a short distance, generally less than 0.5 mile, but with some effort required; or, less than 1.0 mile over flat, non-taxing terrain.

Moderate—less than 1.0 mile over mixed terrain; some effort required.

Moderate to Difficult—less than 1.5 mile over mixed terrain; or, less than 1.0 mile, but involving an appreciable ascent with more effort required.

Difficult—greater than 1.0 mile, with appreciable ascent and increasing effort required; or greater than 2.0 miles, with some effort needed.

Very Difficult—regardless of distance, the hike requires maximum effort because of steep ascent and/or difficult terrain.

Will Rogers once said, in an address given in Boston in 1930, "I never met a man I didn't like." So it is with waterfalls.

The Berkshires

Geology and Geography

Despite their timeless appearance, the Berkshire Mountains have stood for only a short time by geological standards. We know that mountain-building processes have raised them up at least twice before, only to level them back to the ground to await being uplifted again. The Berkshires of today are but a mere shadow of their former selves, with Mt. Greylock, at an elevation of 3,491 feet, being their highest peak. At one time, however, they stood as high as the Rocky Mountains. One can only imagine the waterfalls that must have existed there at that time! Fortunately, although they have lost elevation over the centuries, the Berkshires are not waterfall-shy today. As one nineteenth-century writer stated, "There are 16 major waterfalls in the Berkshires, and more than 1,000 brooks and streams in the county."[1]

The Berkshire Mountains acquired their name from their association with Berkshire County, Massachusetts, which extends across the fifty-mile length of western Massachusetts's borders between Connecticut and Vermont. The county was incorporated in 1761 by Governor Frances Benard.[2] In earlier days the Berkshire area was called *Housatonick*, a Native American expression meaning "a place over the mountains," and was inhabited by the Mahican tribe of the Algonquin Nation.[3]

The Berkshires have always been geologically separated from their neighbors, both by the "Berkshire Barrier," which blocked an easy westward traverse from the Connecticut River Valley, and by the Taconic Mountains, which sealed the Berkshires off from the Hudson River Valley.

Today, "the Berkshires" have come to include the western part of Franklin, Hampshire, and Hamden counties in Massachusetts between the Connecticut River Valley and Berkshire County, a 500-square-mile area known as the Berkshire Hilltowns[4] because of its glacially rounded hills and countless streams dissecting what had once been a relatively flat plateau. Some even count Litchfield County in western Connecticut as part of the Berkshires, referring to

Scenes on Murray Crane's Estate, Dalton, Mass.

Falls have been dammed to create millponds. Postcard circa 1920.

it as the Berkshire foothills, but this waterfall-rich area has not been included in this book. (I am planning, however, another book that will tour the waterfalls of western Connecticut.)

There are a number of major river valley systems in the Berkshires: flowing north to south are the Hoosic and Housatonic rivers; west to east are the Deerfield River, the Westfield River, and the West Branch of the Westfield River. These rivers created passes through the mountains that allowed for the advancement of settle-

A Berkshire Trout Brook near Rockdale, Great Barrington, Mass.

Unnamed cascade near Great Barrington circa 1900.

ment. Where nature wasn't quite so accommodating, workers created the 4.5-mile-long Hoosic Tunnel to connect the Deerfield Valley and the Hoosic Valley.

In terms of underlying bedrock, as a general rule, limestone and marble can be found in the valleys. These are the rocks that you will typically see when visiting many of the waterfalls contained in this book. Schists and gneisses tend to predominate in the highlands.

To ensure that waterfalls can be accessed as easily and efficiently as possible, they have been grouped according to their proximity to the major highways that crisscross western Massachusetts. These highways generally follow along major river valley systems, which means that you will never be far from water when traveling through the Berkshires.

There are seven principal routes that we will consider: the southern section of Route 41, which parallels the Taconic range running north-south from South Egremont to the Connecticut Border; Route 7, extending north-south from Williamstown to Ashley Falls; Route 8, extending north-south from North Adams to south of New Boston; Rockwell Road and Notch Road, which run north-south from North Adams to Lanesborough through the Mt. Greylock State Reservation; Route 2, which runs west-east from Williamstown to Greenfield; Route 9, which runs west-east from Pittsfield to Northampton; and Route 20, which heads west-east from West Pittsfield to West Springfield. All of these routes can be accessed from the westernmost exits of the Massachusetts Turnpike (I-90)—a major, 123-mile-long, interstate highway, completed in 1957, that connects West Stockbridge with Boston.

A number of waterfalls can be accessed from the Appalachian National Scenic Trail, which extends from Connecticut through Massachusetts along the Taconic range to Tyringham, then north through October Mountain State Forest and over Mt. Greylock to the Vermont border northeast of Williamstown.

Art and Culture

Beginning in the early 1800s the Berkshires became a cultural mecca, attracting by its beauty and natural wonders, as well as its relative proximity to Boston and New York, some of the most influential

American writers of the nineteenth century. Henry David Thoreau journeyed on many occasions to the Berkshires from his home on Walden Pond. One of his favorite Berkshire hikes was to The Cascade in North Adams. Herman Melville, author of *Moby Dick*, settled in Pittsfield and converted an eighteenth-century home into an estate named Arrowhead. It was Melville who gave the name October Mountain[1] to a nearby peak with several small cascades.

Nathaniel Hawthorne lived in Tanglewood for a short period of time while writing *The House of the Seven Gables*.[2] The name "Tanglewood" was given to the estate by Hawthorne after he had thrashed about in a patch of thickets by the Stockbridge Bowl. As a young man, Hawthorne also made several trips to Natural Bridge and its small falls in North Adams.

William Cullen Bryant, considered by some to be America's first great poet, had a summer home in Cummington and wrote passionately about the nearby Green River and Monument Mountain.[3] The Reverend Henry Ward Beecher, a prominent social reformer, abolitionist, and brother of *Uncle Tom's Cabin* author Harriett Beecher Stowe, came to Lenox around 1853 and purchased a home there.[4] Oliver Wendell Holmes, physician, writer, and poet, was accustomed to spending summers at his family farm in the Berkshires, and later built a year-round home there, which he called Holmesdale.[5] Henry Wadsworth Longfellow spent two summers in the Berkshires while working on *Kavanagh*.[6]

Mark Twain was a frequent summer visitor at Tyringham and may have hiked past the falls on what is now McLennon Preserve land. Catherine Sedgwick fell in love with the Berkshires and wrote her first novel, *A New England Tale*, while there. One British magazine called A New England Tale "the first utterance of a national mind." It was Sedgwick who named the lake at Lenox "Stockbridge Bowl," changing it from the Native American name *Mahkeenac*.[7] Edith Wharton built a summer retreat at Lenox in 1902, calling it The Mount. Her novel *Ethan Frome* conjures up images of Lenox in winter.[8]

It was a golden age of American literature, and it was in the Berkshires that the greatest literary minds of the century congregated, on occasion getting together to discuss their latest works and spur each other on to greater heights through a camaraderie that was naturally competitive. One of the most well-documented gatherings of famous authors occurred in the summer of 1850 when Nathaniel Hawthorne, Herman Melville, Oliver Wendell Holmes and David Dudley Field (a famous trial lawyer) hiked through the Ice Glen in Stockbridge and then up Monument Mountain towards its summit, Squaw Peak, only to be forced down to seek shelter as a raging thunderstorm struck.[9]

At the same time, landscape painters, particularly those of the Hudson River School, were also bringing to light the splendors of the Berkshires. Thomas Cole and Frederic Church, early luminaries of the Hudson River School, came to the Berkshires to paint the landscape. They were soon followed by many others. John Kensett and Asher B. Durand both painted Bash Bish Falls in the mid-1800s. George Inness is credited with rendering more paintings of the Berkshires than any other nineteenth-century landscapist.

It was inevitable that, as the writers and painters extolled the beauty and natural wonders of the Berkshires, the region began to attract the affluent and well-to-do who longed to experience nature's rugged beauty while remaining safely insulated in a cocoon of comfort. Samuel Gray Ward built the first great estate in Lenox in 1846.[10] By the late 1800s the wealthy were firmly established in the Berkshires. In Lenox and Stockbridge they built large homes modeled on the mansions of Newport, Rhode Island. In the late 1800s the largest private residence in the United States[11] was built in Lenox by Ansen Phelps Stokes, banker and industrialist. He called the 100-room mansion Shadowbrook. It burned to the ground in 1956.[12]

It was only a matter of time, however, before this aristocratic bubble had to burst, for only the fabulously wealthy could afford to maintain such grandiose residences, and wealth has always been a precarious commodity, subject to sudden and dramatic turns of events. In the early 1900s the financial collapse began, and then was accelerated by World War I, the creation of the income tax system, and the Great Depression of the 1930s.[13]

Many of these great homes and estates would eventually have fallen into ruin and ultimately been razed were it not for a renaissance in the Berkshires that began in the late 1920s. Suddenly, the region again began attracting great writers, as well as world-class dancers, musicians, and playwrights. These artistic luminaries lit up the region like a beacon, drawing wealth and prestige back to the Berkshires. In 1928 the Berkshire Playhouse opened in Stockbridge, slowly evolving into the Berkshire Theater Festivals as it is known today. It is now the second-oldest summer stock theater in America.[14]

Jacob's Pillow Dance Festival, organized by Ted Shawn, the father of modern dance, began in the 1930s at nearby Becket.[15] The dance company initially consisted of male performers only, but changed in time to a mixed company of male and female performers, thereby attracting an even wider following. It is now the oldest dance festival in the United States.[16]

In 1934 the Berkshire Music Festival opened its doors. The festival took up permanent residence at Tanglewood in 1936 and became the summer home of the Boston Symphony Orchestra. Today, Tanglewood's fan-shaped open-sided pavilion, called "The Shed," provides the illusion of being part of the natural landscape, and seating on the lawn is available for those who wish to listen to the orchestra under a canopy of stars.

The Berkshires have also attracted folk musicians. The lyrics of James Taylor's "Sweet Baby James" still resonate today: "The first of December was covered with snow/So was the turnpike from Stockbridge to Boston/The Berkshires seemed dreamlike on account of that frosting." And who can forget Arlo Guthrie's "Alice's Restaurant," where "you can get anything that you want"?

The grand nineteenth-century mansions and enormous estates of Lenox and Stockbridge could no longer be sustained as private residences by the 1930s, but they could be made sustainable if converted into elegant inns. This proved to be the perfect symbiosis. The inns provided hundreds of needed rooms to house the crowds of visitors and seasonal residents who came to enjoy the burgeoning performing arts scene, and by providing this needed service, the grand estates saved themselves from eventual destruction.

Over the last half century the Berkshires' cultural heritage has undergone further preservation. In 1980, Edith Wharton's summer home, The Mount, was rescued from destruction by a group of concerned citizens in Lenox.[17] The grounds have now become the home

Tanglewood circa 1940.

of Shakespeare and Company, which gives outdoor summer performances of the Bard's great works. In 1961, Hancock Shaker Village, near West Pittsfield, was in danger of being taken over by a neighboring racetrack when, at the last moment, it was saved, restored, and then opened to the public as a living museum to exhibit the Shakers' nineteenth-century lifestyle.

The Norman Rockwell Museum, which thrived in Stockbridge for twenty-five years, finally outgrew the "Old Corner House" where Rockwell had lived and painted for the last twenty-five years of his life.[18] The museum moved into a much larger facility located north of Glendale.

Daniel Chester French's summer home, Chesterwood, was preserved as a National Trust for Historic Preservation site after French's death in 1931. His workshop contains the actual hand-sized model that French first crafted of what later would become Abraham Lincoln's statue at the Lincoln Memorial.

Today, the Berkshires have a vibrant community of performers, artists, and writers whose presence has been a major reason for the region's success, building on the legacy of the many magnificent nineteenth-century and early-twentieth-century works of art and literature that brought to life many of the area's natural wonders.

Route 41:
THE TACONICS

On road to Mt. Washington circa 1910.

Introduction

The Taconics are a narrow range of mountains, deeply cut into peaks and valleys that straddle the border between New York State and New England, extending all the way from northern Connecticut to central Vermont. Although seemingly beholden to no one for their existence, the Taconics were once part of the Green Mountains, only to be cleaved off millions of years ago and moved by enormous geological forces to their present location, some 10–15 miles westward. Although not an exceedingly high mountainous range when compared to the Green Mountains of Vermont or the Adirondack Mountains of New York State, the Taconics do have some notable peaks, such as Berlin Mountain (2,798 feet), Mt. Everett (2,602 feet), Mt. Race (2,365 feet), Mt. Ashley (2,390 feet), and Mt. Alander (2,240 feet) in Massachusetts, and Mount Frissell (2,380 feet), Mount Brace (2,311 feet), South Brace Mountain (2,304 feet), and Round Mountain (2,296 feet) in Connecticut. Like many of the other mountainous regions of the northeastern United States, the Taconics were at one time many thousands of feet higher than at present.[1]

The section of the Taconics that is of particular interest to us lies in southwestern Massachusetts in an area extending from South Egremont to the Connecticut border. This route closely follows Rt. 41, which is called Under Mountain Road, and justly so, for the road travels virtually within the shadow of Mt. Everett and the Taconic Highlands, the part of the Taconic range that is spanned by the Appalachian National Scenic Trail.

1. Bash Bish Falls

Location: Near Copake, NY (Berkshire Co.)
Mt. Washington State Forest
DeLorme Massachusetts Atlas & Gazetteer: p. 43, I26
Fee: None
Hours: Open daily from sunrise to sunset
Restrictions: No diving, swimming or rock climbing; entrance into upper gorge is not permitted
Views: Head-on
Accessibility: From main parking area, 0.7-mile walk (one way) along old gravel road; from upper parking area, less than 0.3-mile (one way), 300-foot descent
Degree of Difficulty: Easy to Moderate from main parking lot; Moderate to Difficult from upper parking lot

Description: Bash Bish Falls is a massive waterfall[1] formed on Bash Bish Brook, a medium-sized stream that rises from two tributaries—Ashley Hill Brook descending from a swampy area west of Mt. Frissell, and City Brook coming down from between Mt. Everett and Mt. Race. After plunging over Bash Bish Falls, Bash Bish Brook immediately enters New York State, where it soon joins the Roeliff Jansen Kill at the western base of the Taconic Range.

The waterfall looms over fifty feet high and is divided near its top into two rivulets by a mammoth, gray, pulpit-like rock. Below, the waters fall into a large, deep pool. There are small cascades below the pool. Bash Bish Falls is located in a 3,290-acre park that contains a series of hiking trails, most of which lead up into the mountains.

A huge gorge is formed directly above Bash Bish Falls where a number of cascades and drops have been created by the rapidly descending stream. The area is off-limits, however, and posted signs above the falls announce that anyone caught trespassing will be fined $250. So content yourself with just enjoying the main falls and save yourself $250 (as well as possibly your life and limbs).

And please! The falls are called Bash Bish, not Bish Bash as so many people have erroneously referred to them. Undoubtedly the

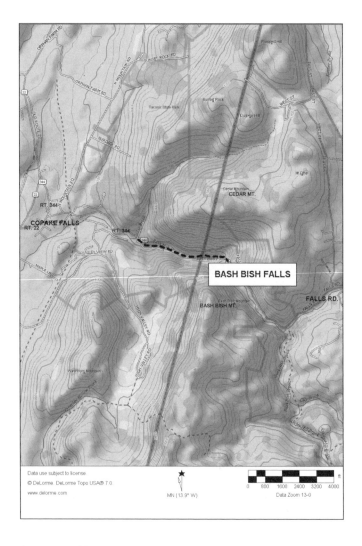

reversing of Bash Bish" to "Bish Bash" arises from the fact that "Bish Bash" rhymes with "mishmash" and "splish-splash."

Like many big waterfalls, Bash Bish Falls has claimed many lives, most often the result of carelessness and needless risk-taking. By the end of the twentieth century, over twenty-five fatalities had been recorded at the falls.[2]

History: According to legend, the fall was named after an Indian maiden named Bash Bish, who was strapped to a canoe and sent over the top of the fall to her death for her unfaithfulness. It is said that if you listen closely enough, you can hear the sound of the falling waters repeating "Bash Bish" over and over again. Legend also has it that if you look into the swirling spray at the base of the fall, and conditions are just right, you can see the serene face of Bash Bish in the rising mist.[3] This tale of an unfaithful Indian maiden is one that is commonly attached to large waterfalls. In fact, Bash Bish Falls even has a secondary legend—the story of Bash Bish's daughter, White Swan, and her tragic fate at the same fall.[4]

In the nineteenth century the fall was painted by artist John Frederick Kensett, a well-known landscape painter of the Hudson River School.

By 1867, eight parcels of land, including the fall, had been acquired by Jean Roemer. In 1874 the property was conveyed to his good friend, Josephine Douglas (wife of the prominent New York City attorney, Alfred Douglas), and a Swiss chalet-style estate was built on the site of what is now the main parking area for Bash Bish Falls. Alfred was never to be significantly involved in his wife's enterprises, however, for he died in 1876. In 1879, Josephine built an inn overlooking the fall but, failing to make a profit, the building was torn down in 1897.

In 1899, John Haldane Flagger acquired the Douglas property. Retaining the area around the fall, he sold 300 acres of land to Margaret and Eugene Vacheron in 1903. In turn, they converted the Douglas residence into an inn and added on an eight-room Swiss chalet guesthouse. The inn failed to prosper, however, and the property went into foreclosure. It was then acquired by Louis Moquin, a French chef. Unfortunately, it later burned to the ground and no attempt was made to rebuild it.

The land and remaining buildings were then purchased by Philip Schick, a New York City attorney who turned it into an auto-

Bash Bish Falls circa 1900.

mobile campground.[5] In 1924 the Massachusetts Department of Conservation (now known as the Department of Environmental Management) purchased 400 acres of land surrounding the fall from Francis R. and Ella R. K. Masters, who had acquired it from John Haldane Flagger with the expressed purpose of reselling it to the Commonwealth of Massachusetts. In the 1960s the state obtained 4,000 additional acres and established the Mount Washington State Forest.[6]

Directions: From South Egremont (junction of Rtes. 23 West & 41 South), drive south on Rt. 41 for 0.1 mile. After passing by Mill Pond, immediately turn right onto Mt. Washington Road. Proceed southwest for 7.5 miles, always staying on the main road. Take note that when you cross the town line, at 3.3 miles, Mt. Washington Road becomes East Street. At the intersection of East Street, with Plantain Road to your left and Cross Road to your right, turn right onto Cross Road and drive west for 0.5 mile. West Road enters from the left. Bear to the right, now on West Road, and continue downhill on what becomes a very winding road. After you have gone 1.6 miles from East Street, you will come to a sharp U-turn and begin following Wright Brook momentarily. The road is now called Bash Bish Falls Road (Bash Bish Brook soon comes in on the left). At 3.0 miles from East Street, you will reach the upper parking lot for Bash Bish Falls. If you park here, a steep trail takes you down to the base of Bash Bish Falls, some 300 feet below, in less than 0.3 mile.

From New York State: Driving south on Rt. 22 to Copake, turn left onto Rt. 344 and proceed southeast for over 0.3 mile. Then turn left again, following Rt. 344 east. In less than 0.3 mile you will come to a fork in the road. Go left here, following signs for Bash Bish Falls. After 0.6 mile from the fork, turn right into the parking area for the fall.

You can also visit the area directly upstream from the gorge by following an old road downhill from the upper parking area for 0.1 mile to Bash Bish Brook. Here, several tiny cascades can be seen and, if you continue walking downstream for several hundred feet, you can see the beginning of the Bash Bish Gorge where the ravine dramatically narrows, with the stream dropping 10 feet over its first

Cascade and gorge below Bash Bish Falls circa 1910.

cascade. Take note of the warning signs (and penalties for trespassing), however, and go no farther than you are permitted.

A better and easier way to access Bash Bish Falls is to continue driving downhill for another 1.0 mile to the lower parking area, which will be on your left. From here, follow a gravel-surfaced carriage road paralleling Bash Bish Brook upstream for 0.7 mile. All at once you will come to an open area, with views of the fall below. Walk down a long flight of stone stairs and you will end up at the base of the fall.

If you wish to avoid the crowds, visit this popular falls midweek.

Additional cascades: From the upper parking area, continue driving uphill on Bash Bish Falls Road for 0.9 mile. Pull over to park into a tiny area on your left. Some small cascades can be seen in the stream below by looking down from the right-hand side of the road.

2. Falls on Cedar Brook

Location: Copake (Columbia County, New York)
DeLorme Massachusetts Atlas & Gazetteer: p. 43, H25
Fee: None
Hours: Open daily from sunrise to sunset
Views: Head-on and lateral
Accessibility: Over 0.5-mile hike one way
Degree of Difficulty: Moderate

Description: This series of falls and cascades is formed on Cedar Brook, a small tributary to Bash Bish Brook. The stream rises northwest of Mt. Ethel and flows into Bash Bish Brook next to the main parking area for Bash Bish Falls. The stream is named after nearby Cedar Mountain.

The first fall you will come to is at the beginning of a narrow, chasm-like gorge where the stream drops 12 feet down through a slot formed between carved sections of the bedrock. From here you will encounter a series of cascades and ledge drops between 3–5 feet high. Then you will pass by an elongated 8-foot-high cascade, and finally several smaller cascades. These falls are located in New York just over the state line from Massachusetts, and are accessed from the same parking lot used for Bash Bish Falls. The falls are not well known or frequently visited, eclipsed as they are by the spotlight glare of attention focused on Bash Bish Falls. Consider this an alternative hike if the area around Bash Bish Falls is too crowded for your tastes.

Directions: Follow the directions given to the main (lower) parking lot for Bash Bish Falls. From the parking lot, walk across Bash Bish Road to a barricaded old road on the east side of Cedar Brook. Follow this blue-blazed road/path north as it parallels the stream. Be prepared for some ascent. In over 0.5 mile you will reach the area of the falls and cascades.

When the path eventually reaches the level of the streambed, you will have reached the end of the gorge and the cascades and falls.

3. Falls on Glen Brook

Location: South of South Egremont (Berkshire County)
DeLorme Massachusetts Atlas & Gazetteer: p. 43, I30
Fee: None
Hours: Open daily from sunrise to sunset
Restrictions: Hikers must park in the visitor parking area next to the tennis courts of the Berkshire School. For anyone planning to leave their car overnight, the school requests that a note be placed on the windshield indicating this intention.
Views: Lateral and head-on
Accessibility: Short hike uphill
Degree of Difficulty: Easy to Moderate

Description: There are three small falls formed on Glen Brook (also known as Glenny Brook), a small stream that rises on the northeast shoulder of Mt. Everett and flows into Willard Brook east of Rt. 41. None of the falls are of any notable size, but they all have one distinguishing feature: they are formed in a muddy-brown or chocolate-colored marble bedrock that is visible at the falls and along sections of the brook upstream from where a deep-cut gully has formed. The coloration of this bedrock is strikingly different from that of most of the other waterfall sites in western Massachusetts.

In ascending order, you will encounter a 6-foot fall (consisting of a plunge onto a cascade), and two 3-foot cascades. All are found within a short distance of each other.

Farther upstream, at the reservoir, the stream cascades down from a considerable height. Near the top of this cascading stream is a 10-foot-high cascade.

History: The Berkshire School is a rigorous college-preparatory institution that was founded in 1907. It boards 380 students, with the goal of providing a "supportive environment where a diverse group of young men and women can develop intellectual foundations and traits of character and leadership that will permit them, in the words of [the] school's motto, to learn not for school, but for life."[1]

Directions: From South Egremont (junction of Rtes. 41 South & 23 West), take Rt. 41 south for 3.2 miles. Turn right onto the paved road leading west up to the Berkshire School. If you continue straight past the Admissions Office (on your right) and then bear left, you will reach the end of the road, which is where the trail for Glen Brook begins. Take note, however, that visitor parking is not allowed here.

To park in the designated area, turn right before the Admissions Office as you drive up Berkshire School Road from Rt. 41, and then turn right again after crossing over a small bridge. Keep following the road as it wends its way around until you come to a stop sign. From here, go straight (north), and then right to the Visitor Parking area next to the tennis courts. You will have gone 0.6 mile from Rt. 41 when you reach the parking area.

To reach the trailhead, walk back through the campus to the southwest end of the school, where Glen Brook flows nearby in the woods to your right. At the end of the paved road, follow the road, now gravel, as it continues. Within 75 feet you will come to a green-and white-marked trail on your left. Take that trail and follow it uphill, going west for 0.1 mile. When you come to a point where the path levels off momentarily, look to your right and you will see Glen Brook only 30–40 feet away. Bushwhack over to the brook and you should be close to the three cascades, which can be observed from the top of the south bank.

If you return to the green/white trail and follow it farther west, it will take you across Glen Brook via a footbridge and then, in less than 0.3 mile, to a glen where the brook can be seen tumbling down from a great height into an artificially created reservoir. It is quiet and scenic here.

There are some cascades farther upstream, high above the reservoir, but there are no trails leading up to them. They are thus, for all practical purposes, inaccessible.

Additional Points of Interest: At an elevation of 850 feet, the area around Berkshire School provides an excellent launching point for a hike up to the higher elevations of Mt. Washington State Forest.[2] Historical records mention a Bridal Veil Falls, located in Royce's Ravine. This may be an earlier name for one of the cascades on Glen Brook, or it may indicate another waterfall in the general area.[3]

Egremont is noted not only for its vistas, but also for its caves. The most famous of these is Growling Bear Cave—one of the Bats' Den group of caves on Jug End Mountain—which sports a 2–3-foot waterfall in its interior.[4]

4. Race Brook Falls

Location: South of South Egremont (Berkshire County)
Mt. Washington State Forest
DeLorme Massachusetts Atlas & Gazetteer: p. 43, J30
Fee: None
Hours: Open continuously
Views: Head-on
Accessibility: An uphill hike of nearly 1.0 mile one way
Degree of Difficulty: Moderate to Difficult to reach the lower and upper falls; Difficult to reach the falls in between

Description: Race Brook Falls are formed on Race Brook, a small stream that rises from a col between Mt. Race and Mt. Everett and flows into Dry Brook just east of Rt. 41. The waterfalls consist of a series of five cascades, with the first (the lowermost) being the largest and most spectacular at nearly 100 feet high.[1] There is a wonderful view of the valley from the top of this cascade.

The second fall, which is 30 feet high and fairly inclined, can be seen just upstream from the top of the first fall. Farther up is the third fall, which is actually a series of smaller cascades totaling well over 30 feet in height. The fourth fall is absolutely gorgeous, with water cascading 60 feet down onto boulders that are brown and covered with algae, with smatterings of green moss. Hikers will marvel at the first fall, but the fourth fall is a close rival in terms of sheer splendor. The fifth fall, like the third cascade, consists of a series of smaller cascades, totaling 30 feet or more.

You'll know when you have reached the top of the ravine, where the fifth fall can be glimpsed, for the stream suddenly flattens out and becomes docile. It is in these wetlands that Race Brook takes form, illustrating the concept behind the word "watershed."[2]

History: The falls were named after William Race, an early pioneer who lived in the valley in the mid-1700s. Race was involved in a rent dispute and was killed by a party of debt-collectors sent by land baron Robert Livingston. The brook seems aptly named, for the

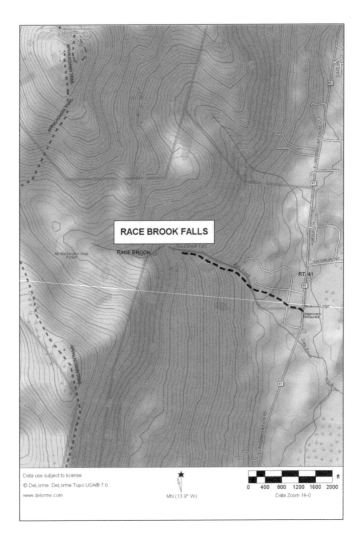

stream truly *races* down the side of the mountain at terrifying speeds during spring's snowmelt.

For those interested in spending time in the area, the ideal place to stay is Race Brook Lodge (Web site, www.rblodge.com), which is located next to Race Brook. The falls can be readily accessed by following Race Brook upstream from the inn.

Directions: From South Egremont (junction of Rtes. 41 South & 23 West), drive south for 5.0 miles. Pull into the parking area for Mt. Race and Mt. Everett, which will be on your right. If you are staying at the Race Brook Lodge, continue south for another 0.4 mile.

A well-marked, heavily used trail proceeds southwest from the parking lot for Mt. Race and Mt. Everett, and begins the long trek up the mountain. After hiking uphill for a distance, you will reach a junction where the Loop Trail (on your right) takes you down to the base of the lowermost fall for great views. This vantage point provides a more than adequate payoff for any hiker with limited time or little inclination to continue climbing farther.

From the base of the lowermost fall, continue along the loop trail, which will lead to the top of the fall. In the process, roughly halfway up, you can walk over to a rocky promontory that affords excellent views of the fall.

From here, try to stay as close as you can to the stream as you continue the hike up so that you won't miss any of the upper falls—all of which take a fair amount of scrambling to get to. If you wish to avoid excessive scrambling, skip the middle two falls and proceed directly uphill along the main trail to the base of the fourth fall.

From the base of the fourth waterfall, the blue-blazed trail temporarily pulls away from the stream, but then returns to follow the stream higher up. From here it is possible to scramble over to a fifth waterfall, which is recessed in the gorge.

Less than 0.2 mile farther upstream, the trail passes by a tiny flume-like cascade. Continuing west along the trail will eventually take you up to the white-blazed Appalachian Trail.

It is also possible to access Race Brook Falls by hiking along the Appalachian National Scenic Trail between Mt. Race and Mt. Everett, and then descending to the falls via the Race Brook trail.

Race Brook Falls, 1998.

5. Bear Rock Falls

Location: South of South Egremont (Berkshire County)
Mt. Washington State Forest
DeLorme Massachusetts Atlas & Gazetteer: p. 43, L29
Fee: None
Hours: Open continuously
Views: Limited; looking down from top of fall
Accessibility: Nearly 3.0-mile hike one way
Degree of Difficulty: Difficult, because of the length of the hike

Description: Bear Rock Falls[1] is formed on Bear Rock Stream, a small brook that rises from the outlet at Plantain Pond and flows into Schenob Brook slightly north of the Massachusetts/Connecticut border.

The cascade is quite high (some sources indicate a height of up to 100 feet), but it is broken up into sections and difficult, if not nearly impossible, to see from the top except for the first section immediately below. At the top, the stream drops through a short chasm before it plummets precipitously over the edge of the escarpment. Fortunately, although you cannot get great views of Bear Rock Falls, there are grand vistas of the valley below from the rocky precipice next to Bear Rock Stream.

There is also an unnamed 15-foot-high waterfall on a little stream that drops over a ledge 0.1 mile south of Bear Rock Falls, downstream from a spur trail that leads from the Appalachian National Scenic Trail to the nearby Laurel Ridge campsite. The stream then continues down nearly vertically, producing additional cascades as it rushes down to the lowlands.

History: Depending on the source, Bear Rock Falls was named either for a bear-sighting at the falls or from the fall's close proximity to Bear Mountain, a huge block of rock that forms the southern slope of nearby Sages Ravine. In either case the falls do cascade over a considerable portion of *bare* rock, if you'll pardon the pun.

Directions: *From the Race Brook Falls trail*—When the Race Brook trail reaches the white-blazed Appalachian National Scenic Trail north of the summit of Mt. Race (see "Race Brook Falls" for directions), turn left and follow the Appalachian National Scenic Trail south for 1.8 miles. When you come to Bear Rock Stream, follow it left for less than 0.05 mile to the top of the falls.

From Upper Sages Ravine—From the crossing over Sages Brook [see "Sages Ravine (Upper)" for directions], follow the white-blazed Appalachian National Scenic Trail east initially and then north for 1.4 miles. When you come to Bear Rock Stream, cross over it and immediately follow the brook downstream to the top of the falls. If you reach the area of Plantain Pond, you have gone 0.3 mile too far north.

The waterfall is best seen from the top, even though the views are limited. Descending to the base of the falls is ill-advised and dangerous. The slopes are nearly vertical. Because the views are limited, this hike is best as a side trip if you are already on the Appalachian National Scenic Trail.

6. Falls on Sages Ravine Brook

Location: Near Massachusetts/Connecticut border
(Berkshire County)
DeLorme Massachusetts Atlas & Gazetteer: p. 43, L30
Fee: None
Hours: Open continuously
Views: Lateral view, looking over from top of bridge
Accessibility: Roadside

Description: This waterfall is formed on Sages Ravine Brook, a small stream that rises in the hills northeast of Mt. Ashley and flows into Schenob Brook in Connecticut just below the Massachusetts border.

The waterfall is 15 feet high and very picturesque, framed by the stone bridge that spans it.[1] Several smaller cascades can be seen upstream from the bridge.

History: The ravine was named after the Sage family, who operated a mill in the 1800s at the terminus of the gorge. The most prominent member of the Sage family was Zachias Sage, a Revolutionary War soldier.[2] Within time other mills were established nearby, including a forge. The foundations of these early mills are visible today from the east side of the bridge.

Directions: From South Egremont (junction of Rtes. 41 South & 23 West), proceed south on Rt. 41 for 7.9 miles. Park immediately at a little pull-off on your right after crossing over a bridge, where a blue-colored sign can be seen that reads "Scenic Road. Next 6.2 miles."

The main cascade can be seen by looking straight down from the east side of the bridge. Smaller cascades directly upstream can be observed from the west side of the bridge.

Sage Brook Falls circa 1910.

7. Sages Ravine (Lower Falls)

Location: Near Massachusetts/Connecticut border
(Berkshire County) Mt. Washington State Forest
DeLorme Massachusetts Atlas & Gazetteer: p. 43, L29
Fee: None
Hours: Open continuously
Views: Head-on and lateral
Accessibility: 1.0-mile hike (one way) up to Appalachian National
Scenic Trail; 1.5-mile hike (one way) to Sages Ravine Campsite
Degree of Difficulty: Very difficult; strenuous climb with much
scrambling. Do not continue into the interior of the gorge unless you
are comfortable scrambling up and down a steep, forested slope.

Description: There are over a dozen falls formed on the lower section of Sages Ravine Brook, a small stream that rises in the hills
northeast of Mt. Ashley and flows into Schenob Brook in Connecticut
just below the Massachusetts border.[1] Of these, the most notable is
Twin Falls, consisting of a 30-foot-high cascade that drops into a pothole-shaped pool of water. This is immediately followed by a lower,
25-foot-high cascade, which goes off diagonally from the upper one.
There is also a 12-foot-high fall farther upstream that drops into
a beautiful pool with high rock walls on both sides. In addition,
there are many smaller but beautiful cascades and falls interspersed
through the ravine.

Sages Ravine is a tortuous gorge cut by Sages Ravine Brook. It
rises steeply, gaining 400 feet in elevation in less than a mile.

Several hundred yards upstream from Under Mountain Road
(Rt. 41) is a phenomenon that is well worth seeing during the summer when the water volume is low. For a distance of several hundred
feet, the brook actually disappears from sight, traveling underground
until it resurfaces again downstream.

Twin Falls, Sages Ravine circa 1910.

Directions: From South Egremont (junction of Rtes. 41 South & 23 West), take Rt. 41 south for 7.9 miles to the Massachusetts/Connecticut border. Just after crossing the border and going over a small stone bridge spanning Sages Ravine Brook, turn into a small pull-off on your right next to a blue-colored sign that reads "Scenic Road. Next 6.2 miles." Follow a trail (more like a road in the beginning) that proceeds west into the woods, paralleling the south bank of Sages Ravine.

After 0.3 mile or so of fairly flat terrain, you will reach the beginning of Sages Ravine. From here, there are no real trails to follow. The hiking can be treacherous and should be avoided by those who are not confident in their ability to negotiate blowdown, rock scrambles, and constantly changing elevation. At the beginning of the ravine, you will see several cascades, which make the hike to this point worthwhile even if you do not explore the main part of lower Sages Ravine.

8. Sages Ravine (Upper Falls)

Location: Near Massachusetts/Connecticut border
(Berkshire County) Mt. Washington State Forest
DeLorme Massachusetts Atlas & Gazetteer: p. 43, L29
Fee: None
Hours: Open continuously
Views: Head-on and lateral
Accessibility: More than 1.5-mile hike
Degree of Difficulty: Moderate to Difficult

Description: Although the falls formed in the upper section of Sages Ravine are not as dynamic and awe-inspiring as those contained in the lower section, neither are they as foreboding and difficult to access. Within a 0.2-mile length of stream, you will see multiple cascades and falls, all from the relative safety of the Appalachian National Scenic Trail.[1]

Directions: From South Egremont (junction of Rtes. 41 South & 23 West), go south on Rt. 41 for 0.1 mile. Turn right onto Mount Washington Road and drive west initially, and then south, for a total of 11.4 miles. Along the way, take note of the following landmarks: at 3.3 miles you will cross over the town line (Mount Washington Road becomes East Street from this point on); at 7.5 miles you will pass through the intersection where Plantain Road comes in on the left and Cross Road comes in on the right; at 8.7 miles you will pass by the headquarters for Mt. Washington State Forest.

When you have gone a total of 11.4 miles, pull into the Appalachian Mountain Club (AMC) parking area on your left. You are nearly at the Massachusetts/Connecticut state line. Take note that the road from this point on (going south into Connecticut) is seasonal, and closed during the winter.

Follow the unmarked trail (which appears more like a road) that leads east from the parking area. In over 0.1 mile you will find yourself paralleling Sages Ravine Brook and will see an impressive AMC cabin off in the woods to your right. By the time you reach 0.7 mile, the trail has pulled away from Sages Ravine Brook. Shortly, you

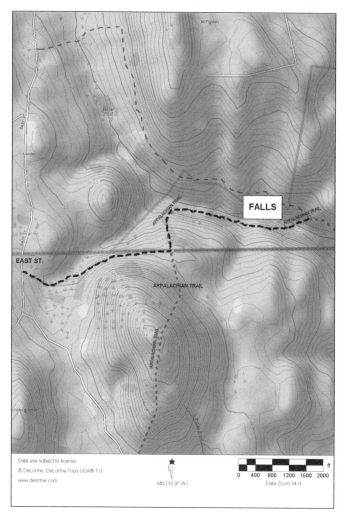

will come out to the white-blazed Appalachian National Scenic Trail. Turn left and begin following the Appalachian National Scenic Trail northeast. In 0.05 mile you will come to a junction where a sign indicates that you are entering Sages Ravine. To the right is the Paradise Lane Trail, which leads to Rt. 41 in 3.2 miles.

Continue straight ahead on the Appalachian National Scenic Trail, going steeply downhill into the depths of the ravine. After 0.2 mile you will be at the level of Sages Ravine Brook. Continue following the trail downstream, now heading east for less than 0.3 mile, and you will reach the Sages Brook Campsite (located on the opposite side of the stream). The waterfalls in upper Sages Ravine are found along the next 0.5 mile of the Appalachian National Scenic Trail.

Continue east along the Appalachian National Scenic Trail, all the time paralleling the south bank of Sages Ravine Brook. Within 0.2 mile you will pass by a pretty cascade on your left where the stream drops into an oval-shaped chasm. A short distance farther downstream, the trail crosses over a tiny log footbridge where a cascading stream comes down the sloping side of the ravine on your right, producing a series of small cascades as it drops into Sages Ravine Brook. As soon as you cross over the footbridge, you will come to a tiny flume fall on your left. Then, in 0.05 mile, you will pass by a pretty, 10-foot-high cascade where Sages Ravine Brook turns left in a bend, allowing you to look back at the fall head-on. Downstream from here, a tiny tributary to Sages Brook Ravine comes cascading in on the left, next to a tiny cascade on the main stream. Within another 0.2 mile or less you will come to where the Appalachian National Scenic Trail crosses Sages Ravine Brook. Just upstream and downstream from the stone crossing can be seen small cascades as well as a small rock shelter cave on the south bank.

This is your turnaround point unless you are committed to hiking farther downstream east into the trailless maw of lower Sages Ravine (if so, avoid the revegetation area next to the crossing) or wish to continue north along the Appalachian National Scenic Trail to Bear Rock Falls, 1.4 miles beyond, or to the top of the Race Brook Falls trail, 3.2 miles distant.

MT. GREYLOCK
STATE RESERVATION
(Berkshire County)

Cascading falls on Mt. Greylock circa 1910.

Introduction

As Massachusetts's tallest and most regal mountain, it seems only fitting that Mt. Greylock (3,487 feet) should possess waterfalls in great abundance—and it does. There are at least four notable cascades that have long histories of regular visitation, as well as numerous other

Summit of Mt. Greylock.

drops and plunges on streams that run down from the upper reaches of Mt. Greylock in all directions of the compass.

The waterfalls are located in the Mt. Greylock State Reservation—a 10,000-acre park that is capped, at Mt. Greylock's summit, by a 90-foot-high granite tower. The tower is a memorial to all Massachusetts veterans who served during wartime. Also to be found on the mountaintop is Bascom Lodge, a small inn that was constructed

Early view of summit, Mt. Greylock circa 1900.

by the Civilian Conservation Corps (CCC) in 1937[1] and which today is run by the Appalachian Mountain Club (AMC) and the Massachusetts Department of Environment Management. The Mt. Greylock State Reservation was Massachusetts's first state park, having been acquired by the Commonwealth in 1898. The Appalachian National Scenic Trail runs right over Mt. Greylock's summit.

Mt. Greylock is surrounded by smaller mountains, including Saddleball (3,238'), Mt. Williams (2,951'), Mt. Fitch (3,110'), Mt. Prospect (2,690'), Stony Ledge (2,580'), and Ragged Mt. (2,451')—all of which are higher than any other peak in Massachusetts, Rhode Island, or Connecticut.

Rockwell Road, leading up to the summit of Mt. Greylock from Lanesborough, was built between 1906 and 1907. It was named after Francis W. Rockwell, one of the original Mt. Greylock commissioners appointed by Governor Roger Wolcott in 1898. Notch Road approaches the summit from the opposite side of Mt. Greylock, coming up from North Adams.

Bear in mind that the roads leading up to Mt. Greylock's summit are closed during the winter and spring until May 14, so schedule your trips accordingly unless you plan to ascend by snowshoes or cross-country skis.

DIRECTIONS TO THE MT. GREYLOCK VISITOR CENTER

From Pittsfield (junction of Rtes. 20 West and 7), drive north on Rt. 7 for nearly 7 miles and turn right onto North Main Street at a sign for Mt. Greylock State Reservation.

From South Williamstown (junction of Rtes. 7 & 43 East), drive south on Rt. 7 for 9.5 miles and turn left onto North Main Street.

Proceed north on North Main Street for 0.7 mile, then bear right at a fork in the road onto Quarry Road. Go east for 0.5 mile and, veering left onto Rockwell Road, continue north, uphill, for another 0.6 mile to the visitor center, on your right. Altogether, you will have driven 1.8 miles from Rt. 7.

9. March Cataract

Location: Upper section of Mt. Greylock State Reservation
DeLorme Massachusetts Atlas & Gazetteer: p. 20, G14
Fee: Modest seasonal fee for parking
Hours: Open continuously
Views: Head-on view from base
Accessibility: Less than 1.0-mile hike one way. Access in winter is more difficult because roads are closed to vehicles.
Degree of Difficulty: Moderate

Description: March Cataract is formed on Hopper Brook, a small stream that rises on the west shoulder of Mt. Greylock and flows into the Green River northeast of South Williamstown. The cascade drops 35–40 feet in a fairly dramatic style.[1] Despite the access roads being closed until May 14, March Cataract—as the name suggests—is best visited in March or early spring when waters are sufficiently vigorous to animate the fall, although you will generally find water running over it year-round. The waterfall is also referred to as March Cataract Falls—an obvious redundancy.

If sufficient water is flowing, the fall can be seen from as far away as the Mt. Greylock Regional High School along Rt. 7 near Williamstown.

On the back of a postcard of March Cataract published by Apple Hill Design, mention is made of an odd natural rock sculpture near the base of the fall that resembles a cat. You can form your own conclusions about this rock when you visit the waterfall.

Directions: From the visitors' center on Rockwell Road (1.8 miles from Rt. 7), continue northeast on Rockwell Road for over 5.2 miles, and turn left onto Sperry Road. Follow Sperry Road downhill, going north, for 0.6 mile until you reach the campsite area. The trailhead for March Cataract is on the side of the road opposite the entrance building (to your right) and leads northeast to the cascade in less than 1.0 mile.

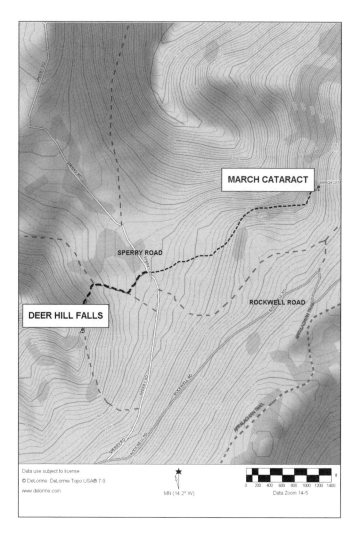

Data use subject to license
© DeLorme. DeLorme Topo USA® 7.0
www.delorme.com

MN (14.2° W)

0   200   400   600   800   1000   1200   1400

ft

Data Zoom 14-5

March Cataract, 1998.

10. Deer Hill Falls

Location: Upper section of Mt. Greylock
DeLorme Massachusetts Atlas & Gazetteer: p. 20, H14
Fee: Modest seasonal fee for parking
Hours: Open continuously
Views: Head-on
Accessibility: 0.5-mile hike one way. Access in winter is more difficult because roads are closed to vehicles.
Degree of Difficulty: Moderate

Description: Deer Hill Falls is formed on Roaring Brook, a small stream that rises on the east slope of Mt. Greylock and flows into the Green River. The fall is 35–40 feet in height.[1] There are smaller cascades that are easily seen from the trail, just downstream from the footbridge.

Directions: From the visitors' center, drive northeast up Rockwell Road for over 5.2 miles and turn left onto Sperry Road. Follow Sperry Road north for 0.6 mile to the campgrounds and park there.

From the entrance building, walk several hundred feet north along Sperry Road until you reach a kiosk. Turn left at the kiosk, following signs to "Roaring Brook, the Circular, and Deer Hill Falls." After a hundred feet you will reach a parking area next to a modern outhouse. The Roaring Brook trailhead starts at the parking area.

Follow the trail gradually downhill for less than 0.2 mile. Cross over Roaring Brook via a footbridge, and then immediately turn left onto the Deer Hill Trail. Look for cascades on your left in less than 0.05 mile as you proceed downhill. Continuing farther, the Deer Hill trail takes you down and around to the base of Deer Hill Falls in less than 0.3 mile. It is a fairly steep descent.

If you wish to undertake a longer and more adventurous hike to the fall, it is also possible to approach the cascade starting from the Roaring Brook Trailhead in the valley below. To access the lower Roaring Brook trailhead, start at South Williamstown (junction of Rtes. 7 & 43 East), drive south on Rt. 7 for 1.6 miles, and then turn left onto Roaring Brook Road. Approaching from Lanesborough, drive 7.8 miles north on Rt. 7 from the entrance road to the Mt. Greylock State Reservation (North Main Street), and turn right onto Roaring Brook Road. Drive uphill on Roaring Brook Road, going east, for 0.5 mile and park in the small designated area on your left. From here, follow the Roaring Brook Trail, which leads steadily and steeply up to the Sperry Campground. At 0.2 mile before you reach Sperry Road, you will arrive at a footbridge spanning Roaring Brook. Turn right before crossing the bridge and follow a steep trail down to the base of Deer Hill Falls in less than 0.3 mile.

11. Falls on Peck's Brook

Location: Mt. Greylock State Reservation
DeLorme Massachusetts Atlas & Gazetteer: p. 21, H16
Fee: None
Hours: Open continuously
Views: Lateral views, looking down
Accessibility: 1.0-mile hike (one way) from near the top of
Mt. Greylock. Access in winter is more difficult because roads
are closed to vehicles.
Degree of Difficulty: Moderate to Difficult, because of change
in elevation

Description: There are multiple falls formed on Peck's Brook, a small
stream that rises near the top of Mt. Greylock and flows into the Hoosic River at Adams. The cascades are formed near the Peck's Brook
shelter, a refuge for campers at the top of the junction of two huge
gorges formed by the confluence of Peck's Brook and its tributary.
It is a spectacular setting, with the streams joining together approximately 80–100 feet below. The setting is even more spectacular if you
visit during times of heavy water flow.

The main falls are formed in the chasm directly in front of the
shelter and are composed of two distinct sections: The upper section
consists of a 10-foot-high cascade[1] followed by several smaller drops
as the stream plunges 25 feet into a chasm. The upper cascade can
be easily viewed from the shelter by looking to your right.

The lower cascade is more difficult to view and can only be
glimpsed in part. The stream gushes out through a narrowing in the
chasm, cascades 25 feet, and then drops another 10 feet through a
series of boulders. To view this cascade you will have to walk away
from the shelter towards Peck's Brook's tributary, and then look
back and down into the gorge.

In early spring, Peck's Brook's tributary also becomes a dynamic, cascading stream, bouncing down a very steep incline as though it were a stairway. A 10-foot-high cascade can be seen about two-thirds of the way down the stream.

There are more falls on Peck's Brook upstream from the shelter. These range in height from 3–6 feet and total 7 or 8 in number, depending upon how you count them. At 0.1 mile upstream from the shelter, you will come to the base of a towering 35–40-foot-high cascade.

History: The Gould Trail was named after Charles Gould, who operated a farm at the end of Gould Road.[2] Previously the trail was known as Peck's Brook Trail.[3]

Directions: From the visitors' center, drive steadily uphill on Rockwell Road, going northeast for 6.7 miles (or 1.5 miles beyond Sperry Road). From the junction of Rockwell Road and Notch Road (near the summit of Mt. Greylock), park in the dirt lot opposite Notch Road. Follow the blue-blazed Gould Trail steadily downhill for 1.0 mile until you reach the sign pointing to Peck's Brook Shelter, on your right. Follow the side path downhill for 0.1 mile to the shelter.

12. Money Brook Falls

Location: Upper section of Mt. Greylock
DeLorme Massachusetts Atlas & Gazetteer: p. 20, F15
Fee: None
Hours: Open continuously
Views: Head-on view from base
Accessibility: 0.8-mile hike one way. Access in winter is more difficult because roads are closed to vehicles.
Degree of Difficulty: Moderate to Difficult because of elevation change

Description: Money Brook Falls is formed on Money Brook, a small stream that rises on the southwest shoulder of Mt. Williams and flows into Hopper Brook northwest of Mt. Greylock. The waterfall is approximately 40 feet high.[1] Like March Cataract, Money Brook Falls can be seen from the valley, especially during early spring.

History: Money Brook Falls has an interesting history associated with it, which Clay Perry, in *New England's Buried Treasure*, narrates at some length. Between 1765 and 1783 a gang of counterfeiters allegedly built a makeshift cabin by the stream, where they secretly minted Spanish dollars and Pine Tree shillings. According to the story, which may be more fanciful than factual, a hunter overheard the crooks busily at work and reported their activities to the authorities. The thieves were never apprehended, however. By the time the sheriff arrived, there was nothing to take into custody except the tool chest.[2]

In earlier days the stream was called Spectre Brook, supposedly because ghosts of dead rogues kept watch at the entrance to the glen.[3] The upper part of Money Brook Falls has also been called Sky Falls.[4]

Directions: From North Adams (junction of Rtes. 8 South & 2), take Rt. 2 west for 1.3 miles. Turn left onto Notch Road and drive south for 5.0 miles, going uphill most of the time. The parking area for Money Brook Falls will be on your right.

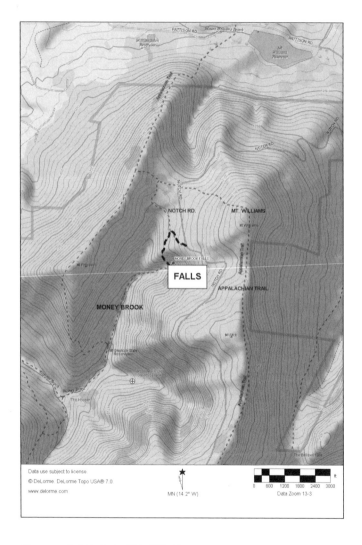

If you are approaching from the summit of Mt. Greylock after coming up Rockwell Road, proceed north along Notch Road. As soon as you pass by the trailhead for the Thunderbolt Trail, continue north for roughly another 2.0 miles. Shortly after you cross over a small stream (which is Money Brook) and wind around a series of curves, look for a trailhead on your left. You will see signs pointing the way to Money Brook Falls. Follow the trail downhill for 0.8 mile to the fall.

Money Brook Falls can also be accessed from the base of Mt. Greylock. From Williamstown (junction of Rtes. 2 & 43), drive south on Rt. 43 for 2.4 miles and turn left (southeast) into the entrance for Mt. Hope Park. Cross over a stone bridge spanning the Green River and continue southwest on Hopper Road for roughly 1.0 mile. Then turn left and drive 0.5 mile southeast to the end of the road, where parking is available. Begin the hike from the gate, following the main trail east for 0.2 mile. When you come to the junction of Money Brook Trail and the Hopper Trail, bear left and follow the Money Brook Trail uphill for over 2.0 miles to the fall.

Cascading falls on Mt. Greylock circa 1910.

ROUTE 7

Campbell Falls circa 1920.

Introduction

Route 7 is a major highway that runs north-south through western Massachusetts, extending 55 miles from Williamstown to Sheffield. Part of the northern section of the road follows along the Green River; the southern section parallels the Housatonic River.

In past centuries the route was a footpath used by the Mahicans, an Algonquin people, enabling them to reach the seashore during summers to gather clams and catch fish. Later, the section of the road near Great Barrington became known as the Great Road because it was so heavily traveled by expeditions and warring parties during the French and Indian War. In 1920 the road became known as the New York-Berkshire-Burlington Way. Finally, in 1926, the federal government changed the name to US Route 7.

13. Falls at Mt. Hope Park

Location: Sweets Corner (Berkshire County)
Mt. Hope Park
DeLorme Massachusetts Atlas & Gazetteer: p. 20, E13
Fee: None
Hours: Open daily from sunrise to sunset
Views: Head-on
Accessibility: 100-foot walk one way
Degree of Difficulty: Easy

Description: This small cascade is formed on the Green River just upstream from the river's confluence with Hopper Brook.[1] The Green River rises south of New Ashford from two branches. After 11 miles it flows into the Hoosic River in Williamstown.[2] Its name derives from the supposed greenish hue of the water. Native Americans, however, called it *Waumpaniksepoot*, meaning "White River."[3] Hopper Brook was named for the notch it rises from, which was thought to resemble a grain hopper.[4]

The cascades total just 4–5 feet, but despite their diminutive size they have a pleasing quality because of the nearby presence of Hopper Brook, whose cascading waters along with those of the Green River create a stereophonic effect.[5]

For those wishing to reach the higher regions of the Mt. Greylock State Reservation, Hopper Road can be taken to its end to access the Hopper Trail and Money Brook Trail.

History: Mt. Hope Park was once part of Mt. Hope Farms, a 1,300-acre working farm that served as a major driving force in Williamstown's economic development during the early 1900s. The farmers used genetic science to improve the yield of potatoes and to increase the production of dairy cattle and poultry.[6] Mt. Hope Park is located near what used to be the entrance gate to the farm.

Earlier, from 1767 until after the Civil War, the cascades powered gristmills and sawmills.[7]

The beauty and majesty of the Green River was extolled by William Cullen Bryant in a sixteen-line poem called "Green River," the first four lines of which go as follows:

> Yet pure its waters—its shallows are bright
> With colored pebbles and sparkles of light,
> And clear the depths where its eddies play,
> And dimples deepen and whirl away,[8]

Bryant, who lived in Cummington for parts of his life, was very familiar with the river, and obviously enchanted by it.

Directions: From Williamstown (junction of Rtes. 2 & 43), drive south on Rt. 43 for 2.4 miles. From South Williamstown (junction of Rtes. 7 & 43), go northeast for 2.3 miles.

Turn east on Hopper Road into the entrance for Mt. Hope Park. Cross over a stone bridge spanning the Green River, and immediately turn left. Drive less than 100 feet to the end of the road and park to your right. The cascades are 100 feet away and can be clearly viewed from a point near the confluence of Hopper Brook and the Green River.

Green River circa 1900.

14. Falls on Ashford Brook

Location: New Ashford (Berkshire County)
DeLorme Massachusetts Atlas & Gazetteer: p. 20, I11
Fee: None
Hours: Open continuously
Restrictions: Posted land; stay at roadside
Views: Limited lateral view
Accessibility: Roadside

Description: The falls are formed on Ashford Brook, a small stream that rises southeast of New Ashford and flows into the Green River. The waterfall consists of several drops, beginning directly under the bridge.[1]

History: The falls on Ashford Brook are located next to the Mill on the Floss Restaurant, which is historically significant, having once been part of a seventeenth-century farmhouse. The name of the restaurant is taken from the title of a novel by the Victorian English author George Eliot.

The falls and the restaurant are not the only points of interest in New Ashford. The hamlet is also home to Red Bat Cave, which during its heyday was a well-promoted and popular natural wonder.[2] Unfortunately, the cave has been closed to the public for many years now and has fallen into obscurity.

In earlier days New Ashford was referred to as the "Switzer-land of the Berkshires"[3] because of its proximity to the Mt. Greylock massif and the Taconic Range. This sobriquet was also applied to Florida, a much loftier nearby town,[4] which suggests that the analogy was probably generic to the area, rather than specific to one village.

Directions: The falls can be reached either by driving south on Rt. 7 for 4.1 miles from South Williamstown (junction of Rtes. 7 & 43), or heading north on Rt. 7 for 5.4 miles from the Mt. Greylock Auto Road intersection.

The falls are posted as private and can only be viewed from roadside along Rt. 7, or by looking down from the top of the tiny bridge that crosses Ashford Brook and leads to the Mill on the Floss Restaurant and Carriage House Motel.

Nearby Red Bat Cave was also a popular attraction. Postcard 1920.

15. Lulu Cascade

Location: Northwest of Pittsfield (Berkshire County)
Pittsfield State Forest
DeLorme Massachusetts Atlas & Gazetteer: p. 32, A7
Fee: Seasonal park entrance fee
Hours: Open sunrise to sunset
Restrictions: Observe rules and regulations posted at park.
Accessibility: 0.1-mile walk one way
Views: Lateral
Degree of Difficulty: Easy to Moderate

Description: Lulu Cascade is a small falls formed on Lulu Brook, a little stream that rises between Berry Mountain and Honwee Mountain and flows into Onota Lake (the "Lake of the White Deer")[1] after merging with Parker Brook and Hawthorne Brook.[2] The falls are located in the Pittsfield State Forest, which today encompasses nearly 10,000 acres of land.[3]

The main cascade is over 6 feet in height and drops into a pretty pool. There are several smaller cascades populating the stream, but none are able to match the main waterfall in size or charm.

History: The roads and buildings that intersperse the park today were constructed by the Civilian Conservation Corps (CCC), an organization created by President Franklin D. Roosevelt during the Great Depression to provide employment to thousands of out-of-work laborers. At the same time, the program also served to improve the country's forest and recreational resources. The program lasted from 1933 to 1941 and, during its peak, supervised 10,000 workers in 51 camps throughout Massachusetts. The workers were called "Pine Cone Johnnies," a tribute to that legendary American tree-planter, Johnny Appleseed.

The name of the cascade arose from a tragedy that occurred many years ago, when a logger's daughter named Lulu drowned at the base of the cascade.[4]

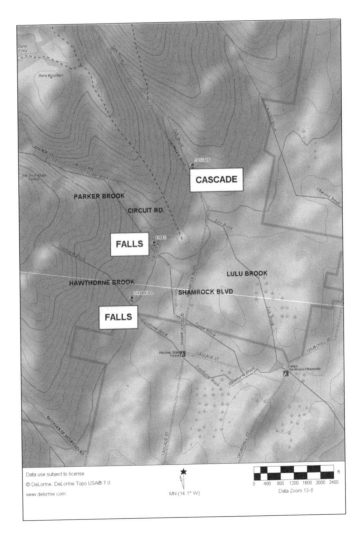

Onota Lake circa 1910.

Directions: From Pittsfield (junction of Rtes. 7 and 20 West), drive west on Rt. 20 (West Housatonic Street) for 0.7 mile, then turn right onto Merrium Street and drive north for 0.5 mile. When you come to West Street, turn left and proceed west for 1.9 miles. Then turn right onto Churchill Street and drive north for 1.6 miles until you reach Cascade Street (note: ignore the first left-hand turn for Cascade Street, at 0.6 mile). Turn left onto Cascade Street and drive west. At 0.5 mile, bear right where a road comes in on your left and continue for less than 0.2 mile to the contact station (entrance booth) to Pittsfield State Forest. From the entrance, drive straight ahead for 0.6 mile. Park in an area on your left before a little bridge that spans Lulu Brook.

From the parking area, walk up to the bridge and follow the "Lulu Brook Foot Trail" (marked by blue-colored triangles) along the east bank of the stream. The cascades are encountered within 0.1 mile.

The trail continues beyond the first grouping of cascades, following the stream uphill. Additional small cascades can be seen as you make your way upstream, but none are of any significant height. If you do continue up this trail—which is a lovely walk—it is possible, at any time, to climb uphill for 10–20 feet and reach the wide and well-maintained Honwee Circuit Trail (marked by yellow-colored triangles), which parallels the Lulu Brook Trail and provides a much easier walk back to the parking lot.

Additional Point of Interest: While visiting the Pittsfield State Forest, a worthwhile side trip takes you up to Berry Pond, which, at an elevation of 2,150 feet, is the highest natural body of water in Massachusetts (analogous to Lake Tear-of-the-Clouds in the High Peaks Region of the Adirondacks). The pond was named after William Berry, a Revolutionary War soldier.[5]

To get there from the parking lot at Lulu Cascades, drive across the bridge spanning Lulu Brook and follow a one-way paved road, which takes you high above the west side of the Lulu Brook Ravine. After a little over 1.5 miles, the road turns left and then begins to descend. At 2.2 miles you will pass by Berry Pond on your left. Parking is available if you wish to explore the area more fully. In 4 miles you will return to the main part of the park and down to the Forest Headquarters.

16. Parker Brook Cascades

Location: Northwest of Pittsfield (Berkshire County)
Pittsfield State Forest
DeLorme Massachusetts Atlas & Gazetteer: p. 32, A7
Fee: Seasonal entrance fee
Hours: Open daily sunrise to sunset
Restrictions: Observe rules and regulations posted at park.
Views: Head-on and lateral
Accessibility: 0.5-mile walk one way
Degree of Difficulty: Easy to Moderate

Description: This pretty waterfall is formed on Parker Brook, a small stream that rises from Tilden Swamp and flows into Onota Lake.[1] The waterfall consists of a 5-foot drop followed immediately by a long, 6-foot-high cascade covered in luscious moss. When viewed from the bottom, the cascade is very picturesque and, in many ways, much prettier than the more heralded Lulu Cascade.

Just downstream from the falls and at the beginning of the Parker Brook ravine is a little chasm, where a slab of rock has slid into the stream creating a roofed tunnel under which the stream passes.

Although additional cascades are located farther upstream near Tilden Swamp,[2] these are no more pronounced than the other tiny cascades formed on the streams in the Pittsfield State Forest, and none truly call out to be visited.

Virtually all of the paths in the Pittsfield Forest lead up to the white-blazed Taconic Crest Trail, which runs along the crest of the Taconic Range for 35 miles in a north-south orientation, with the average elevation of the trail being 2,200 feet.

Directions: See "Lulu Cascade" for directions to the entrance station to Pittsfield State Forest.

Immediately after entering into the park, turn left and drive 0.1 mile to the parking area on your right by the Forest Headquarters/Ski Lodge.

There are two easy ways to get to the falls: the scenic way, or by following the main road.

1) The scenic way follows part of the Tranquility Trail, which is a 0.7-mile long, paved walkway designed for all levels of ability, including those who are wheelchair-dependent (note: electric wheelchairs are permitted). The paved walkway has an almost fairy-tale quality to it, with sections covered in a thick coating of green moss that looks like a green carpet.

On the side of the road opposite the parking lot, follow the Tranquility Trail as it crosses Parker Brook and immediately bears right. Proceed northwest on the walkway, with Parker Brook to your right, avoiding any initial turns to the left. After 0.2 mile the walkway begins to curve to the left (ultimately returning to the parking area). This is as far as wheelchairs will be able to go. From here, walk straight ahead into the woods, following an unmarked old road/path. In less than 0.2 mile you will come to views of the falls on your right and then up to an intersection with the blue-triangle-blazed trail. Turn right, cross over the wide footbridge, and then make your way down to the base of the falls, which is just downstream from the footbridge.

2) From the parking lot, walk northwest along the main automobile road, keeping to the side, for nearly 0.5 mile. You will eventually see signs for the Parker Brook Campsite. Just before you get to where the road becomes one-way with a sign stating "Do not enter," turn left onto a blue-triangle-marked secondary road leading past campsites 16R and 15R. Fifty feet after passing by campsite 15R, turn left and proceed straight towards Parker Brook. When you reach a wide footbridge spanning Parker Brook, scramble downstream to the base of the falls before crossing the stream.

If you walk downstream 50 feet from the base of the falls, you will reach a little chasm where a wide slab of rock lies on top of the streambed, forming a natural tunnel through which the stream passes.

Additional Point of Interest: If you are visiting Parker Brook when limited water is flowing, take note that the stream goes completely underground in the area by the outdoor stadium (near the forest headquarters/ski center). There is no obvious fissure in the stream-bed; the stream merely seeps through the rock and is gone. It serves as a ready reminder of just how predominant and porous the limestone bedrock is in the Berkshire valleys.

17. Hawthorne Brook Cascades

Location: Northwest of Pittsfield (Berkshire County)
Pittsfield State Forest
DeLorme Massachusetts Atlas & Gazetteer: p. 32, A7
Fee: Seasonal parking fee
Hours: Open daily from sunrise to sunset
Restrictions: Observe rules and regulations posted at park.
Views: Lateral, and head-on views from base
Accessibility: 0.3-mile walk (one way) from Parker Brook Cascades; additional 0.1-mile walk (one way) to see upper cascades
Degree of Difficulty: Moderate

Description: The cascades are formed on Hawthorne Brook, a small stream that rises from the southern shoulder of Pine Mountain and later combines with Parker Brook and Lulu Brook to flow into Onota Lake. Hawthorne Brook, unlike Parker Brook and Lulu Brook, is still in its infancy. Its walls are fairly steep and not as rounded and mature-looking as its cousins positioned to its north, whose more powerful streams have cut much deeper and wider ravines.

The main cascade (the one farthest downstream) is 30 feet high and consists of two main tiers. The stream is narrow as it drops over the top, but rapidly spreads out during its descent. The two cascades farther upstream are less distinctive, being considerably more elongated. They are essentially exposed sections of inclined bedrock. Neither cascade is much over 25 feet in height.

Take note of the decaying ruins of an old wooden structure near the edge of the ravine by the upper cascades.

History: The Hawthorne Brook Cascades are located in the Pittsfield State Forest. Pittsfield was originally called Pontoosuc Plantation, *Pontoosuc* being a Mohegan name meaning "land of the winter deer." The name of the area was later changed to honor British statesman

William Pitt.[1] The old name has not been entirely lost, however. To the northeast (north of Pittsfield) lies Pontoosuc Lake.

It seems reasonable to assume that the brook was named after Nathaniel Hawthorne, who lived nearby in Lenox.

Directions: See "Lulu Cascade" for directions to reach the entrance station to Pittsfield State Forest. Then follow the directions given to "Parker Brook Cascades."

From the footbridge above the Parker Brook Cascades, cross over Parker Brook and immediately turn right onto the Parker Brook Trail. Go uphill for 0.05 mile, then turn left, following a spur trail that leads to the Hawthorne Trail in 0.3 mile. The Hawthorne Trail goes both right and left from the spur trail and parallels Hawthorne Brook. Instead of taking the trail, continue straight ahead, bushwhacking down the gradual slope of the ravine for 100–200 feet to Hawthorne Brook. If you have veered slightly to the left, you will end up close to the bottom of the main cascade that has formed on Hawthorne Brook.

Return to the junction of the spur trail with the Hawthorne Trail. This time, take the Hawthorne Trail uphill, heading towards Pine Mountain (2,220 feet). In 0.1 mile you will see a tiny ditch on your left and will quickly come to where the trail veers to the right. At this point go left from the trail, bushwhacking to the stream, which is no more than 50–75 feet away. There are two cascades that can be seen once you have reached the stream.

18. Daniels Brook Chasm & Cascades

Location: West of Lanesboro (Berkshire County)
Pittsfield State Forest
DeLorme Massachusetts Atlas & Gazetteer: p. 20, O8
Fee: None
Hours: Open daily sunrise to sunset
Views: Lateral view from top
Accessibility: 0.5-mile hike one way; longer in winter when access road becomes seasonal 0.1 mile before the trailhead parking
Degree of Difficulty: Moderate

Description: This impressive chasm and its cascades are formed on Daniels Brook, a small stream that rises north of Honwee Mountain and flows into the north end of Onota Lake. The chasm is 100 feet in length and, like a bolt of lightning, zigs and zags as it makes its way through the bedrock, which has been turned upright at a sharp angle. The chasm is deep, very narrowly cut, and unlike anything you would expect to see on a stream that, up until this point, has been modest and unassuming.

A small slide fall leads into the mouth of the chasm. Midway, the stream drops over a 6-foot cascade. At the very end of the chasm is an 8-foot-high cascade that is not easy to see from above, but it can be readily seen from below at the end of the chasm.

Directions: From Pittsfield (junction of Rtes. 7 and 20 West), drive west on Rt. 20 (West Housatonic Street) for 0.7 mile. Turn right onto Merrium Street and drive north for 0.5 mile. When you come to West Street, turn left and proceed west for 1.9 miles. Turn right onto Churchill Street and drive north for 3.7 miles (along the way, at 1.6 miles, you will pass by the left-hand turn for the Pittsfield State Forest). When you come to Potter Mountain Road, turn left and drive uphill, northwest, for 0.4 mile. Turn left into a parking area before crossing over Daniels Brook.

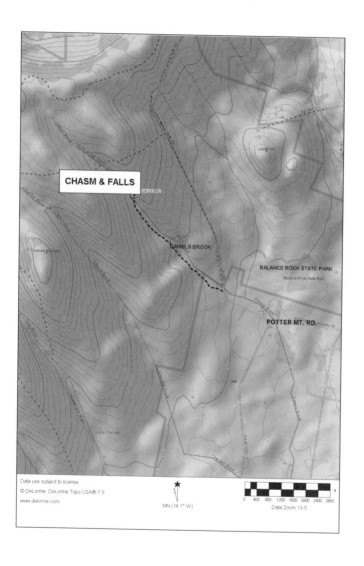

CHASM & FALLS

CHASM FALLS

DANIELS BROOK

Long Hill

BALANCE ROCK STATE PARK

Balance Rock State Park

POTTER MT. RD. MOUNTAIN RD

Howes Mountain

Little Cascade

Data use subject to license.
© DeLorme. DeLorme Topo USA® 7.0
www.delorme.com

MN (14.1° W)

0 400 800 1200 1600 2000 2400 2800
Data Zoom 13-5

If you are approaching from Rt. 7 in Lanesboro, drive to the south end of Pontoosuc Lake, where you will come to a stoplight. Turn onto Hancock Street and drive west for nearly 1.9 miles. When you come to Churchill Street, turn right and drive north for 1.0 mile. Then turn left onto Potter Mountain Road and drive uphill for 0.4 mile to the parking area.

Take note that Potter Mountain Road becomes seasonal and is not plowed 0.1 mile before you reach the trailhead parking.

From the parking area, follow the path/old logging road upstream that parallels Daniels Brook. When you come to a fork in the road, always take the trail that keeps you closest to the stream. In 0.4 mile the trail will take you past the rim of a spectacular chasm on your right, where cascades can be seen.

The bottommost cascade cannot be readily viewed from the top, but can be accessed if you make your way to the bottom of the chasm by backtracking for 50 feet to where the slope becomes much less precipitous and by scampering down the hillside to the level of the stream.

19. Cascades on Shaker Brook

Location: Hancock (Berkshire County)
Hancock Shaker Village
DeLorme Massachusetts Atlas & Gazetteer: p. 32, D5
Fee: None for walk to cascade; fee to tour Shaker Village
Hours: Open daily, 9:30 AM to 5:00 PM
Restrictions: Check in at visitors' center before proceeding on trail.
Views: Lateral
Accessibility: 0.5-mile walk one way.
Degree of Difficulty: Easy

Description: This small, 3-foot-high cascade is formed on Shaker Brook, a small stream that rises on Shaker Mountain and flows into Southwest Brook, north of Richmond Pond. What makes the cascade worth visiting is the vital role it played in the history of Shaker Village, providing a consistent source of power for the Shaker community.[1] Directly above the cascade can be seen a 3-foot-high dam (the Lower Dam), which furnished waterpower to the village. An old rusted pipe next to the cascade and dam is a reminder of the fall's heritage.

One hundred feet farther upstream is the Upper Dam which, though breached, still looms imposingly. Judging by the rock wall set into the east bank, the dam must have topped out at nearly 20 feet high. Foundation ruins are visible along the east bank just downstream from the dam.

A visit to the cascade would not be complete without touring the Shaker Village (fee charged) and gaining a perspective on the dam, the fall, and its relationship to the Shaker community.

History: Hydropower was of vital importance to the Shakers, not only for being a labor-saving device in itself, but for enabling them to produce other labor-saving devices. The Shakers are credited with inventing the screw propeller, the automatic spring, the turbine waterwheel, the common clothespin, the threshing machine, a planing machine, a fertilizing machine, the circular saw, an improved washing machine, a revolving oven, the first flat brooms, and metal pens, just to mention a few of the more recognizable items.[2]

Directions: The trailhead is located at the Hancock Shaker Village on Rt. 20. To get to Shaker Village, drive west from Pittsfield (junction of Rtes. 7 & 20 West) on Rt. 20 for 4.8 miles (0.5 mile west of the intersection with Rt. 41 South). Turn left into the designated parking area for the village.

From the visitors' center, cross over Rt. 20 and then follow an old farm road north across an open field. In 0.3 mile you will come to the edge of the woods. Turn right at a T-intersection and follow the road, now marked by green triangles, as it comes up to and begins paralleling Shaker Brook. Within 0.2 mile you will reach the lower dam and cascade.

Dammed fall on Shaker Brook, 2004.

20. Fall on Roaring Brook

Location: Northeast of Lenox (Berkshire County)
October Mountain State Forest
DeLorme Massachusetts Atlas & Gazetteer: p. 32, G12
Fee: None
Hours: Open continuously
Views: Lateral view, looking down
Accessibility: Less than 0.3-mile walk one way
Degree of Difficulty: Easy to Moderate

Description: This fall is formed on Roaring Brook, a medium-sized stream that rises from the upper regions of the October Mountain State Forest and flows into the Housatonic River after joining with Mill Brook, a much smaller stream.[1] The fall is over 5 feet in height and formed in a section of the gorge that has been cut deeply by the stream. Twenty feet downstream from the base of the waterfall is a row of stones placed across the stream by hikers and campers to form a crude dam and deepen the waters.

On the north bank of the stream and close to the fall is Tory Cave. The cave can be seen only by crossing to the other side of the stream and looking back towards the north bank. Tory Cave is tectonic (formed in a fractured zone in the quartzite) and not solutional (formed by water dissolving the bedrock).[2] It was named after Gideon Smith, a Tory who sought refuge in the cave after being chased from his home in Stockbridge by patriots. Smith later emerged from the cave and was captured, but he managed to survive the Revolutionary War.[3] The cave was later used for a variety of nefarious purposes. Finally, around 1970, the entrance was dynamited. What you see today are the remnants of this historic cave.[4]

A stone wall lines the opposite bank upstream from the cascade, making the stream look channel-like at that point. Then, 0.05 mile farther upstream, are the breached ruins of an old stone dam.

History: October Mountain State Forest is the largest state forest in Massachusetts,[5] encompassing 16,127 acres of land.[6] Originally the land was owned by William C. Whitney, who was Secretary of the Navy under President Grover Cleveland. At that time, 1,000 acres of Whitney's land were used as a game preserve for exotic animals. In 1915 a group of Pittsfield philanthropists pledged $25,000 for the purchase of the Whitney estate. The state added another $35,000, and the lands were eventually purchased for a total price of $60,000.[7]

The name "October Mountain" is attributed to Herman Melville, whose home, Arrowhead, on nearby Holmes Road near Pittsfield, provided a commanding view of the 1,984-foot mountain.[8]

Directions: From Pittsfield (junction of Rtes. 7 & 20 West), go south on Rt. 7 for 3.4 miles. Turn left onto New Lenox Mountain Road at a traffic light and drive east for 1.7 miles (crossing over the Housatonic River at 1.5 miles). Then turn right onto Roaring Brook Road and drive south for 0.4 mile. When you come to a bridge spanning Roaring Brook, park on either side.

Proceeding on foot, follow the blue-blazed trail (an old road) upstream as it parallels the north side of the brook. After over 0.2 mile the trail begins to climb as the walls of the ravine become compressed. In several hundred feet you will reach the main cascade, which is 25 feet below you.

The trail/road follows the stream for well over 0.7 mile farther upstream until it reaches the yellow-blazed ATV trail (which is much more road-like). The hike along this stretch is exceptionally scenic, and you will find yourself deep in the gorge at times. You will see many 1–2-foot cascades, but there are no other significant falls should you continue past the main cascade.

21. Cascades on Mill Brook

Location: Northeast of Lenox (Berkshire County)
October Mountain State Forest
DeLorme Massachusetts Atlas & Gazetteer: p. 32, G12
Fee: None
Hours: Open continuously
Views: Lateral
Accessibility: Roadside

Description: There are a number of small cascades formed on Mill Brook, a small stream that rises from Farnham Reservoir and, along with Roaring Brook, flows into the Housatonic River. The main cascade is 8–10 feet high, quite elongated, and not all that well-defined. The substantial ruins of an old, breached, stone dam can be seen at the top of the cascade.

Although Mill Brook doesn't contain even a single medium-sized waterfall, it does possess a number of 1–2-foot-high cascades and chutes that make a walk along New Lenox Mountain Road (which is dirt-based and eroded if you continue on foot up from the parking area) very enjoyable. If you hike up to the two-tier, 8-foot-high dam (0.4 mile upstream from the parking area), take note that the height of the streambed changes markedly from the top of the dam to the base. This difference in height suggests that there was once a natural waterfall here that was obscured when the dam was constructed.

Directions: From Pittsfield (junction of Rtes. 7 & 20 West), go south on Rt. 7 for 3.4 miles. Turn left onto New Lenox Mountain Road at the traffic light and drive east for 1.7 miles (crossing over the Housatonic River at 1.5 miles). At the intersection with Roaring Brook Road, continue straight ahead (east) for 0.5 mile farther, passing by the main cascade at 0.4 mile. Pull into the small parking area on your right. Take note that there are several small cascades near the parking area. To see the main cascade, walk back down the road for 0.05 mile.

There are also a number of 1–2-foot-high cascades that can be seen by hiking up the road from the parking area. If you have a four-wheel-drive vehicle, there is also the option of continuing by car, but you will then miss out on a pleasant walk and the sound of cascading waters. In less than 0.2 mile from the parking area, you will come to a block-shaped building that may have been an old pump house. Look around and you will see some small cascades here. If you continue hiking uphill for over 0.2 mile farther, you will come to a two-tiered, 8-foot-high dam.

22. Cascades along Overbrook Trail

Location: North of Lenox (Berkshire County)
Pleasant Valley Wildlife Sanctuary
DeLorme Massachusetts Atlas & Gazetteer: p. 32, G7
Fee: Modest fee for nonmembers
Hours: Trails are open dawn to dusk on all days that the nature center is open. The office is open Tuesday through Friday, 9:00 AM to 5:00 PM, and on Saturday, Sunday, and Monday holidays from 10:00 AM to 4:00 PM; on Mondays from the end of June to Columbus Day, the hours are 9:00 AM to 4:00 PM.
Restrictions: Check with office
Views: Head-on and lateral
Accessibility: 0.8-mile hike one way
Degree of Difficulty: Moderate

Description: There are at least 5 distinct cascades formed on a tiny brook that rises from the upper region of Lenox Mountain and flows into one of the several ponds contained at the Pleasant Valley Wildlife Sanctuary.[1] The cascades range in height from 10–20 feet. The first one encountered is a 20-foot-high cascade located where the stream zigzags as it races down the mountain. The second cascade is 15 feet high, and the next two are both 12 feet in height. The last waterfall is a 10-foot-high cascade that typically carries little water because of the limited watershed above it.

History: The Pleasant Valley Wildlife Sanctuary is a 1,300-acre nature and wildlife center that is owned and maintained by Massachusetts Audubon Society. The sanctuary has created a different kind of trail-marking system from those found elsewhere in this guidebook: blue markers lead outward from the center; yellow markers return you to the starting point.

Directions: From Pittsfield (junction of Rtes. 7 & 20 West), go south on Rt. 7 for 4.6 miles. Turn right onto West Dugway Road and proceed northwest. At 0.8 mile you will come to a fork in the road. Bear left on West Mountain Road and continue southwest for a total of 1.6 miles from when you turned off of Rt. 7.

From the main building (the gift shop and office), follow the Bluebird Path for 0.3 mile as it leads through fields and downhill to the edge of the woods. From there, continue on the Bluebird Trail as it takes you over two streams via footbridges. As soon as you cross over the second footbridge, continue straight ahead, heading uphill, on the Ovenbird Trail for 0.05 mile. When you come to the Overbrook Trail, turn left and begin climbing uphill at a steady rate. The trail parallels the stream, which is on your left, providing an opportunity to see several small cascades along the way. Within 0.3 mile you will reach the first of the main cascades, where the trail crosses the stream below the waterfall.

The trail pulls away momentarily from the stream and then returns at a higher point on the stream. Two more cascades soon come into view as you continue the uphill climb, with the stream now on your right. Once again the trail crosses over the stream and, continuing uphill, you will come to the last two cascades, both of which will be on your left.

23. Stevens Glen

Location: Near West Stockbridge (Berkshire County)
Stevens Glen Preserve
DeLorme Massachusetts Atlas & Gazetteer: p. 32, I5
Fee: None
Hours: Open daily from sunrise to sunset
Views: Lateral view from viewing platform
Accessibility: 0.8-mile hike one way; 320-foot descent.
Degree of Difficulty: Moderate

Description: The waterfall in Stevens Glen is formed on Lenox Mountain Brook, a small stream that rises from a little reservoir and flows into the Williams River at West Stockbridge. The fall is formed in a narrow fissure, dropping approximately 30–40 feet.[1] An observation platform has been constructed halfway down into the interior of the ravine to allow easy access and viewing. A sign on the platform asks visitors not to bypass the platform and descend farther into the ravine, to protect the fragile layers of duff (a mixture of decaying plant material, small roots, and delicate fungi) that make the glen so distinctive and attractive.

History: Stevens Glen has been a popular attraction since the 1800s, when visitors came from near and far by foot, horseback, and buggy to visit the falls. In the early 1900s a farmer named Romanzo Stevens, whose family had owned the land since 1760, decided that the glen could be turned into a commercial attraction. Stevens proceeded to build stairways and bridges to make the glen safer and more accessible, and began charging tourists twenty-five cents for admission—a considerable amount of money in those days. With the business thriving, Stevens decided to branch out into the entertainment field and built a dance pavilion with an oak floor. In 1918 over 900 people attended a gathering at the pavilion. Romanzo kept a guest book and was able to impress others by revealing that Mrs. Grover Cleveland, wife of the president, visited the glen in 1901 while staying in Tyringham.[2]

Nevertheless, Stevens's business started going into decline. With the advent of the trolley, people began using public transportation more and more instead of the older, slower forms of travel; unfortunately, no mass-transit route was established near Stevens's lands. Business dwindled as the months went by. In 1919, heavy snows collapsed the roof of the pavilion, and no attempt was made to preserve the structure. For more than seventy years, the glen fell into obscurity and was infrequently visited. Even the forest itself changed. An infestation of chestnut blight led to the cutting down of all mature trees in 1924 in an attempt to control the spread of the contagion.[3]

In 1995, Millard and Frederic Pryor and their wives, Claire and Zora, donated the land to the Berkshire Natural Resources Council, with the Richmond Land Trust maintaining a perpetual conservation restriction. Work soon began on creating the present trail system, and in 1998 the foot trail was dedicated to the Pryors.

Directions: From West Stockbridge (junction of Rtes. 41 North & 102 East), drive southwest on Rtes. 41 & 102 for 0.2 mile. As soon as you cross over the bridge leading into West Stockbridge, turn left onto Swamp Road. Then immediately turn right onto Lenox Road and drive uphill, going northeast, for 1.5 miles. You will see a pull-off on your left for Stevens Glen.

At the parking area, an informative kiosk gives historical information about the glen and includes a map of the trails and the spur trail to the fall. Walk downhill several hundred feet, following the red-blazed markers. You will come to a junction where the trail branches off to the left and right, ultimately completing a circuit that, if you include the distance covered by the side trail to the glen, totals 1.2 miles.

For purposes of this hike, take the right-hand trail, which crosses over a tributary to Lenox Mountain Brook several times while making its way downhill. In less than 0.7 mile you will come to a junction. Bear right, following the spur trail to Stevens Glen. The trail leads down to a footbridge spanning Lenox Mountain Brook, and then up and around the side of a hill. Within 0.2 mile from the junction, you will arrive at your destination, descending via a flight of metal stairs to a platform overlooking the gorge and fall.

Stevens Glen fell rapidly into obscurity during the 1900s. Postcard circa 1910.

24. Hawthorne Falls

Location: Between Stockbridge and Great Barrington
(Berkshire County) Monument Mountain Reservation
DeLorme Massachusetts Atlas & Gazetteer: p. 44, A5
Fee: None
Hours: Open daily from sunrise to sunset
Restrictions: Observe rules and regulations posted at park.
Views: Head-on
Accessibility: 0.5-mile hike (one way) uphill
Degree of Difficulty: Moderate

Description: This small waterfall is formed on a tiny unnamed
stream that rises from the upper section of Monument Mountain and
flows into Konkapot Brook.[1] During most of the year, Hawthorne

Hawthorne Cave and Waterfall, 1997.

Falls is less a waterfall and more a shelter cave; when little water is flowing, it is the 5-foot-deep cavity extending under the overhanging lip of rock, and not the waterfall itself, that draws hikers in for further exploration.

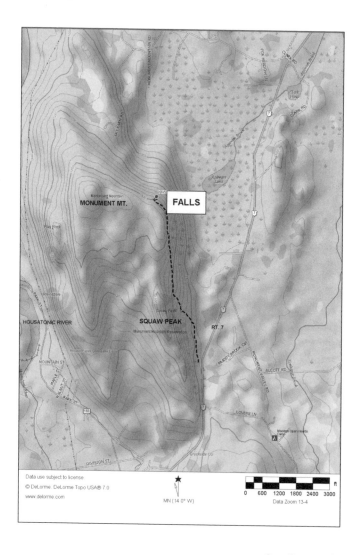

History: The waterfall and cave were named after writer Nathaniel Hawthorne. Hawthorne, along with a group of friends including William Cullen Bryant, Herman Melville, and David Dudley Field, climbed the mountain one afternoon in the late 1800s and got caught in the rain. Legend has it that it was at this cave, with its overhanging waterfall, that they sought shelter.

Directions: From Stockbridge (junction of Rtes. 7 & 102), take Rt. 7 south. After driving for 3.1 miles, pull into the designated parking area for Monument Mountain, which will be on your right.

From northeast of Great Barrington (junction of Rtes. 7 & 183 North), drive north on Rt. 7 for 1.6 miles. Pull into the designated parking area for Monument Mountain on your left.

Take the Hickey Trail from the north end of the parking lot and follow it uphill for roughly 0.5 mile. Along the way you will come to a steeply cut ravine on the right, containing a small stream. Shortly after, you will cross over the stream, traversing a small log bridge. From here, you will quickly come to the fall and shelter cave, which will be on your left.

Craggy rock face on Monument Mountain circa 1930.

25. Fall in South Egremont

Location: South Egremont (Berkshire County)
DeLorme Massachusetts Atlas & Gazetteer: p. 44, F1
Fee: None
Hours: Open continuously
Restrictions: Remain on road; the fall is on private property
Views: Lateral
Accessibility: Roadside

Description: This tiny cascade is formed on Hubbard Brook, a small stream that rises from Mill Pond west of South Egremont and flows into Mill Pond northwest of Sheffield. The cascade is only 3–4 feet high, but very pretty.

History: South Egremont is located just north of Jug End, a section of the Taconic Range that juts out east into Egremont and Sheffield. It was called *Jugend* (meaning "youth" or "a new beginning") by Palatine Germans. Early local mills dependent on Hubbard Brook's hydropower included a chair factory, cheese factories, sawmills, and an axle works.[1] The Old Mill Restaurant, which is just downstream from the cascade, is a restored 1797 mill and blacksmith's shop.[2]

Adding to this area's interest are the local caves, of which Bat's Den Cave is the most famous.[3]

Directions: From South Egremont (junction of Rtes. 41 & 23 West), drive northeast on Rtes. 41 & 23 for 0.2 mile. The cascade will be visible on the right-hand side of the road, just downstream from The Old Mill Restaurant.

26. Fall on Konkapot River

Location: West of Monterey (Berkshire County)
DeLorme Massachusetts Atlas & Gazetteer: p. 44, E11
Fee: None
Hours: Open continuously
Views: Lateral and head-on
Accessibility: 75-foot walk (one way) from roadside
Degree of Difficulty: Easy

Description: This pretty cascade is formed on Konkapot River, a medium-sized stream that rises from Lake Garfield and flows into the Housatonic River near Ashley Falls. The cascade consists of a long flume, approximately 15 feet in total height, that plunges into a pool of water.[1]

History: The river is named after Konkapot, chief of the Stockbridge Mahicans.[2] By the time that Konkapot was an elder in the tribe, the northeastern United States was already substantially colonized by European settlers. The Mahicans' days of glory were long past, thanks to repeated military defeats at the hands of the Iroquois. When the colonists offered Konkapot their god to worship, Konkapot was quick to convert to Christianity, believing that the Great Spirit no longer had any power to help the Mahicans. Despite Konkapot's conversion, however, the Mahicans continued to decline. By the time of Konkapot's death in 1749, the Mahicans' total fall from power and influence was inevitable.[3]

During the eighteenth century, the Konkapot River was called the Iron Works River because of a bar-iron forge that was established in the 1730s near the river's terminus at Ashley Falls.[4] It has also been called Mill River, a fairly common name for a stream or brook in Massachusetts.[5]

There are other falls on the Konkapot River. A small cascade, memorialized in an oil and acrylics painting by Edward Lazansky,[6] is reputed to be located at the tiny hamlet of Mill River, and at Ashley Falls there is a small, inaccessible cascade 0.2 mile downstream from the Rt. 7 bridge (where the top of a dam is visible).

Directions: From Great Barrington (junction of Rtes. 23 East & 7), drive east on Rt. 23 & Rt. 183. When Rtes. 183/57 go off to the right, at 3.5 miles, stay left on Rt. 23, continuing east. At 5.8 mile from the junction with Rt. 7, turn right onto River Road (also called The Hatchery). Cross over a small bridge, and in less than 0.3 mile from Rt. 23 you will see a pull-off on the right between sets of guardrails. Park here.

Follow one of two paths that lead down 75 feet to the stream, where the cascade can be seen from its base.

Konkapot Falls circa 1920.

27. Umpachene Falls

Location: Near Marlborough (Berkshire County)
Umpachene Municipal Park
DeLorme Massachusetts Atlas & Gazetteer: p. 44, J9
Fee: None
Hours: Dawn to dusk.
Restrictions: Use of the park is limited to residents of New Marlborough and their guests.[1]
Views: Head-on view
Accessibility: Short, level, 0.05-mile walk one way
Degree of Difficulty: Easy

Description: Umpachene Falls is formed on Umpachene River, a medium-sized stream that rises in the hills east of New Marlborough and flows into Konkapot River southwest of New Marlborough. The falls consist of a long series of cascades and ledges, totaling over 35 feet high,[2] which are located only a short distance upstream from the Umpachene River's confluence with the Konkapot River.

History: The river and falls derive their name from an Indian chief named Umpachene (pronounced *Um-pa-che-knee*).

The falls are located in an 8-acre municipal park that was donated by Mr. and Mrs. Robert K. Wheeler, who at one time owned a summer camp by the falls. The camp was repeatedly damaged by fire. For a time, the land was leased to the New Marlborough Sporting Club[3] before it became a municipal park. Along the way to the falls, you will pass by the ruins of an old lodge on your left, just before reaching the falls.

Much earlier, a gristmill used the falls for hydropower.

The waterfall is noted for having attracted at least one famous visitor. In 1977, Senator Edward Kennedy and his family picnicked at the park.[4]

Umpachene Falls was used early on to power a gristmill.
Postcard circa 1910.

Directions: From Great Barrington (junction of Rtes. 7 & 23 East), take Rt. 23 east for 3.5 miles. Turn right onto Pixley Road (Rtes. 183 & 57) and follow it southeast to New Marlborough. In the hamlet of New Marlborough, turn right onto New Marlborough/Southfield Road (look for the green sign indicating the way to Southfield and Canaan) and drive south for 1.3 miles. Bear right at the fork in the road and take Mill River/Southfield Road west for 1.1 miles. At the end of this road, turn left, then continue straight where the road divides, driving south on Hadsell. At 0.8 mile, just before crossing over Umpachene River via an old metal bridge, turn right onto a dirt road and drive downhill for 0.5 mile. Pull into a parking lot for Umpachene Falls directly on your left.

To get to the falls, walk across the playground and outdoor picnic area. The falls are 0.05 mile from where you parked.

Umpachene Falls during its industrial heyday. Postcard circa 1910.

28. Campbell Falls

Location: Near Southfield (Berkshire County)
Campbell Falls State Park
DeLorme Massachusetts Atlas & Gazetteer: p. 44, M11
Fee: None
Hours: Open daily from sunrise to sunset
Views: Head-on
Accessibility: Short, less than 0.2-mile hike one way down
a steep trail
Degree of Difficulty: Easy to moderate

Description: Campbell Falls is formed on Whiting River, a medium-sized stream that rises north of Thousand Acres Swamp and East Indies Pond, and flows into the Blackberry River near East Canaan, Connecticut.[1] The falls consist of a dramatic plunge through a cleft in the rocks, pouring down for over 60 feet in two steps, with the upper step being the larger of the two.

Upstream, above the falls, the Whiting River flows under an old stone bridge. Small cascades can be seen on both sides of and directly under the bridge.

History: The waterfall is located in Campbell Falls State Park and has been one of the most frequently visited natural wonders in western Massachusetts. The falls were a gift to the State of Connecticut and the Commonwealth of Massachusetts from the White Memorial Foundation of Litchfield, Connecticut, and were placed under the permanent protection of both states in 1923.[2]

Long ago a sawmill was located at the rocky top of the falls and used the stream for waterpower.[3]

Directions: *From New Marlborough*—From Rt. 57, in the center of New Marlborough, turn onto Marlborough/Southfield Road and

Campbell Falls circa 1920.

proceed south. When the road forks, at nearly 1.4 miles, bear left towards Southfield. When you reach Southfield, continue right on Norfolk Road and proceed south for 4.4 miles until you come to Campbell Falls Road, which will be on your right (just before the Massachusetts/Connecticut border). Turn right onto Campbell Falls Road and proceed west for nearly 0.4 mile until you reach the parking area for Campbell Falls, which will be on your left.

From Connecticut—From the junction of Rtes. 44 East & 272 North (north of Norfolk), drive north on Rt. 272 for 4.2 miles and turn left onto Campbell Falls Road. Proceed west for less than 0.4 mile to the parking area on your left.

Follow the white-blazed trail downhill for less than 0.2 mile to the base of the falls.

To see the small upper cascades, follow Campbell Falls Road west on foot from the parking area for several hundred feet. A number of small cascades can be seen on both sides of the old stone bridge. Cross over the bridge and follow a path to your left for 30 feet to see the cascade directly under the bridge.

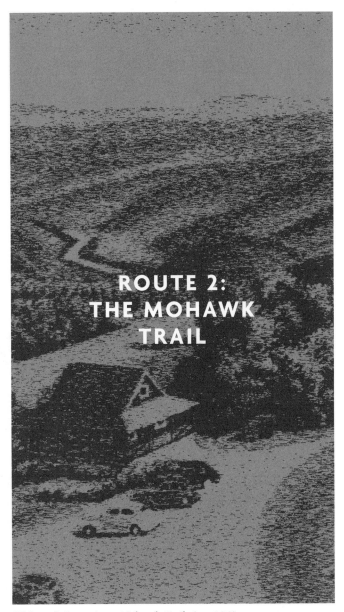

ROUTE 2:
THE MOHAWK
TRAIL

Whitcomb Summit on Mohawk Trail circa 1940.

Introduction

Route 2 (the Mohawk Trail) has a rich history. Centuries ago it consisted of a faint path through dense woods, used by Native Americans for foraging expeditions between the Hudson River Valley in New York State and the Connecticut River Valley in Massachusetts and Connecticut. Although the name of the trail suggests strong Mohawk ties to the area, it was actually the Algonquians who occupied the region—the Pocumtucs to the east of the Hoosic Range, and the Mahicans to the west. The Mohawks did use the trail, but primarily to wage battles or to attend gatherings.

In 1759 a primitive road was hacked out for colonial travelers. This provided the first substantial means for crossing over the Hoosic Mountains—a range that served as a natural barrier between the Hoosic River Valley and the Deerfield River Valley. The highest point of the Hoosics is Spruce Hill, at an elevation of 2,588 feet. In 1786 this road, the Mohawk Trail, became America's first toll-free inter-

state road and was called a "shunpike" (meaning that it shunned the toll roads).

The present highway was opened in 1914 and became the first roadway in Massachusetts designated for automobile touring. It has grown from a 15-mile mountain road in western Massachusetts to 165 miles of highway (now identified as Rt. 2) from Boston to Troy, New York (with the latter section—the Taconic Trail—a westward extension of the Mohawk Trail).

The Appalachian National Scenic Trail crosses Rt. 2 squarely between Williamstown and North Adams.

The section of Rt. 2 that stretches for 60 miles between Williamstown and Millers Falls is dotted with relics such as Indian souvenir shops and trading posts from the 1950s heyday of automobile touring. Its highest point is Whitcomb Summit (2,173 feet), where views of the adjacent states of Vermont, New York, and New Hampshire can be seen from a wooden tower. East of North Adams is an unusually sharp and notorious hairpin turn halfway up the face of Forbidden Mountain.[1]

Horseshoe turn on Mohawk Trail circa 1920.

29. Haley Brook Falls

Location: South of Williamstown
DeLorme Massachusetts Atlas & Gazetteer: p. 20, C10
Fee: None
Hours: Open continuously
Views: Head-on view from downstream viewing platform
Accessibility: 0.2-mile hike one way
Degree of Difficulty: Easy to Moderate

Description: Haley Brook Falls is formed on Haley Brook, a small stream that rises north of Berlin Mountain and flows into Hemlock Brook. The waterfall is located on lands under the purview of Williamstown Rural Lands Management. The fall is 15 feet high and shaped like a punch bowl, with the cascade dropping into the bowl like a ladle. Several small cascades can be seen above the main one.

Nearby Berlin Mountain, at an elevation of 2,798 feet, is the highest peak along the Taconic Range in Massachusetts and is part of the Taconic Crest Trail system.

History: The waterfall is contained in a 35-acre parcel on the shoulder of Berlin Mountain. It was dubbed a "mini-Stevens Glen" (see chapter on "Stevens Glen") for the excellent work done on erecting the observation platform. The construction project was spearheaded by Peter Jensen and the crew from Open Space Management. Major funding came from the Field Pond Foundation.[1]

Directions: From Williamstown (junction of Rtes. 2 & 7 North), drive southwest on Rtes. 2 & 7 for 2.4 miles. At the junction of Rtes. 2 West & 7, where Rt. 7 continues south, turn right on Rt. 2 and head northwest towards New York State. After 0.3 mile, turn left onto Torreywoods Road and drive northwest. At 0.4 mile, Oblong Road comes in on the left. Continue straight ahead on what now becomes Berlin Road. Within 1.2 miles from Rt. 2, you will come to a fork in the road where Treadwell Hollow Road goes off to the right. Continue straight (left) on Berlin Road, going west. In just over 2.1 miles from Rt. 2, you will come to a small parking area on your left where a sign states "Class of '33 Trail Parking." Pull in here.

Follow the blue-blazed Williamstown Rural Land Foundation Foot Trail west for less than 0.1 mile. As soon as you cross over a tiny footbridge, turn left at a junction and follow the blue-blazed trail steadily downhill for less than 0.1 mile to a platform overlooking the waterfall, which is approximately 100 feet downstream.

30. Cascades at Green River Linear Park

Location: Williamstown (Berkshire County)
Green River Linear Park
DeLorme Massachusetts Atlas & Gazetteer: p. 20, C14
Fee: None
Hours: Open continuously
Views: Head-on, but from a considerable distance
Accessibility: 100-foot walk one way
Degree of Difficulty: Easy

Description: These small cascades are formed on the Green River, a medium-sized stream that rises south of New Ashford and flows into the Hoosic River at Williamstown.[1] The closer cascades are less than 1 foot high. The larger cascades, slightly farther upstream, are more substantial in size, being 3–4 feet in height.

Green River Linear Park is almost like an island, for the river momentarily does a U-turn here before resuming its more northerly course towards the Hoosic River.

History: "Green River Linear Park: Mt. Pleasant" serves as a playground today, but its history goes back nearly 250 years. Water Street (Rt. 43) was laid out along the west bank in 1761. Soon after, a tannery and cheese factory were established. The tannery, to accommodate its increasing workforce, built a bridge across the river where the stream makes a U-turn and erected two large tenements for its workers. The workers, with a sense of humor, named this area Snob Hill. Later the name was changed to the more agreeable "Mt. Pleasant." A gristmill, the last standing factory on Water Street, was demolished in 1952.[2]

Directions: From Williamstown (junction of Rtes. 2 & 43), drive south on Rt. 43 (Water Street) for over 0.1 mile. Turn left onto a bridge that crosses over the Green River and drive to a parking lot at the playground for Green River Linear Park: Mt. Pleasant, less than 0.1 mile from Water Street.

The cascades can be glimpsed from the east end of the bridge, or by walking upstream for 100 feet from the parking area. The smaller cascades are just a short distance upstream from the bridge; the larger cascades, just barely visible from the bridge, are 0.05 mile farther.

The best views of the cascades may be from the parking lots for several businesses just south of where nearby Latham Street intersects with Water Street.

Dammed falls in Williamstown circa 1910.

31. The Cascade

Location: Southwest of North Adams (Berkshire County)
Cascade Park
DeLorme Massachusetts Atlas & Gazetteer: p. 21, D18
Fee: None
Hours: Open daily sunrise to sunset
View: Head-on
Accessibility: 0.6-mile walk one way
Degree of Difficulty: Moderate

Description: The Cascade is a historically well-known waterfall formed on Notch Brook, a small stream that rises on the northeast slope of Mt. Greylock and flows into the Hoosic River at Brayton-ville.[1] The brook is dammed farther upstream from The Cascade to create the Notch Brook Reservoir.

The Cascade has also been known as Notch Brook Cascade[2] and The Notch Cascade.[3] The fall is over 40 feet in height and drops into a small chasm. Under normal water flow, the fall consists of two tiers, with the stream running diagonally between the two. During heavy water flow, however, the drops become one continuous cascade. The hike up to the waterfall is entrancing and is enhanced by beautiful white boulders along the streambed.

History: The Cascade is contained in an 85-acre park that was acquired in the 1970s by the North Adams Conservation Commission and the Berkshire Natural Resource Council. The bridge crossing Notch Brook midway along the hike was installed in 2002, thanks to a lead grant provided by Dr. Richard Ziter.[4]

Jeremiah Wilbur, an early settler, built a sawmill, cider mill, and gristmill on Notch Brook.[5] In 1794, Joseph Darby set up a blacksmith shop on Notch Brook in close proximity to Fort Massachusetts, farther downstream from the falls.[6]

The Cascade was a favorite haunt of Henry David Thoreau, who appreciated the area's natural beauty and no doubt was attracted by the waterfall's close proximity to North Adams.

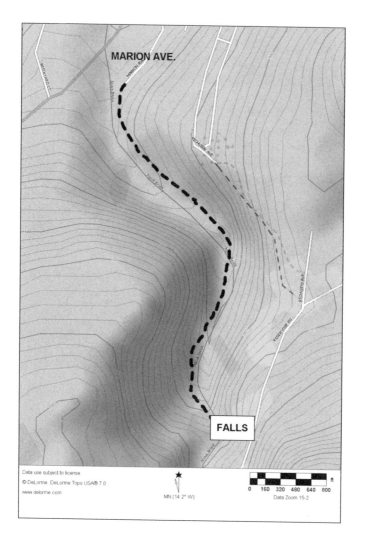

MARION AVE.

FALLS

MN (14.2° W)

0   160   320   480   640   800   ft
Data Zoom 15-2

The Cascade circa 1920.

Directions: *From North Adams*—From the junction of Rtes. 2 & 8 South, drive west on Rt. 2 for 1.2 miles. Just before Notch Road (which leads into the Mt. Greylock State Reservation), turn left onto Marion Ave. and drive 0.3 mile southwest to its end. Park in a small pull-off on your right before the last house. Be careful not to block any driveways, and don't park on any of the private homeowners' lawns.

From Williamstown—From the junction of Rtes. 2 & 43 South, drive 3.8 miles east on Rt. 2 and turn right onto Marion Ave. just after you pass by Notch Road. Drive 0.3 mile southwest and park near the end of the street.

From the end of Marion Ave, follow the trail (an old road), which parallels Notch Brook, for 0.6 mile to the cascade. About half-way along, a footbridge will take you across the stream to the west bank. After this, the going may be tricky in a couple of places. At one spot you will have to edge along the side of the bank in order not to get your boots wet. Then, near the end of the trek, you will have to scramble along the bank of the stream to get down for a closer view of the cascade.

32. Natural Bridge & Dam

Location: Clarksburg (Berkshire County)
Natural Bridge State Park
DeLorme Massachusetts Atlas & Gazetteer: p. 21, C20
Fee: Modest seasonal parking fee; no fee during off-season
Hours: Open daily
Restrictions: Park closes at 5:00 PM
Views: Head-on view of dam from footbridge; downward view
into chasm to see lower cascades
Accessibility: Short walk from parking area to the chasm; 0.3-mile
hike (one way) in winter when road is closed
Degree of Difficulty: Easy

Description: Natural Bridge contains a narrow, deeply carved marble chasm formed on Hudson Brook, a small stream that rises in the hills north of North Adams and flows into the North Branch of the Hoosic River near the center of North Adams.[1] The stream is named after Seth Hudson, who visited the site in the eighteenth century while stationed at nearby Fort Massachusetts.[2] There are a number of small falls and cascades that can be viewed from the top of the chasm via a series of walkways and observation stations. Most of the falls are formed just downstream from the dam. The chasm is 475 feet long with vertical walls that are over 20 feet high. During its days of commercialization, the chasm was promoted as being "150 million years older than Niagara Falls."[3] The chasm has also been called Adams Falls and Adams Cave. Nathaniel Hawthorne referred to it as Hudson's Cave, in honor of its discoverer, Seth Hudson.[4]

The 30-foot-long, 15-foot-thick, natural stone bridge spanning one part of the chasm is reputed to be the only one of its kind in North America. With the exception of the natural bridge in Virginia, it is the largest natural bridge east of the Mississippi River.

At the mouth of the chasm is a beautiful white marble dam—supposedly the only one of its kind at the time it was built—that produces a pretty, stone-faced waterfall.

Downstream from the chasm, Hudson Brook drops over two small dams and produces a little cascade at its confluence with the North Branch of the Hoosic River. All of this is visible from the road leading up from the McCauley Street Bridge to the parking area.

History: From 1810 to 1947, the area around Natural Bridge was an active site for quarrying marble. Early on, a mill was established next to Hudson Brook and cut marble into slabs. Generally, the mill was able to extract hydropower from Hudson Brook eight months out of the year. Over many years the North Adams Marble Dust Company did an extensive amount of excavating near the chasm, the long-term effects of which are evident today. In fact, the quarry's expansion was so extensive that it nearly broke into Hudson Brook. The mill was destroyed by fire in 1947, and with that came the end of quarrying at Natural Bridge.

Marble Dam at Natural Bridge circa 1940.

The property was sold to a couple who turned Natural Bridge into a commercial tourist attraction from 1950 to 1983. In 1984 it was taken over by the state and became a 47-acre park.[5] The old stone foundations and supports for the mill, however, are still visible just downstream from the end of the chasm.

The white marble dam, so prominently visible at the head of the gorge, was completed in 1850.

In August 1838, Nathaniel Hawthorne visited the chasm and was understandably impressed by its rugged beauty.[6] Indeed, he was so smitten that he spent extra time at the chasm collecting background information for his novel *Ethan Brand*.[7] Hawthorne wrote eloquently about Natural Bridge: "The fissure is very irregular, so as not to be describable in words and scarcely to be painted—jutting buttresses, moss-grown, impending crags, with tall trees growing on their verge, nodding over the head of the observer at the bottom of the chasm, and rooted, as it were, in the air. ... The marble crags are overspread with a concretion which makes them look as gray as granite, except where the continual flow of water keeps them of a snowy whiteness."[8]

Directions: From North Adams (junction of Rtes. 2, 8 South, & 8A South), go east on Rtes. 2 & 8 (which is Main Street) for 0.7 mile. When you come to a flashing yellow light (junction of Rtes. 2 & 8), follow Rt. 8 (Beaver Street) to the left and proceed northeast for 0.5 mile. Look for a road on your left just past a red brick factory building. This will be McCauley Road. Turn left and cross over the North Branch of the Hoosic River. Then turn right and follow a small road uphill past a huge quarry, and then up still farther to the parking area.

If you are visiting during the winter when the road is closed, park your car below and walk up to the chasm, approximately 0.3 mile uphill.

Natural Bridge & Chasm circa 1910.

33. Twin Falls (Historic)

Location: South of Florida (Berkshire County)
Accessibility: Inaccessible; entrance land is posted

Description: Twin Falls consist of two large cascades. One is formed on Cascade Brook, and the other on its tributary. Both are located near the confluence of the two streams.[1]

Cascade Brook is a small stream that rises on the northeast slopes of Whitcomb Summit and flows into the Deerfield River 0.5 mile downstream from the cascades. Several writers have attributed the falls as being on Fife Brook and its tributary,[2] but this would appear to be inaccurate, since Fife Brook comes into the Deerfield River farther north of the Hoosic Tunnel.

The waterfall on Cascade Brook is over 40 feet high; the cascade on its tributary is nearly double that in height. Slightly downstream is a 10-foot-high stone dam that at first glance almost looks like a natural waterfall. Farther downstream are a number of small cascades and one 10-foot-high cascade.

One of two Twin Falls circa 1920.

34. Cascades on Dunbar Brook

Location: Southwest of Monroe (Franklin County)
Monroe State Forest
DeLorme Massachusetts Atlas & Gazetteer: p. 21, C27
Fee: None
Hours: Open continuously
Views: Head-on and lateral
Accessibility: Over 1.0-mile hike one way
Degree of Difficulty: Moderate

Description: Several scenic cascades are formed on Dunbar Brook, a medium-sized stream that rises in the Hoosac Range and flows into the Deerfield River.[1] The cascades are contained in the 4,321-acre Monroe State Forest, in a boulder-strewn gorge where huge rocks populate the streambed and sloping walls.

The first cascade is over 6 feet in height and rushes into a small pool at its base. Just upstream, several small cascades are encountered and then, above them, an enormous boulder sits directly in the middle of the stream, splitting the creek momentarily into two rivulets. A short distance farther upstream is a 6-foot cascade.

Directions: From North Adams (junction of Rtes. 2 & 8 North), drive east on Rt. 2 for 6.7 miles. Turn left onto Whitcomb Hill Road and drive downhill, going southeast for 2.5 miles. When you reach the bottom of the long hill, turn left onto River Road and drive northwest, initially, and then northeast, following along the course of the Deerfield River. At 0.8 mile you will pass by the entrance to the Hoosac Tunnel, on your left. Continue northeast along River Road for another 4.0 miles (or a total of 4.8 miles from Whitcomb Hill Road). Turn left into a parking area for the Dunbar Brook trailhead. Be sure to take note of the enormous white marble boulder at the edge of the parking area.

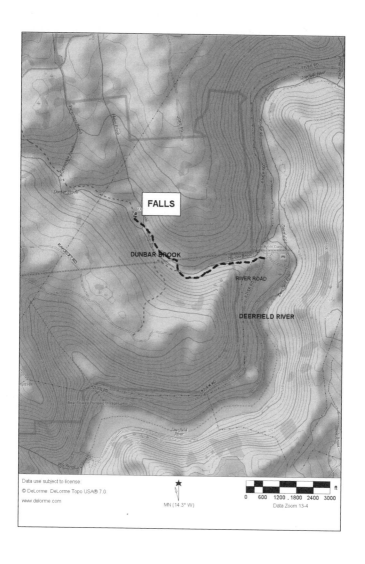

FALLS

DUNBAR BROOK

RIVER ROAD

DEERFIELD RIVER

Data use subject to license.
© DeLorme DeLorme Topo USA® 7.0
www.delorme.com

MN (14.3° W)

0   600   1200 . 1800 2400 3000   ft
Data Zoom 13-4

From the parking area, walk along an old road going uphill for 100 feet, and then bear right onto a blue-blazed path that leads into the woods, paralleling Dunbar Brook to your right. The initial 0.1-mile length of Dunbar Brook is dammed. In a moment or two, however, you will begin to hear the gurgling and splashing sounds of rapids and little cascades ahead as you leave the impoundment behind and begin following the actual creek.

After 0.7 mile you will reach the junction of the Dunbar Brook Trail and the Raycroft Trail (which veers left). Bear right and immediately cross over Dunbar Brook via a well-constructed footbridge. At the end of the footbridge, turn left and follow the brook upstream, passing campsites along the way. In 0.3 mile after crossing the footbridge, you will reach the Dunbar Brook shelter, which is commandingly situated at the confluence of Dunbar Brook and its tributary, Haley Brook. Cross over a footbridge spanning Haley Brook and continue past the shelter, following a trail west for a couple of hundred feet. Along the way, take note of an old stone foundation on your right that is set into the hillside. As soon as you pass by the stone foundation, you will come to a fork in the trail. Take the path to the left, which leads down to Dunbar Brook and begins following it, heading upstream. In less than 0.1 mile you will come to a gorge where the lowermost cascade is visible.

The trail comes to an end at this point, so the upper cascades can only be accessed by bushwhacking upstream for several hundred feet.

35. Cascades in Cold River Gorge

Location: Southeast of Drury (Berkshire County)
DeLorme Massachusetts Atlas & Gazetteer: p. 21, G27
Fee: None
Hours: Open continuously
Views: The first waterfall is viewed head-on while driving by; the second fall is seen in the distance from roadside.
Accessibility: Roadside

Description: Two large cascades, both visible from roadside, have formed on tiny creeks that drop precipitously into a deep gorge formed by the Cold River—a medium-sized stream that rises on the west shoulder of Crum Hill along the Hoosic Range and flows into the Deerfield River several miles east of the falls.

The westernmost cascade is 25–30 feet high. It can only be glimpsed in passing while driving by in your vehicle. The easternmost cascade is over 40 feet high and is a series of steep drops that can be seen from a bridge spanning the Cold River. The cascade is formed on Wheeler Brook, a small tributary to the Cold River that rises in the hills east of Drury. The waterfall is best viewed in the early spring or late fall when the trees are stripped of their foliage.

The stupendous gorge that Rt. 2 passes through provides motorists a unique opportunity to experience the thrill of driving along the bottom of an exceptionally rugged, deep chasm.

History: Centuries ago, the nearby confluence of the Cold River and the Deerfield River served as a camping ground for Native Americans. Fish were plentiful, and the springs offered water uncontaminated by stream runoff.[1]

Nathaniel Hawthorne was obviously deeply moved by the Cold River valley when he wrote, "I have never ridden through such romantic scenery, where there was such variety and boldness of mountain-shapes as this; and though it was a broad sunny day, the mountains diversified the scene with sunshine and shadow, and glory, and gloom."[2]

Directions: From North Adams (junction of Rtes. 2 & 8 North), drive east on Rt. 2 for nearly 10.4 miles. Look for the first cascade on your left as you wind your way downhill. It can be viewed only in passing, since there is no pull-off on the right-hand side of the road.

Continue east for 1.0 mile farther (or a total of 11.4 miles from the junction of Rtes. 2 & 8 North in North Adams). As soon as you cross over the bridge spanning Black Brook and pass by Black Brook Road, pull over into a parking area on your left.

Carefully walk back up Rt. 2 to the bridge. The cascade can be seen by looking across the Cold River to its opposite bank. It is several hundred feet downstream from the bridge.

From Charlemont (junction of Rtes. 2 & 8A North), drive west on Rt. 2 for 7.0 miles. Just before you cross over a bridge spanning Black Brook, pull into a parking area on your right.

From here, walk carefully up Rt. 2 to the bridge, from where the cascade can be seen by looking downstream a couple of hundred feet and across to the opposite bank. It is probably best to look for this cascade when the trees have cast off their leaves.

To reach the second roadside cascade, drive uphill on Rt. 2 for 1.0 mile farther and look to your right as you pass by the fall. Although there is enough space by the cascade for several cars to park, it is probably not a good idea. You would then have to pull back out into traffic at a spot where visibility is poor.

Bridge near cascades circa 1940.

36. Tannery Falls

Location: North of Savoy (Berkshire County)
Savoy Mountain State Forest
DeLorme Massachusetts Atlas & Gazetteer: p. 21, H25
Fee: None
Hours: Open sunrise to sunset
Views: Head-on view from base
Accessibility: Fairly short walk down a descending path to base of falls
Degree of Difficulty: Moderate

Description: Tannery Falls is formed on Ross Brook, a small stream that rises east of Lewis Hill and becomes Tannery Brook at its confluence with Parker Brook. The waterfall is 100 feet high and quite picturesque.[1] In earlier days the waterfall was known as High Falls.

There are several smaller cascades on Ross Brook between the parking area and Tannery Falls.

History: The waters of Tannery Brook powered a small mill until 1870. From all accounts this early mill was a tannery, which accounts for the name of the waterfall.[2]

Tannery Falls is located in the Savoy Mountain State Forest, an 11,000-acre forest preserve[3] that was created in 1918 after an initial 1,000 acres of abandoned farmland were acquired by the state.[4] In the 1930s the Civilian Conservation Corps (CCC) built a new concrete dam at Tannery Pond to replace an older one,[5] and did much to reforest the area following its days as farmland.[6] The state forest is named after the hamlet of Savoy, a colonial village that was established in 1771.

Directions: From North Adams (junction of Rtes. 2 & 8 North), proceed east on Rt. 2 for 11.4 miles. As soon as you cross over a bridge spanning Black Brook, turn right onto Black Brook Road and drive uphill for 2.5 miles, going south. Then turn right onto Tannery Road and drive downhill, going northwest, for 0.7 mile. Park in the area to your right as soon as you cross over the outlet stream that originates from a small pond on your left. Follow the path downstream to the falls.

Tannery Falls can also be accessed from Savoy (near junction of Rtes. 116 & 8A). From the junction of Rtes. 116 & 8A, continue east on Rt. 116/8A for 0.5 mile into Savoy, and then turn left onto Center

Tannery Falls. The sign should read "No rock climbing."
Photograph 2000.

Road. Proceed north on Center Road for 2.8 miles until you come to Adams Road, which is at Savoy Center. Turn left onto Adams Road and drive west for 0.2 mile. Then turn right onto New State Road and continue northeast for 1.3 miles. At this point you will see a dirt road on your right, which is Tannery Falls Road. Turn right and follow Tannery Falls Road east for 1.9 miles. Look for the parking area on your left as you approach Tannery Pond.

37. Parker Brook Falls

Location: North of Savoy (Berkshire County)
Savoy Mountain State Forest
DeLorme Massachusetts Atlas & Gazetteer: p. 21, H25
Fees: None
Hours: Open sunrise to sunset
Views: Head-on and lateral views
Accessibility: Fairly short walk down a descending path
Degree of Difficulty: Moderate

Description: The path leading down to Tannery Falls (see previous chapter) passes by Parker Brook Falls, a pretty, narrow-cut waterfall that, like Campbell Falls (see chapter on Campbell Falls), slices through towering slabs of rock, descending at a steep angle.[1] The waterfall is 40 feet in height.

Parker Brook Falls is formed on Parker Brook, which rises from Shakey Pond east of Borden Mountain. The stream has also been called Tannery Brook.[2] Parker Brook flows into Ross Brook just downstream from Tannery Falls, and together the two become Tannery Brook.

Directions: Follow the directions given for Tannery Falls. On your way down to the base of Tannery Falls, you will pass by Parker Brook Falls to your right.

At left: Parker Brook Falls, 1997.

38. Whirley Baths

Location: West of Charlemont (Franklin County)
DeLorme Massachusetts Atlas & Gazetteer: p. 22, G1
Fee: None
Hours: Open continuously
Restrictions: Note sign at pull-off: "Live parking only—unattended vehicles will be towed after 30 minutes"
Views: Lateral view from side of river
Accessibility: Less than 0.05-mile scramble (one way) to the stream and cascade
Degree of Difficulty: Moderate

Description: The Whirley Baths contain a small cascade and a number of granite potholes (or tubs) formed on the Deerfield River, a large stream that rises in Vermont and flows into the Connecticut River in Greenfield.[1] The cascade consists of a 4-foot-high block that spans the entire length of the river. Although small, the cascade is worth visiting because of the plethora of potholes formed in the nearby bedrock, which can best be seen when the water level is low.

History: The Whirley Baths are located just downstream from the Mohawk Trail State Forest, a camping area encompassing more than 6,000 acres spread along the banks of Deerfield and Cold rivers.[2]

Directions: From North Adams (junction of Rtes. 2 & 8 North), drive east on Rt. 2 for nearly 14.4 miles (or nearly 0.4 mile after you pass by the bridge leading left into the campgrounds for the Mohawk Trail State Forest). Park in the large pull-off on your left where a sign states: "Live Parking Only. Unattended vehicles towed after 30 minutes." Undoubtedly this restriction is intended to discourage swimmers and party-goers from misusing the grounds. Designate someone to stay in the car in order to comply with the rules and not get towed.

From Charlemont (junction of Rtes. 2 & 8A North), drive west on Rt. 2 for nearly 4 miles. (If you come to the Mohawk State Forest Campgrounds, you have gone too far). Pull into a parking area on the right, just before crossing over a small tributary to the Deerfield River.

Follow a short trail down to the river, and then scramble upstream along the bank, immediately crossing over a little tributary. In less than 0.05 mile you will reach the fall and the potholes.

39. Cascades on Pelham Brook

Location: Rowe (Franklin County)
DeLorme Massachusetts Atlas & Gazetteer: p. 21, F29
Fee: None
Hours: Open continuously
Views: Lateral view from bank of stream
Accessibility: Roadside

Description: These little cascades are formed on Pelham Brook, a small stream that rises from Pelham Lake, northeast of Rowe, and flows into the Deerfield River east of Drury.1 The cascades range in height from 2–4 feet. The name of the creek may refer to its past association with the blacksmith shop that once stood by the mill-pond in Rowe,2 or it may have been the name of a mill operator.

History: Near Rowe, as you follow Pelham Brook upstream, are a series of historical roadside markers identifying past mill sites. In ascending order the sites are: Snows Wagon Shop, 1866–1922; Foliated Talc Mill, 1902–1922; Eddy's Casket Shop, 1846–1948; Scotts Boot Shop, 1844–1885; and, by the bridge on Kings Highway Road, Sibley-Richards Blacksmith Shop, 1882–1941.

Additional Point of Interest: On the south side of the road just west of Indian Bridge (which crosses over the Deerfield River), resting on a 9-ton boulder, is Hail to the Sunrise—a 900-pound bronze casting of a native Mohawk with upraised arms. The statue is a memorial to all Native Americans and a reminder that the Berkshires and its waterfalls were once under the stewardship of these early Americans. The statue was sponsored by Old Deerfield Conference in 1926 and placed on an acre of land donated by Mr. and Mrs. Cecil Kennedy.

Directions: From North Adams (junction of Rtes. 8 North & 2), drive east on Rt. 2 for 16 miles. As soon as you cross over the Deerfield River on Indian Bridge, turn left onto Zoar Road (following the green-colored signs for Monroe & Rowe) and drive northwest for 2.3 miles. Then turn right onto Rowe Road and begin heading north. In 0.8 mile you will cross over a bridge, where cascades can be seen upstream. If you pull over next to the roadside sign that welcomes you to Rowe, you can see the cascades by walking over to the stream bank, about 30 feet away.

Back in the car, continue northeast up Rowe Road. As you approach the hamlet of Rowe, a series of roadside historical markers point out the various factories that once populated the creek, illustrating how even a small stream like Pelham Brook was heavily industrialized in past years.

At 3.6 miles you will reach the turnaround point, which is where Kings Highway Road comes in on your right. Turn right, and from the Kings Highway Bridge you can see a small millpond cascade upstream, as well as several small cascades downstream.

The Indian on the Trail and Wishing Well, Charlemont, Mass.

"Hail to the Sunrise" circa 1940.

40. Falls on Mill Brook

Location: Charlemont (Franklin County)
DeLorme Massachusetts Atlas & Gazetteer: p. 22, H3
Fee: None
Hours: Open continuously
Restrictions: Limited parking options
Accessibility: Roadside

Description: The 10-foot-high dam and the cascades are located in a little gorge formed on Mill Brook, a small stream that rises in the hills north of Charlemont and flows into the Deerfield River 0.3 mile downstream from the falls.[1] Waterfall purists will be disappointed, for most of the effect of falling water is created by the 10-foot-high dam next to the Bissell Covered Bridge. Small natural cascades, however, can be seen starting from the base of the stone dam and continuing downstream below the bridge.

The main attraction is the bridge itself, which spans the stream directly above the cascades.[2] It was recently closed to traffic, and a replacement bridge was built several yards upstream.

History: This waterfall and covered bridges have had a long association. In 1951 the present 92-foot-long, Long Truss covered bridge, built by T. J. Harvey & Sons, replaced an earlier version that had served for 70 years.[3] To celebrate the occasion, the town held a dance festival on the newly constructed bridge.[4] In the early 2000s the bridge was retired from active duty and is preserved today for its historic value.

Charlemont mills once produced axes, hats, cloths, shoes, pottery, stoves, lumber, chairs, and wool.[5]

Directions: From Charlemont (junction of Rtes. 2 & 8A North), turn north onto Rt. 8A North (Heath Road) and drive uphill. In 0.2 mile you will come to a stoplight, where Rt. 8A goes left, crossing over a one-lane bridge. The Bissell Covered Bridge and cascades are found at this point. Guardrails have been placed seemingly everywhere in the immediate vicinity, so there is no nearby place to park if you wish to leisurely view this historic bridge and its cascades. You will have to park either farther up Rt. 8A and walk back to the bridge, or stay on Heath Road, go past the stoplight, and turn immediately left into a small dirt road where it might be possible to park.

41. Salmon Falls

Location: Shelburne Falls (Franklin County)
DeLorme Massachusetts Atlas & Gazetteer: p. 22, I11
Fee: None
Hours: Open continuously
Restriction: Access to streambed is no longer allowed
Views: Lateral
Accessibility: Roadside

Description: Salmon Falls is formed on the Deerfield River, a large stream that rises from the Harriman Reservoir southeast of Wilmington in Vermont and flows into the Connecticut River near Greenfield.[1] The falls were named for the salmon that once flourished and spawned by the cascades and ledges. The waterfall is also known as Shelburne Falls.

Three distinct cascades, contained in a field of over 50 glacial potholes, can be seen below an expansive dam. The largest, and lowermost, cascade is nearly 15 feet in height. The upper cascade falls along a large expanse of zigzagging bedrock and is approximately 10 feet high.

The glacial potholes are known as the Buckland Potholes and range in size from a few inches to 30 feet in diameter.[2]

History: Shelburne Falls, named after the second Earl of Shelburne,[3] was first settled in 1712, and its waters powered a number of early factories. The principal industries were the Lamson and Goodnow Manufacturing Company, Mayhew Silk Company, H. H. Mayhew and Co. Hardware Manufactory, Silver-plating Factory, Shelburne Falls Co-operative Creamery, Frost & Bartlett's Grist Mill, H. A. Bowen's Paper Box Works, Richmond Sash and Blind Factory, and Rush Brothers Cutlery.[4]

Today the village is best known for its Bridge of Flowers—a 400-foot-long, five-arch trolley bridge built in 1908. The bridge was taken over by the Woman's Club of Shelburne Falls in 1929 and transformed into a footbridge decorated with flowers and bushes.

The first traffic bridge at Shelburne Falls was built in 1821 and lasted until 1869, when it was washed away by a freshet. That bridge was followed by a more substantial iron bridge, erected in 1872.[5]

A historic marker next to the observation walkway overlooking the falls and dam states: "'Salmon Falls' Site of Potholes. Indian Fishing Treaty between Mohawks and Penobscots 1708–1758. Recognized by the Colonial Court in 1744, preserving in perpetual peace the area within one day's journey of this site, for hunting and fishing."

In 1844 the falls were visited by Henry David Thoreau, who found the potholes to be a curious phenomenon.[6]

Directions: From the junction of Rtes. 2 and 2A East (just north of Shelburne Falls), turn onto Rt. 2A and drive south for less than 0.8 mile into Shelburne Falls. Turn left onto Bridge Street, cross over the Deerfield River, and take the first right onto Deerfield Avenue. In 0.05

Salmon Falls circa 1910.

mile you will be at the historic Mole Hollow shopping area, where parking is available for customers. If you park here, you must spend some time in the stores. The falls and potholes can be readily seen from a stone observation walkway.

Shelburne Falls can also be reached from the junction of Rtes. 2 & 2A West (east of Shelburne Falls). From this entry point, turn west onto Rt. 2A West. The main part of town will be reached in 0.6 mile.

Land of potholes, Salmon Falls, 1997.

42. Sluice Brook Falls

Location: Southwest of Shelburne (Franklin County)
DeLorme Massachusetts Atlas & Gazetteer: p. 22, K13
Fee: None
Hours: Open continuously
Views: Head-on view of upper fall; view from top of lower fall
Accessibility: Over 1.0-mile hike one way
Degree of Difficulty: Difficult, because the trail meanders up and down along the bank of the Deerfield River

Description: This attractive set of falls is formed on Sluice Brook, a small tributary that rises to the north by Patten Hill and flows into the Deerfield River at the base of the falls.[1] The upper cascade is 10 feet high. From its base the stream races off at a right angle, arriving at the top of the lower fall within 30 feet. From here the stream drops down 30 feet to the Deerfield River through a long, irregularly shaped, narrow cleft in the bank.

History: In 1992 a group of Williams College students decided to recreate part of a Native American trail that once joined the Connecticut River Valley with the Hudson River Valley. The result is the Mahican Mohawk Trail, which is 9 miles long and follows Old Deerfield to Shelburne along the Deerfield River.[2] It is evident that a considerable amount of work went into creating and maintaining the Mahican Mohawk Trail, and those who have worked on it so diligently deserve the highest accolades. It is not easy to maintain a trail where over half of it follows along the steep, erosion-prone bank of a river. The precipitous and narrow walls of this part of the gorge were remarked upon by early historians as far back as the beginning of the nineteenth century.[3]

Directions: From Shelburne Falls (junction of Rtes. 2 & 2A West), drive southeast on Rt. 2 for 1.0 mile. Turn right at a sign for Wilcox Hollow and follow a dirt road downhill, initially paralleling a tiny creek, for less than 0.5 mile. You will come to an area by the Deerfield River where several cars can be parked. Additional parking is available along the road before you reach its end.

Follow the trail that leads downstream from the parking area. It is marked by yellow disks that read "Mahican Mohawk Trail." You will also see an occasional blue-colored triangle. The trail will

The Deerfield River, Shelburne Falls, Mass.

take you up and down repeatedly along the sloping bank of the river, periodically crossing ravines formed by incoming tributaries. Some of these tributaries produce tiny cascades of their own. After well over a mile, you will emerge from a deep ravine created by a small tributary to the Deerfield River (where a log bridge and handheld cable provide support) and cross under a set of power lines; then back into the woods. Less than 0.05 mile farther, you will return to the power lines, where a space cleared of trees allows for sweeping views of the river below. From here, follow the trail

Deerfield River circa 1900.

back into the woods for one final time and, within 75 feet, you will be at the falls.

The upper cascade can be viewed head-on from the west bank of the stream. The lower cascade can be only partially glimpsed, from midway down the bank.

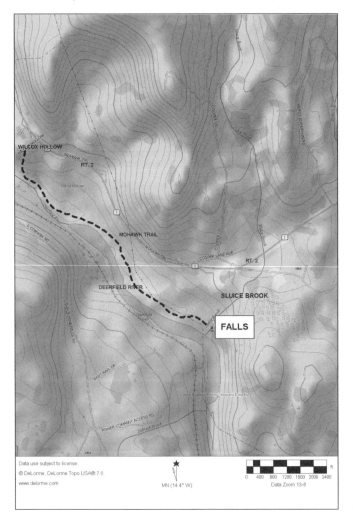

ROUTE 8

Pettibone Falls circa 1910.

Introduction

Route 8 runs north to south from Clarksburg to New Boston, taking advantage of the valley created by the Hoosic River in the northern Berkshires and of the valley created by the Farmington River's west branch in the southern Berkshires. Along the way, Route 8 passes through the towns of North Adams, Adams, and Dalton, and by a number of bodies of water, most notably the Cheshire Reservoir and the Otis Reservoir.

43. Falls along the Bellows Pipe Trail/Thunderbolt Ski Trail

Location: West of Adams (Berkshire County)
Mt. Greylock State Reservation
DeLorme Massachusetts Atlas & Gazetteer: p. 21, G16
Fee: None
Hours: Open continuously
Views: Lateral and head-on
Accessibility: Over 1.5-mile hike one way
Degree of Difficulty: Difficult, because of length and ascent

Description: There are a number of falls contained on a small creek paralleling the Bellows Pipe Trail/Thunderbolt Ski Trail. The first one is located at the end of a small, 0.05-mile-long side path and is over 50 feet high. The path takes you to the midway point of this waterfall, where 30 feet of cascades loom above you and 20 feet of cascades and chutes drop below you into a ravine.

The second grouping of waterfalls consists of an 8-foot-high cascade, followed 100 feet farther upstream by two 6-foot-high ledge falls at a point where the stream begins narrowing and enters a small chasm.

The third site is less than 0.1 mile farther upstream and can be seen by looking across the ravine at the point where the main stream comes in from the opposite bank of the gorge. A large cascade, over 40 feet high, is visible in the near distance.

The last cascade is next to the junction of the Bellows Pipe and Thunderbolt Ski Trail and looms 40 feet high.

Like many of the other cascades on Mt. Greylock, these falls need to be visited during the spring or following significant rainfall in order to be fully appreciated.

History: The Thunderbolt Ski Run was developed in 1934 by the Civilian Conservation Corps (CCC), which cut a nearly 2-mile-long trail that started near the top of Mt. Greylock and continued all the way to the bottom of the mountain, emerging near the town of Adams. The trail was called "the Thunderbolt" after a heart-pounding roller coaster ride at Revere Beach in Massachusetts. When built, the ski trail was criticized for being too steep and too narrow. Many also thought that it would be too hard for skiers to keep climbing back up to the top. It would take 90 minutes to struggle up Mt. Greylock's steep slope just to ski the 1.6 miles back down in as quickly as 2 minutes, a descent of about 2,175 feet![1] But skiers loved it. After WWII, however, the Thunderbolt was essentially abandoned as skiers turned to other, more user-friendly ski centers.[2]

The Bellows Pipe Trail was named for the sound the wind made (like a blacksmith's bellows) as it swirled through the notch formed between Ragged Mountain and Mt. Greylock.[3] The trail has also been known as Thoreau's Ascent, after Henry David Thoreau, who ascended Mt. Greylock via this route in 1844.[4]

Directions: From Adams (junction of Rtes. 8 & 116), drive south on Rt. 8 for less than 0.4 mile. Turn right onto Prospect Street. At 0.1 mile bear left onto Harmony Street. When you come to a fork in the road at 0.1 mile, veer left and continue uphill on Fisk Street (in doing so, take note of the beautiful, two-tiered, dam-created falls near the fork). After driving west for another 0.5 mile, you will reach West Road. Turn right and drive northeast on West Road for 0.2 mile (in the process, crossing over Peck's Brook), then turn left onto Gould Road. After 0.3 mile you will come to another fork in the road. Go right on Thiel Road (currently unmarked) and drive northwest for 0.5 mile until you reach the end of a cul-de-sac. At one time the dirt road that continues to the right led to the Thiel farm.

From the center of the parking area, follow the trail straight ahead, heading uphill between signs stating: "To Bellows Pipe Mt. Bike Trail" and "Thunderbolt Foot & Ski Trail. 2m summit." All of the trails seem to be blue-blazed, so you cannot rely upon colors to guide you to your destination—as you will soon discover.

The trail quickly comes to Hoxie Brook, on your right, and then parallels the stream. In less than 0.2 mile you will pass by large cement ruins on your left. These are probably relics from the

Cascade on Bellows Pipe Trail, 1999.

Thunderbolt Ski Run, which once occupied this section of the mountain. Some of the trails you will be following were originally built as downhill ski runs.

In another 0.2 mile you will reach a junction. Take the trail to the left (and not the one marked "Thunderbolt Foot & Ski Trail," which goes to the right), and in 0.05 mile you will reach another junction. Bear left here, proceeding downhill for 0.1 mile. You will quickly come to yet another junction. Continue straight ahead. (left leads to the "Gould Road & Parking Lot"). In 50 feet you will pass by more relics from the ski center—floodlights and towers. In another 100 feet the trail passes by a cement-block structure set into a stone wall on your right.

Continue south for another 0.05 mile and you will come to the last important junction. Bear right and begin climbing uphill again, this time on the Bellows Pipe Trail. In 0.1 mile, look for a faint path that goes off to your left. After less than 0.05 mile it will lead you to a magnificent waterfall.

Back on the main path again, continue up the Bellows Pipe Trail for less than 0.2 mile. Off to your left will be an 8-foot-high cascade, followed one hundred feet farther upstream by two 6-foot-high ledge falls at a point where the ravine narrows.

After ascending for another 0.1 mile, look for a large pit on your left (perhaps the excavation for an old foundation). From this point, look across to the opposite side of the ravine and you will glimpse an enormous cascade where the main stream enters the ravine from the side.

Continue uphill for less than 0.3 mile farther and you will come to the junction of several trails. Walk left, into the woods, and in less than 100 feet you will see a large cascade to your right as you look uphill.

Return the same way that you came.

44. Falls on Peck's Brook
(Mt. Greylock State Reservation)

Location: Mt. Greylock State Reservation (Berkshire County)
DeLorme Massachusetts Atlas & Gazetteer: p. 21, H16
Fee: None
Hours: Open continuously
Views: Lateral views of lower falls, looking down; head-on view of upper cascade
Accessibility: 2-mile hike one way
Degree of Difficulty: Difficult, because of length and steady ascent

Description: There are a number of waterfalls formed on Peck's Brook and its tributary where the two streams come together forming a deep canyon on the upper slope of Mt. Greylock. For specific details, see "Falls on Peck's Brook" in Mt. Greylock State Reservation section.

Directions: From Adams (junction of Rtes. 8 & 116), drive south on Rt. 8 for less than 0.4 mile. Turn right onto Prospect Street immediately after crossing over Peck's Brook. At 0.1 mile go left onto Harmony Street. When you come to a fork in the road in another 0.1 mile, bear left and continue uphill on Fisk Street. After driving west for 0.5 mile farther, you will reach West Road. Turn right and drive north on West Road for 0.1 mile. Then turn left onto West Mountain Road and drive uphill, going west, for over 0.8 mile. Turn right into the parking area for the Gould Trail (and Old Adams Road), from where excellent views of the summit of Mt. Greylock and the War Memorial Tower can be obtained.

From the back of the parking area, follow the Gould Trail (an old road) west for nearly 0.1 mile. When you come to a footbridge crossing Peck's Brook, take note of the seasonal 20-foot-high cascade formed on a tiny tributary along the west bank just upstream.

Continue on the Gould Trail for 1.5 miles as it climbs steadily uphill. When you arrive at the junction with the "Cheshire Trail. E. Harbor" connecting trail on your left, bear right and continue on the Gould Trail for another 0.2 mile until you see a sign for the Peck's Brook shelter. Turn left and follow the path as it crosses over Peck's Brook's tributary and quickly leads down to the shelter, 0.1 mile from the Gould Trail.

The upper cascade is visible from the shelter and from along the top of the gorge. A short path leads down to it from the shelter. The lower cascade is best glimpsed by walking southeast from the shelter towards the tributary and then looking down. It is inadvisable to attempt to climb down to the bottom of the gorge.

The cascades on Peck's Brook's tributary can be viewed by walking towards the junction of the two gorges.

The multiple cascades farther upstream on Peck's Brook, culminating in one large cascade, can be viewed by walking upstream for 0.1 mile.

The waterfalls can also be accessed from near the summit of Mt. Greylock. See "Falls on Peck's Brook" in Mt. Greylock State Reservation section.

45. Cascades on Upper Bassett Brook #1 & #2

Location: Southeast of Adams (Berkshire County)
Mt. Greylock State Reservation
DeLorme Massachusetts Atlas & Gazetteer: p. 20, I15
Fee: None
Hours: Open continuously
Views: Head-on and lateral
Accessibility: 1.7-mile hike one way
Degree of Difficulty: Difficult, because of length and steady ascent

Description: A number of small cascades are formed on the North Branch of Bassett Brook, a relatively small stream that rises on the southern slopes of Saddleball Mountain and flows into the Hoosic River south of Adams. A couple of tiny cascades, 1–2 feet in height, are visible upstream from the wooden bridge crossing Bassett Brook. Just below the bridge is a very pretty 6-foot-high cascade where the stream glides over the exposed bedrock, which is smooth and curved. Tiny cascades are evident as far as 100 feet downstream from the bridge.

There are also a number of cascades formed on the South Branch of Bassett Brook, and these are located in a gorge that is considerably deeper and more rugged than the one encountered on the North Branch. From the rim of the gorge can be seen, in descending order, a 3-foot-high cascade, an 8-foot-high cascade, and a 6–8-foot-high cascade. Immediately downstream the brook drops over several 4-foot-high cascades and then races through a deeply cut, narrow canyon.

Undertake this hike in mid-May and you will be rewarded with a trail lined with red and white trillium and trout lilies. There will also likely be sufficient water flowing to enjoy the smaller cascades.

Directions: Follow the directions given in the previous chapter, "Falls on Peck's Brook, Mt. Greylock State Reservation," to reach the main parking area (which is 0.8 miles up West Mountain Road from West Road).

From the parking lot, follow the blue-blazed trail southwest, where a sign indicates the way to "Old Adams Road." In less than 0.1 mile you will come to a junction. Continue straight, following the blue-blazed trail where a sign states "Foot Trail 1/2 mile to Old Adams Road." The path initially parallels Peck's Brook (to your right), and then pulls away, climbing steadily.

In 0.5 mile you will reach Old Adams Road and the end of the blue-blazed trail. Follow the road, going uphill. After another 0.5 mile you will come to a junction where a less identifiable road proceeds straight ahead and the main road veers left. You will also see two signs, one indicating that it is 1.0 mile back to the parking area, and the second stating "To Redgate & Adams Rd." Bear left, staying on the main road. In less than 0.2 mile you will come to a wooden bridge crossing over the North Branch of Bassett Brook. Small cascades are visible upstream, and a pretty cascade can be seen downstream from the bridge.

From the North Branch of Bassett Brook, continue southwest along the Old Adams Road for 0.4 mile farther. You will soon reach a point where the road bears to the right at a deep gorge created by the South Branch of Bassett Brook. Look down from the road and you will have excellent views of the interior of the gorge and its cascades.

The road soon curves to the left and then crosses over Bassett Brook, but there are no further views should you continue on the road.

46. Peck's Falls
(Upper, Middle, and Lower)

Location: Adams (Berkshire County)
DeLorme Massachusetts Atlas & Gazetteer: p. 21, H17
Fee: None
Hours: Open continuously
Views: Head-on and lateral
Accessibility: 0.05-mile walk one way to upper falls; 0.1-mile walk to lower falls
Degree of Difficulty: Easy to Moderate

Description: Peck's Falls are formed on Peck's Brook, a small stream that rises at an elevation of 2,900 feet[1] on the south shoulder of Mt. Greylock and flows into the Hoosic River at Adams.[2] The upper waterfall consists of two drops and totals 12 feet in height. The fall cascades into a pretty pool that has been deepened by a line of stones placed by visitors near the base. Fifty feet downstream can be found moss-covered stone blocks from an old foundation. Peck's Falls begins at the mouth of a deeply cut gorge whose steepness and depth increases as you proceed downstream from the fall.

The middle and lower falls on Peck's Brook are wilder and more scenic than the upper falls.[3] When the stream reaches the middle falls, it tumbles over a 4-foot-high cascade and then immediately races down a 6-foot cascade that is surrounded by enormous boulders and contained in a deep gorge.

Several hundred feet farther downstream, the brook reaches the end of the gorge, where it is compressed into a slot canyon, dropping 10–15 feet, and then bounces down two cascades into a pool of water. It is an incredibly wild and scenic area, with the limestone bedrock weirdly sculpted by the action of the stream. It is reminiscent of parts of Huntington Gorge in Huntington, Vermont. Look for the large pothole that the stream's erosive power has carved into the north bank rock wall near the top of the lower falls.

Forty feet downstream from the pool, the stream pours over a 5-foot cascade and then, finally, over a tiny cascade before reaching equilibrium where the gorge suddenly opens up into a valley.

Directions: From Adams (junction of Rtes. 8 & 116), drive south on Rt. 8 for less than 0.4 mile. Turn right onto Prospect Street immediately after crossing over Peck's Brook. At 0.1 mile turn left onto Harmony Street. When you come to a fork in the road in another 0.1 mile, bear left and continue uphill on Fisk Street. After driving west for 0.5 mile farther, you will reach West Road.

To Upper Falls: Turn right and drive northeast on West Road for 0.2 mile, in the process crossing over Peck's Brook, then turn left onto Gould Road. After 0.3 mile you will come to a fork in the road in an area called Greylock Glen. Bear left, continuing on Gould Road, and drive over 0.3 mile farther to the parking area on the right for Peck's Falls.

Walk across the road to the "Peck's Falls" sign and follow the path downhill as it descends to the stream. Within 200 feet you will be at the base of the falls.

To Middle and Lower Falls: Turn right at West Road and drive north for 0.1 mile. Turn left onto West Mountain Road and drive uphill for 0.2 mile, parking over to the right by a white- and orange-colored gas pipe.

To access the middle falls, follow the road back uphill and then go west on the trail/road from the parking area for over 100 feet. At the point where you can clearly hear the cascades, follow the slope downhill for a short distance until you can obtain a good view of the two middle falls. Do not attempt to enter the gorge; it is a treacherous descent.

You can access the upper fall by remaining on this road/path for less than 0.1 mile. You will end up with excellent views of the upper fall, this time from the south bank.

To access the lower falls, follow the trail downhill (east) for several hundred feet to a series of overlooks.

47. Bellevue Falls

Location: Adams (Berkshire County)
DeLorme Atlas & Gazetteer: p. 21, I18
Fee: None
Hours: Daily, 8:00 AM to 9:00 PM
Views: Head-on and lateral
Accessibility: 0.05-mile walk
Degree of Difficulty: Easy to moderate

Description: Bellevue Falls is formed on Dry Brook, a small stream that rises from a swampy area southwest of Savoy and flows into the Hoosic River at Adams. The stream and waterfall are located next to the Bellevue Cemetery, whose interment records go back as far as 1890.[1] Bellevue Falls is a 6-foot-high cascade that drops into a huge circular pool of water.[2] It has also been known as Dry Brook Falls.[3]

The surrounding exposed bedrock makes for a very scenic area. Several smaller cascades can be seen as you walk upstream for the next 100 feet. Take note of the grouping of large boulders on the left, upstream from the cascade, where the stream bends to the right.

Directions: From Adams (junction of Rtes. 8 & 116), go south on Rt. 8 for over 0.7 mile until you reach Leonard Street (on your left). If you are approaching from Cheshire (junction of Rtes. 8 & Church Street at a stoplight), drive north on Rt. 8 for 4.0 miles. Turn east onto Leonard Street and drive for 0.2 mile, crossing over Dry Brook in the process. At Bellevue Avenue, turn right and drive south for less than 0.2 mile to the entrance gate to Bellevue Cemetery. Once inside the cemetery, keep turning right at every intersection. When you come to your third right-hand turn, at 0.3 mile, pull over to your right into a tiny pull-off large enough for one car, opposite the sign indicating "Section L." Follow a deep, well-worn path that leads into the woods and down to the waterfall in less than 200 feet.

48. Falls at Tophet Chasm (Historic)

Location: Little Egypt (Berkshire County)
Accessibility: Inaccessible; falls are located on private land

Description: These small cascades are formed on Tophet Brook, a little stream that rises in the Savoy Mountain State Forest and flows into the Hoosic River at Adams. Although the cascades are fairly small—4–6 feet—the chasm containing them is impressive. A small tributary (the north branch) comes in on the opposite side of the chasm, forming a noticeable cascade of its own.[1]

The abutment on the northwest bank of the chasm is all that remains of a bridge that once spanned the gorge and connected Little Egypt to Savoy Center

History: Tophet Brook is historically connected to Susan B. Anthony, one of the twentieth-century founders of the Women's Suffrage Movement. Anthony was born on the corner of East Road and East Street in Adams. Her Quaker father, Daniel, erected a three-and-a-half-story-high textile mill on Tophet Brook near the village that had a twenty-six-foot-diameter waterwheel.[2]

It is believed that the area was originally named Egypt because of the pyramid-shaped mounds of sawdust and slab wood that loggers had left scattered about on the hillside.[3] By 1894, the name of the hamlet had changed to Little Egypt, possibly because two exotic dancers in the 1880s named Ashea Wabe and Mazar Syropoubs had popularized the stage name "Little Egypt."[4]

Tophet Brook also suggests a Middle Eastern connection. Tophet is a shrine near Jerusalem where children were offered as sacrifices to Moloch. Tophet has also been used as a synonym for Hell, which some imaginative person may have fancied the deep dark chasm on Tophet Brook to represent.[5]

49. Cascades at Bassett Reservoir

Location: Cheshire Harbor (Berkshire County)
DeLorme Atlas & Gazetteer: p. 21, J17
Fee: None
Hours: Open continuously
Views: Lateral view looking down
Accessibility: Roadside

Description: This pretty cascade is formed on Bassett Brook, a small stream that rises on the southeast slopes of Saddleball Mountain and flows into the Hoosic River just downstream from the falls. Bassett Brook is one of many minor streams rising from the shoulder of Mt. Greylock. At a total length of only 1.9 miles, it is one of the shortest, but it is blessed with waterfalls (see "Cascades on Upper Bassett Brook").

The cascade begins at the base of the 15–20-foot-high dam that impounds Bassett Reservoir, starting off quite broad and then narrowing as it enters a ravine. In the process the cascade drops a total of 20 feet.

History: The Bassett Reservoir, elevation 1,085 feet, was created to supply water to the Town of Adams.

Directions: From Cheshire (junction of Rt. 8 & Church Street at a stoplight), proceed north on Rt. 8 for over 2.5 miles. Turn left opposite East View Street and drive northwest, going uphill, for less than 0.2 mile. The reservoir, dam, and cascades are visible from a paved pull-off on your right, just before you come to West Road/Fred Mason Road.

If you are approaching from Adams (junction of Rtes. 8 & 116), drive south on Rt. 8 for 2.3 miles and turn right onto an unnamed road, which leads up to the reservoir in less than 0.2 mile.

Cascade on Bassett Brook circa 1910.

50. Cascade on South Brook

Location: Southeast of Cheshire (Berkshire County)
Stafford Hill Wildlife Management Area
DeLorme Atlas & Gazetteer: p. 21, L17
Fee: None
Hours: Open sunrise to sunset
Views: Head-on
Accessibility: 100-foot walk from parking lot
Degree of Difficulty: Easy to moderate

Description: This 8-foot-high cascade is formed on South Brook, a medium-sized stream that rises northwest of Weston Mountain and flows into the Hoosic River at Cheshire. The cascade is situated at the mouth of a rugged gorge, 0.3 mile downstream from the confluence of South Brook and McDonald Brook. Below the fall, the stream turns sharply right and continues through a deeply cut ravine.

The fall is only 0.7 mile north of the summit of The Cobble (1,850 feet), a favorite destination for hikers coming up from Cheshire or along the Appalachian National Scenic Trail.

History: The cascade is located in the Stafford Hill Wildlife Management Area, a 1,592-acre nature preserve that, along with the Chalet Wildlife Management Area to the south and the Eugene Moran Wildlife Management Area to the southeast, are part of the larger Chalet Wildlife Management Area. These parcels of wilderness are on lands that formerly consisted primarily of farms and open fields, and now protect a vast natural habitat for indigenous wildlife.

Directions: From Cheshire (junction of Rt. 8 & Church Street), turn onto Church Street and drive east for 0.5 mile. When the main road veers left, continue straight ahead on East Main Street (which quickly becomes Windsor Road). Drive southeast, proceeding uphill for 0.4 mile with South Brook to your right. When you come to Notch Road, turn right, and in 0.1 mile you will cross over a bridge. At the end of the bridge, turn immediately into a large parking area on your right.

The top of the cascade can be seen from the bridge, but the best approach is to cross over a tiny rivulet at the back of the parking area and then follow a path to your right, which leads down into the ravine. From the bottom of the ravine, you will have good views of the cascade, 50 feet upstream.

51. Pettibone Falls (Historic)

Location: Farnhams (Berkshire County)
Accessibility: Inaccessible; the falls are on private property

Description: Pettibone Falls is formed on Pettibone Brook, a small stream that rises in the hills northwest of the Cheshire Reservoir and flows into the reservoir south of Camp Mohawk. The falls consist of a chute-like plunge into a small gorge.[1]

In a book written in the late 1800s, mention is made of a stream called Northrup Brook emptying into the Cheshire Reservoir near Farnhams. The source notes that a 75-foot-high waterfall, called Barker's Falls, could be found there.[2] It's possible that Barker's Falls may be a larger-than-life version of what is known today as Pettibone Falls.

History: The fall is historically significant because of its association with nearby Pettibone Falls Cave, which is the birthplace of the National Speleological Society (NSS). The society's inaugural meeting was held at the cave in December 1940.[3]

Pettibone Falls circa 1910.

52. Wahconah Falls

Location: Dalton (Berkshire County)
Wahconah Falls State Park
DeLorme Massachusetts Atlas & Gazetteer: p. 33, A18
Fee: None
Hours: Open from sunrise to sunset
Views: Head-on view of lower fall; lateral view of upper falls
Accessibility: Short walk to base of main fall
Degree of Difficulty: Easy to main fall; Easy to Moderate to upper falls

Description: Wahconah Falls is formed on Wahconah Falls Brook, a medium-sized stream that rises from the Windsor Reservoir and flows into the Housatonic River at Dalton.[1] The falls are located in a 53-acre oblong-shaped park that follows Wahconah Falls Brook all the way up to a 40-foot-high dam at the Windsor Reservoir.[2] The park was given to the Commonwealth of Massachusetts in 1942 by the Crane Company of Dalton, manufacturers of paper.[3]

The main waterfall is 35–40 feet in height, with a pretty pool at its base, and is formed out of Becket gneiss. Near the top of the fall can be seen the remnants of a talc-producing mine shaft.[4]

Upstream from the main fall are a number of cascades and falls, including (in ascending order): a 5-foot ledge fall; two 6-foot ledge falls encased in a rocky gorge; and a 6-foot-high cascade. Several smaller cascades are interspersed among the larger upper falls.

The entire series of falls is showcased in a magnificent rocky gorge with enormous, green-colored boulders and rock slabs strewn everywhere.

History: Near the uppermost cascade, over 0.1 mile upstream from the main waterfall, is the largely intact foundation of an old mill built in the early 1800s. An early gristmill, built by William Cleveland around 1770, operated at the base of the main fall.[5] Cleveland dammed Wahconah Falls Brook above the main fall to power an overshot waterwheel for his mill. Later, around 1800, Jacob Booth erected a sawmill.[6]

The falls are named after Wahconah, the daughter of Chief Miahcoma, who settled in Dalton after being driven out of Connecticut by the English. Unlike most other stories of Indian maidens and waterfalls (see "Bash Bish Falls"), this one has a happy ending. Wahconah's father promised her to Yonnongah, an older Mohawk chief for whom Wahconah had little feelings. The brave she wanted to marry was Nessacus, who, unlike Yonnongah, was young and handsome. To settle the matter, a canoe was pushed into the river above the falls, with Yonnongah standing on one side of the stream and Nessacus on the other. It was agreed that the side of the stream where the canoe came to rest after going over the falls would determine the winner. There is more to the story (which goes on in great detail), but suffice it to say that the canoe ended up next to Nessacus, and he and princess Wahconah lived, as they say, happily ever after.

This is just one of several versions of the story; some do not end so happily.[7]

The following concluding stanzas are from a seven-stanza poem on Princess Wahconah written by Chloe Woodworth:

> 'Tis said that an Indian maiden,
>   Whose love was wooed and won,
> Against her father's wishes,
>   By a hostile chieftain's son,
> Had her fortune told in this rushing tide,
>   That hurries adown the mountain side.
>
> So they called the Falls Wahconah,
>   By the Indian maiden's name,
> And I love their picturesque beauty
>   Though they never reach to fame,
> For they lift the soul from the common clod,
>   To a broader sense of Nature's God.[8]

Directions: From Dalton (junction of Rtes. 8 & 9/8A), go northeast on Rt. 9/8A for 2.3 miles. Turn right onto North Street. At 0.1 mile, bear right at a fork and continue east for another 0.4 mile to the large parking area on your right.

The main fall is less than 0.05 mile downhill from the parking lot, heading south into the gorge. As you walk down to the main fall, you will see a blue-blazed trail to your left that runs along the stream above the main fall. The trail wends its way upstream past a number of scenic waterfalls and cascades.

Upper Wahconah Falls circa 1910.

53. Becket Gorge Falls (Historic)

Location: Becket (Berkshire County)
Accessibility: Inaccessible; the falls are on private land

Description: The falls in Becket Gorge are formed on Shaker Mill Brook, a small stream that rises northwest of Bald Top (2,040 feet) and flows into the West Branch of the Westfield River at Becket. The main fall is a 20-foot drop into a sculpted rock channel.[1]

History: Becket was settled in 1740. Nearby West Becket is best known for Jacob's Pillow Dance Theatre, the oldest dance festival in the United States.

Becket Gorge circa 1910.

54. Falls on Camp Brook

Location: Tyringham (Berkshire County)
McLennan Reservation
DeLorme Massachusetts Atlas & Gazetteer: p. 44, B15
Fee: None
Hours: Open daily from sunrise to sunset
Views: Head-on and lateral
Accessibility: 2.4-mile (one way) loop trail
Degree of Difficulty: Moderate

Description: There are several small cascades formed on Camp Brook, a small stream that rises in the hills east of Round Mountain and flows into Hop Brook south of Tyringham.[1] The main cascade is located just a slight distance downstream from Hale Swamp, which at one time was a much larger pond until a beaver dam gave way and returned the area to a marshland habitat. The cascade is roughly 15 feet high, falling over slabs of rock. A second stream, considerably smaller, comes in near the top of the falls.

History: The falls are located in the McLennan Reservation, a 594-acre preserve that was established in 1977 by the Trustees of Reservations from land donated by John McLennan. The name of the community, Tyringham, was suggested by the Englishman Lord Howe, who owned an estate in Tyringham, England.

Camp Brook got its name from the Mahicans, who built their maple sugar camp along its banks each spring.[2] Hop Brook, which Camp Brook flows into, is cited as one of the five best trout streams in the country, and President Grover Cleveland is said to have fished on the creek while visiting a friend in Tyringham.[3] Fenn Road is named for the Fenn House, which once stood at the end of the road and was the farmhouse of Julius Beach and his son Edmund.[4]

Directions: From the junction of Rtes. 20 & 102 in Lee (directly by Exit 2 of the Massachusetts Turnpike), proceed west on Rt. 102 and then immediately turn left onto Tyringham Road, going southeast. After driving 4.0 miles you will reach the village of Tyringham. From the junction of Tyringham Road and Jerusalem Road, continue south-

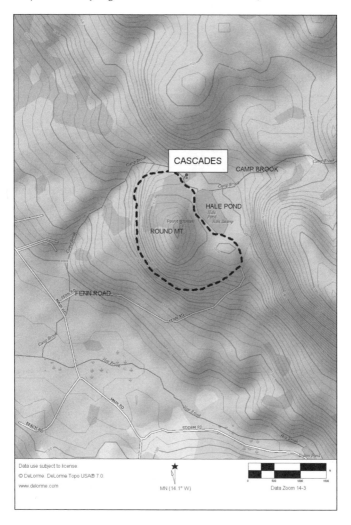

east on Tyringham Road for 1.9 miles farther. Look for Fenn Road on your left. (Note: The turn can be difficult to see. If you cross over Camp Brook, then you have gone too far.) Park off the road at the beginning of Fenn Road.

Walk up the road for nearly 0.5 mile. When you come to the trailhead on your left, follow the white trail markers to the left, which lead clockwise around Round Mountain. Eventually, the trail ends up paralleling Camp Brook. Soon after, a secondary trail leads off to the left, taking you over to the falls at roughly 0.8 mile from Fenn Road.

55. Otis Falls

Location: South of Otis (Berkshire County)
DeLorme Massachusetts Atlas & Gazetteer, p. 45, F22
Fee: None
Hours: Open continuously
Views: Lateral
Accessibility: Less than 0.05-mile walk one way
Degree of Difficulty: Easy to Moderate

Description: The falls at Otis are formed on Fall River, the outlet stream from the Otis Reservoir. Fall River flows into the West Branch of Farmington River west of the reservoir.[1] The cascade is in close proximity to the dam, yet it is far enough away that it retains its natural look.

The waterfall's appearance is entirely dependent upon how much water is being released from the reservoir. When little water is flowing, the fall can look anemic and step-like. When a significant amount of water is being discharged from the reservoir, however, the waterfall becomes a dynamic 40-foot-high cascade, and the stream below it becomes one huge water chute. If you stand at the rock promontory by the top of the falls during times of heavy flow, you will have the illusion of the stream bearing down on you, only to drop precipitously into the depths below at the very last second before engulfing you.

History: The Otis Reservoir was built in 1866, expanding a 318-acre pond into a 1,050-acre reservoir. When full, its water level is 26 feet above the pond's original surface.[2] In 1888 the dam was reinforced by granite blocks. It remains one of the largest bodies of water in western Massachusetts.[3]

At left: Otis Falls circa 1940.

The town and the waterfall were named after Harrison Gray Otis, who represented Massachusetts in the U.S. Senate from 1829 to 1832.[4]

Directions: From Otis (junction of Rtes. 23 East & 8), drive south on Rt. 8 for 2.9 miles, following the West Branch of Farmington River, which will be on your left. Turn left onto Reservoir Road and drive uphill, going northeast. At 1.3 miles bear right when the road divides. When you have gone a total of 1.6 miles from Rt. 8, turn right onto Tolland Road and drive south for 0.8 mile. Pull over to the right at a small parking space before crossing over the one-lane bridge at the dam.

From the parking area, a path leads down into the woods. Go slightly away from the dam initially, and then head towards the stream, either proceeding directly over to a view at the top of the falls, or descending 40 feet farther down, to where a path leads past a rock face on your left to an excellent view of the falls from its base.

The Buck River circa 1910.

56. Cascades on Buck River

Location: West New Boston (Berkshire County)
DeLorme Massachusetts Atlas & Gazetteer: p. 45, 119
Fee: None
Hours: Open continuously
Views: Lateral
Accessibility: Roadside

Description: These two, 4-foot high, elongated cascades are formed on the Buck River, a medium-sized stream that rises from Morley Hill in the Sandisfield State Forest and flows into the Clam River at West New Boston.[1] Buck River is named for Buck Hill, around which it flows.[2]

Directions: From New Boston (junction of Rtes. 57 West & 8), drive northwest on Rt. 57 for 2.1 miles. As soon as you cross over a small bridge spanning the Buck River, pull into a parking area on your right.

Watching out for traffic, walk across the road and then uphill for 50 feet, staying close to the side of the road. The first cascade will be visible in the stream below.

To see the second waterfall, avoid passing traffic by crossing back to the other side of the road (where there is plenty of shoulder), and then walk uphill for another 50 feet. Carefully cross over to the stream side of the road again, from where the second fall can be seen.

57. Marguerite Falls

Location: South of New Boston (Berkshire County)
DeLorme Massachusetts Atlas & Gazetteer: p. 45, K22
Fee: None
Hours: Open continuously
Views: Head-on
Accessibility: Roadside
Description: This pretty, 40-foot-high cascade is formed on a small stream that flows into the West Branch of Farmington River just before the river widens and turns into Coldbrook River Lake in Connecticut.[1] The fall is named after Lake Marguerite, from which the stream rises. Lake Marguerite has also been known as Simons Pond.[2] The cascade is quite picturesque, falling all the way down to the base of the bridge.

Although the name of the waterfall may seem distinctive, there is a 60-foot-high cascade by the same name in northeast Tennessee.

Directions: From New Boston (junction of Rtes. 57 East & 8), go south on Rt. 8 for 3.5 miles. Pull over into a truck pull-off on your left after crossing over a bridge spanning the outlet stream from Lake Marguerite.

Walk back along the road for a couple of hundred feet and cross over to the west side of the bridge. The cascade can be safely appreciated from the bridge because of the road's wide shoulder.

58. Hubbard River Gorge & Falls

Location: Near West Granville (Hampden County)
Granville State Forest
DeLorme Massachusetts Atlas & Gazetteer: p. 45, L28
Fee: None
Hours: Open continuously
Restrictions: The campground is open from mid-May to mid-October. Office hours are 8 AM to 10 PM. When the office or campground is closed, an additional 0.6-mile of hiking will be required to reach the trailhead at the road's cul-de-sac.
Views: Many lateral views
Accessibility: 1.0-mile hike one way (or 1.5-mile hike one way if you start from the parking area by the bridge)
Degree of Difficulty: Moderate to Difficult

Description: The falls are formed on the Hubbard River, a medium-sized stream that rises from the hills north of Tolland and flows into Barkhamsted Reservoir in Connecticut.[1] Along the way the river drops 450 feet as it travels 2.5 miles through the gorge.[2] Although seven main waterfalls are described on this hike, there are actually untold numbers of smaller cascades and drops, and you will be accompanied by the sound of cascading water for virtually the entire length of the trek.

Waterfall #1—This 6-foot-high cascade surrounded by bedrock drops into a beautiful pool. It is a favorite swimming hole for campers, but please obey the sign that states: "Jumping or diving from cliffs prohibited."

Waterfall # 2—This cascade is a 4-foot drop near the opposite bank of the stream. A towering wall of bedrock nearly 8 feet high rises up on the trail side of the river.

Waterfall # 3—This very elongated cascade totals over 8 feet in height, but spans a considerable horizontal distance. When you walk out onto the bedrock to look back at the cascade, you will be standing next to a 2-foot-high cascade that drops into a pool and then exits via another tiny cascade.

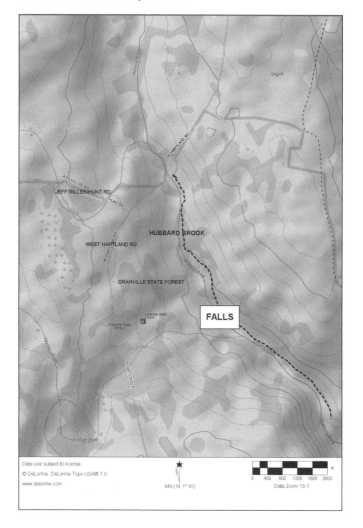

Waterfall # 4—This is an 8-foot-high cascade located where the stream rushes past on the trail side of the bedrock and then drops diagonally towards the center.

Waterfall # 5—This cascade is close to 5 feet in height and encompasses nearly the full width of the stream.

Waterfall # 6—This very pretty 3-foot-high cascade is formed near the center of the stream because of the sloping V-shaped bedrock on both sides.

Waterfall # 7—The last waterfall is equal to the first in terms of scenic value. Here, the stream is compressed between raised bedrock on the side of the river closest to you and an enormous boulder on the opposite side. Accelerated as it is compressed, the river drops over a 4-foot-high cascade and then rushes down a 4-foot chute, arriving at the bottom of the fall 8 feet lower than when it started.

History: The Hubbard River Gorge and Falls are located in the 2,830-acre Granville State Forest. The river is named after Samuel Hubbard, who was the first white settler in this area. Hubbard erected a homestead along the bank of the river in 1749.[3] If you look closely along the trail, you will see remnants from the old days, including faint cellar depressions, a sluiceway, and an old 8-foot-long metal cylinder 3 feet in diameter.

Directions: From New Boston (junctions of Rtes. 57 East & 8), go east on Rt. 57 for 6.7 miles. Turn right onto West Hartland Road and proceed south for 0.6 mile, at which time you will see a sign on your left for the Granville State Forest. At 1.0 mile cross over a bridge spanning Hubbard River and park in a large parking area on your left.

Walk back over the stone bridge and immediately turn right onto a paved road that parallels the river. Stay on the road for the next 0.6 mile. (Note: if you are visiting when the park is open, you will be able to drive down this paved road and park near its end).

When you come to the cul-de-sac, follow the blue-blazed trail to the left. The trail is actually an old road that parallels the river. In less than 0.1 mile the road begins to pull away from the river. At this point follow a fairly noticeable trail that leads off to the right. This will take you over to the river and to waterfall #1, less than 0.05 mile away.

The next waterfall is less than 0.1 mile farther downstream. Stay on the path paralleling the river as best as you can, proceeding downstream. The path fades in and out, and part of the trek will seem like a bushwhack, but the river will always be within sight to your right. In a couple of minutes you will come to waterfall #2.

From here, follow the path downstream for a short distance farther and you will come back out onto the main trail/road. Waterfall #3 is encountered near this point. What is special about this waterfall is that you can walk out onto a rocky part of the streambed and look back upstream at this extremely elongated cascade.

Continue along the old road for less than 0.2 mile. You will pass by a huge metal cylinder lying along the trail side to your left. This is a good reference point for determining where you are on the hike. After passing by the metal cylinder, you will encounter a wide section of stream that appears almost as though it were dammed. Here the river is pushed to the opposite side of the bank and then down. In times of high waters, the section of bedrock that you're standing on may be overrun by the river, forming a 3-foot-high cascade of its own.

As you continue downstream for less than 0.1 mile farther, the streambed begins to become increasingly rocky, and suddenly an island forms at its center, splitting the river momentarily into two sections. After a little more than a hundred feet, look across to the opposite bank and you will see a 2-foot-high cascade, formed where the far divide of the stream has produced its own tiny waterfall.

In 0.1 mile you will come to waterfall # 4, a pretty, 8-foot-high cascade. A jutting extension of bedrock below the waterfall allows you to scamper out to the middle of the stream for a look back at the cascade.

Fifty to seventy-five feet farther downstream, the river plunges over waterfall #5, this one nearly 5 feet high and extending almost the entire width of the stream. Once again it is possible to get a good look at the waterfall from the bedrock below.

From here, the character of the hike begins to change, with the surroundings becoming more gorge-like. You will see more boulders and cliffs of bedrock on both sides now.

In less than 0.1 mile you will come to waterfall #6, a pretty, 3-foot-high cascade that has formed near the center of the stream. The best view of this waterfall is from the trail/road itself.

Then, in less than another 0.1 mile, you will come to waterfall #7, the final distinctive waterfall on this hike, located where the stream is compressed between the bedrock on your side and a huge boulder on the opposite side.

From here, the trail climbs up along the river, and the numerous little cascades and rapids below look more flattened. The trail quickly descends again, however, and comes back to the bank of the river where you will see a pretty, 3-foot-high cascade. From here on, you will find yourself walking out of the main part of the gorge. Although the cascades and rapids continue, none are particularly noteworthy.

But the best is yet to come. When you turn around and walk back along the trail, you will get to see all of the waterfalls in reverse order and facing them head-on.

ROUTE 9:
THE BERKSHIRE
TRAIL

Westfield River circa 1910.

Introduction

Route 9 (less commonly known as the Berkshire Trail) runs west to east, beginning in Pittsfield and ending at Northampton. From West Cummington, the road follows along the Westfield River and then along the West Branch of the Mill River.

59. Windsor Jambs

Location: Windsor (Berkshire County)
Windsor State Forest
DeLorme Massachusetts Atlas & Gazetteer: p. 21, N26
Fee: None
Hours: Open daily from sunrise to sunset
Views: Mostly lateral views looking down
Accessibility: Fairly short trek along rim of gorge
Degree of Difficulty: Easy to moderate

Description: Windsor Jambs is a narrow-cut chasm formed on Windsor Jambs Brook, a small stream that is a tributary of the Westfield River.[1] The stream has also been called *Boundary Brook* in the past.[2]

The chasm is unusually narrow, with nearly vertical walls. This extreme narrowness is the result of the chasm's gray, fissile schist bedding tending to break off in 90-degree pieces, leaving straight, vertical sections of walls behind.

The chasm, located in a 1,626-acre state forest,[3] contains several cascades and many rapids. At the mouth of the gorge can be seen an 8-foot-high cascade split into two sections by a protuberance of bedrock at the center of the creek. Just downstream is encountered the main waterfall, over 10 feet in height. Farther below are several smaller cascades.

History: The area has seen much lumbering and sheep-raising in the past.

Directions: From Dalton (junction of Rtes. 8 & 9/8A), drive east on Rt. 9 for 11.6 miles to West Cunningham. Turn left onto West Main Street. Drive northeast for nearly 0.2 mile and turn left onto Savoy Road (also called River Road). You will see a State Forest sign at the beginning of the road. Proceed northwest for 3.0 miles, paralleling

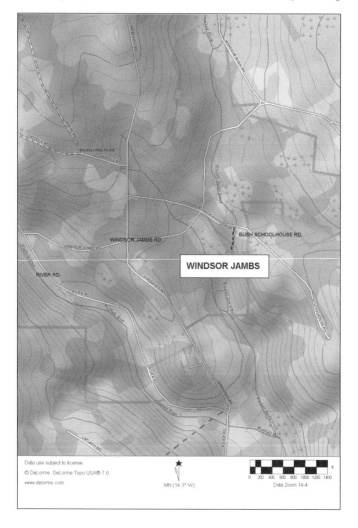

Windsor Jambs, 1999.

the river all the way. When you get to Lower Road (which is dirt-packed), turn right and proceed east for 0.6 mile to Bush Cemetery Road (your second right-hand turn). Turn right and, after 0.1 mile, turn right again into a parking area.

The gorge begins virtually next to the parking lot where the first fall comes readily into sight. A green metal fence parallels the top of the gorge, keeping the unwary from getting too close to the edge and inadvertently tumbling in. I leave it to you to decide as to the aesthetics of this.

If you are approaching from west of Savoy (junction of Rtes. 8A & 116), drive southeast on Rt. 8A/116 for 1.2 miles. Turn right onto River Road and drive south for 2.9 miles.

60. Falls on Basin Brook

Location: Northwest of Plainfield (Franklin County)
Kenneth Dubuque Memorial State Park
DeLorme Massachusetts Atlas & Gazetteer: p. 21, K29
Fee: None
Hours: Open daily from sunrise to sunset
Views: Head-on and lateral
Accessibility: 1.5-mile hike one way
Degree of Difficulty: Moderate to Difficult

Description: Basin Brook and its tributary rise in the hills southeast of West Hawley[1] and flow into King Brook just before joining with the Chickley River. Basin Brook is aptly named, for the stream rushes down from one drop to the next as though each were contained in a basin. King Brook is probably named after Warriner King, who along with Jonathan Fuller established a sawmill in the area.[2]

There are a number of small cascades ranging from 2–6 feet in height along Basin Brook and its tributary, and this hike, which parallels first the tributary and then Basin Brook, is almost magical as it passes by enormous outcroppings of rock, always within the sound of cascading water.

History: The cascades are located in the Kenneth Dubuque Memorial State Park, a 7,822-acre preserve named after a former forest supervisor who played a major role in the park's establishment. The park was previously known as Hawley State Forest, with the name attributed to Joseph Hawley, a Revolutionary War hero.[3] One hundred and eighty years ago this area was a thriving agricultural center and considerably more populated.

The area was also highly industrialized in the past. When you drive along West Hawley Road as it parallels King Brook, look for numerous stone foundations of past mills and factories. Industries in the Hawley area included mines, sawmills, wood-turning mills, tanneries, and gristmills.[4]

Directions: From west of Savoy (junction of Rtes. 116 & 8A), drive southeast on Rt. 116/8A for 5.8 miles. When the two routes divide, turn left onto Rt. 8A (West Hawley Road) and drive north for less than 2.1 miles, going steadily downhill, to Kings Corner. Opposite Stetson Road (on your left), turn right into the parking area for the Kenneth Dubuque Memorial State Park.

From the parking area, walk along the abandoned Hallockville Road down across King Brook and east up the side of a large hill for over 0.5 mile. Shortly after you begin to descend, you will cross over a small stream. Immediately, take a blue-blazed path that goes off to the left. This is the Hawley Pass Trail. After 0.1 mile you will cross over Basin Brook's tributary via a small footbridge. Follow the blue-blazed trail as it turns sharply left and begins following this tributary downstream. After 0.2 mile from the footbridge, you will pass by a 3-foot-high cascade on your left. The trail quickly takes you around and past a 20-foot-high outcropping of rocks from whose base you can look back for a head-on view of the small cascade.

In another 0.1 mile you will pass by an elongated, 6-foot-high, mossy cascade. Next to it, on the opposite side of the trail, is an enormous split boulder.

One hundred feet farther downstream, a footbridge takes you across the brook. From here, the trail leads down a long, fairly steep hill for 0.2 mile, with the cascading stream descending to your right. At the bottom of the stream, you will come to the confluence of the tributary and Basin Brook. Cross over the stream via a footbridge and bear right on the trail. (The blue-blazed trail also goes left, paralleling Basin Brook as it flows downstream towards West Hawley, but there are no significant cascades on that part of the creek). In 50 feet you will come up to a shelter from where, looking upstream, you can see a pretty, 5-foot-high cascade tumbling into a shallow pool of water.

Begin heading upstream, following the blue-blazed trail. Within 0.05 mile you will have to cross over Basin Brook (which can be a bit tricky if there is a lot of water flowing). With Basin Brook now on your left, you will encounter one 3–4-foot cascade after another as you proceed upstream. After 0.4 mile you will pass by a 6-foot cascade, which marks the end of the hike. From here, the stream becomes placid and there are no further cascades of any note. If you wish to continue upstream, be prepared to ford the brook again in less than 0.05 mile.

When you leave the parking area and begin driving back up West Hawley Road (Rt. 8A), after 0.5 mile be sure to look for several small but pretty cascades to your right, on King Brook.

61. Fall in East Windsor

Location: East Windsor (Berkshire County)
DeLorme Massachusetts Atlas & Gazetteer: p. 33, B26
Fee: None
Hours: Open continuously
Views: Head-on
Helpful Hint: Include as a side trip while in the general area
Accessibility: Roadside

Description: This 8-foot high-waterfall is formed on a small stream that passes through East Windsor. The falls are block-shaped and located just upstream from an old bridge. Under normal water flow the falls are divided at the top into two descending rivulets. A series of small cascades can be seen farther upstream, partially visible from roadside.

History: Nathaniel Hawthorne wrote, in *American Notebook,* "the highest point of our journey was at Windsor, where we could see leagues around over the mountains—a terribly bare, bleak spot, fit for nothing but sheep and without shelter of woods."[1] Fortunately, the environment has changed substantially since 1850 and the forests, which had been ravaged and stripped, have grown back.

Directions: From the junction of Rtes. 8 & 8A/9 in Dalton, drive east on Rt. 9 for 10.8 miles. Turn right at a green-colored sign stating "To Rt. 143. Worthington. Peru. E. Windsor" and drive south on Worthington Road for less than 0.5 mile. At the intersection of Worthington Road and Old Rt. 9, you will see the River Street Bridge on your right. The falls are just upstream from the bridge and are visible from the top of the bridge or from Worthington Road before you reach the first private home on your right.

62. West Worthington Falls

Location: West Worthington (Hampshire County)
DeLorme Massachusetts Atlas & Gazetteer: p. 33, E26
Fee: None
Hours: Open continuously
Restrictions: Stay on the road or bridge.
Views: Limited view looking over top and down into the gorge
Accessibility: Roadside view from top of gorge

Description: West Worthington Falls are formed on the Middle Branch of the Westfield River, a medium-sized stream that rises north of West Worthington and flows into the Westfield River at Huntington.[1] The falls drop a total of 50 feet.

History: The town and falls were named after Col. John Worthington of Springfield, an early landowner in the area.[2]

Legend has it that a Native American brave and his beloved, Gerwadeta, leaped to their deaths at the falls. Similar legends are associated with many waterfalls.[3]

Directions: From Dalton (junction of Rtes. 8 & 8A/9), drive east on Rt. 9 for 10.8 miles. Turn right onto West Worthington Road (where a sign points the way towards Rt. 143) and drive south for 3.6 miles. Then turn right onto Rt. 143 and drive southwest for over 1.6 miles. When you come to River Road, turn left and go south for 0.4 mile. The falls are 40 feet downstream from where a little bridge crosses the Middle Branch of the Westfield River.

Bear in mind that only the top of the falls can be glimpsed from roadside. The adjacent land is privately owned.

63. Glendale Falls

Location: East of Middlefield (Hampshire County)
Glendale Falls Reservation
DeLorme Massachusetts Atlas & Gazetteer: p. 33, J27
Fee: None
Hours: Open daily from sunrise to sunset
Views: Lateral views; difficult to see as a whole
Accessibility: Short walk to top of falls; fairly arduous scramble to bottom
Degree of Difficulty: Easy to top; Moderate to Difficult to bottom

Description: Glendale Falls is formed on Glendale Brook, a medium-sized stream that flows into the Middle Branch of the Westfield River.[1] A kiosk by the parking lot provides information on the Westfield River, which in 1993 was designated Massachusetts's first national wild and scenic river.

The waterfall is formed out of granite and located in the Glendale Falls Reservation, a 60-acre park that was established in 1964 by the Trustees of Reservations.

The fall is a massive, hulking block of vertically inclined bedrock whose top begins at an elevation of 1,060 feet. The rock is loaded with chutes and drops, and even has a 20-foot-long flume at its center roughly one-third of the way down. When the water comes over the top, it is as though it has entered a pin-ball machine. The water encounters so many ricochets, bounces, and zigzags during its descent that there is no way to predict where a twig or leaf swept over the top might end up at the bottom. No matter how you try, it is virtually impossible to see the waterfall in its entirety.

History: Along the northern bank are the foundations of two structures that were part of the eighteenth-century Glendale Farm and gristmill.

Directions: From Dalton (junction of Rtes. 8 & 8A/9), drive east on Rt. 9 for 10.8 miles. Turn right onto West Worthington Road and drive south for nearly 3.6 miles. Then turn right onto Rt. 143 and drive southwest for 1.6 miles. When you come to River Road, turn left and drive south for 5.6 miles, paralleling the Middle Branch of the Westfield River (taking note that at 3.4 miles you will bear left where the road forks). Turn right onto Clark Wright Road and drive uphill steeply, going southwest for 0.4 mile. Just before you cross over a small bridge, turn into a parking area on your right.

It is less than 50–100 feet to the top of the falls, but it is a considerable descent on a barely defined path if you wish to scramble down to the bottom of the cascade.

Glendale Falls circa 1940.

64. Chapel Falls

Location: Near South Ashfield (Franklin County)
Chapelbrook Reservation
DeLorme Massachusetts Atlas & Gazetteer: p. 34, B10
Fee: None
Hours: Open daily from sunrise to sunset
Views: Head-on and lateral
Accessibility: 0.1-mile walk one way
Degree of Difficulty: Moderate

Description: Chapel Falls (also called Chapelbook Falls) is formed on Chapel Brook, a medium-sized stream that rises south of Ashfield and flows into Poland Brook, a tributary to the South River.[1] The Falls are located in a 173-acre reservation established in 1964 by the Trustees of Reservations, and consist of a series of drops over rock ledges 10, 15, and 25 feet in height. The lowermost waterfall is, by all accounts, the prettiest. The stream plunges nearly vertically for 20 feet over this fall, and then cascades the rest of the way down. Below the lowermost cascade is a tiny 2–3 foot cascade.

Not all nature lovers come to the reservation to look at its waterfalls, however. From the main parking area, many visitors take the half-mile trail up to the summit of Pony Mountain. Along the trail is a massive, 100-foot rock face called Chapel Ledge.

History: Chapel Falls has been the site of at least two gristmills. The stone foundation of an old mill is visible at the site. According to the Chapelbrook Reservation kiosk, a two-room schoolhouse stood above the falls in the 1800s. The school doubled as a Methodist chapel on Sundays, which is how the stream and falls came to be named.

The Trustees of Reservations is a membership-supported nonprofit organization that preserves, for public use and enjoyment, properties of exceptional scenic, historic, and ecological value in Massachusetts. The original acreage for the Chapelbrook Reservation was a gift, with endowment, from Mrs. Curtiss in memory of her late husband, Henry T. Curtiss. Further land purchases were made in 1981 and 1989 with additional money donated by Mrs. Curtiss. In 1992 more lands were obtained through the generosity of Edward Preissler, Deborah Thomas, and Michael and Jane McCusker.[2]

Chapel Falls, 2006.

Directions: From Ashfield (junction of Rtes. 112 & 116 East), drive southeast on Rt. 116 for 2.4 miles until you reach South Ashfield. When Rt. 116 veers sharply left, continue straight ahead (following a sign that points the way to Rt. 9) and you will quickly come to a stop sign. Go straight, following Williamsburg Road south uphill for 2.3 miles. Just before crossing over a bridge spanning Chapel Brook, turn right into a small parking area for Chapelbrook Reservation.

If you are approaching from Williamsburg (junction of Rt. 9 and the Williamsburg/Ashfield Road), drive north on Ashfield Road (which turns into Williamsburg Road) for 9 miles. As soon as you cross over the Chapel Brook bridge, turn left into the parking area.

Walk across the bridge and then turn left, following an old road. After less than 100 feet, take a path to the left that leads down to the stream and the uppermost fall.

Some scrambling is required to access all three falls.

65. Chesterfield Gorge

Location: South of West Chesterfield (Hampshire County)
Chesterfield Gorge
DeLorme Massachusetts Atlas & Gazetteer: p. 34, G3
Fee: None
Hours: Open daily from sunrise to sunset
Views: From top of chasm
Accessibility: Less than 0.2-mile walk (one way) along top of gorge
Degree of Difficulty: Easy

Description: The Chesterfield Gorge is an impressive granite chasm that was carved out by the Westfield River during the course of many thousands of years.[1] The Westfield River is a substantial, 85-mile-long stream[2] that rises northwest of Savoy and flows into the Connecticut River by Agawam.

There are no large waterfalls in the gorge, just several little cascades and the ever-present sound of rushing water, but the Chesterfield Gorge reveals what the power of moving water can accomplish if you give it enough time—the creation of a 100-foot-wide canyon with vertical walls up to 70 feet high extending for over 0.1 mile

The gorge is located in a 166-acre park created in 1929 by the Trustees of Reservations. Initially, the size of the park was fairly modest. This changed in 1949 when additional lands were purchased through funds provided by Sidney L. Beals and Mrs. Stanley King. Then more land was acquired thanks to the Pioneer Valley Association in 1950, the Quinnehtuk Company in 1955, and Stanley and Mildred Greimann in 1994.[3]

History: At the upper end of the gorge (called The Narrows), are the surviving stone abutments of High Bridge, which was built in 1739. British troops crossed the bridge in 1777 as they returned to Boston

Chesterfield Gorge circa 1900.

following their defeat at the battle of Saratoga. A tollgate was erected in 1779 at the east end of the bridge. You can still see remnants of the gatekeeper's house.

Directions: From West Chesterfield (3.9 miles southeast of the junction of Rtes. 143 & 112), turn south onto Ireland Street (also shown on the *Gazetteer* as River Road) and drive southwest for less than 0.8 mile. Then turn left onto River Road (a dirt road), which leads south in over 0.1 mile to a parking area for the Chesterfield Gorge.

The gorge is located next to the parking area. A fairly unobtrusive railing consisting of posts and interconnecting cable provides a measure of safety.

Additional Points of Interest: If you wish to explore more of the Westfield River and view its myriad of rapids, follow River Road south, downstream, as it parallels the river. The trek is most enjoyable if done on foot, although it is possible to drive along the road if you have a four-wheel-drive vehicle that can handle rough roads. This is called the East Branch Trail.[4] Were you to stay on this road to its end, you would ultimately end up at the Knightville Dam, approximately 11 miles distant. You will pass by many impressive rapids, but there are no significant drops to be seen on this section of the river. A tiny tributary called Whiteside Brook produces a small cascade as it comes down into the Westfield River. You will encounter this stream and cascade on your right within 0.4 mile after you start down River Road from the Chesterfield Gorge parking area.

Although the Westfield is a river of immense natural beauty, it has also been heavily industrialized. Farther downstream, in Woronoco and Russell, impressive waterfalls have been dammed at their tops and pressed into service for power generation. Unfortunately, neither of these waterfalls can be seen up close, nor are there any satisfactory views from afar. The falls in Woronoco can be glimpsed from the east end of the Valley View Avenue bridge, and the falls in Russell can be spotted through fencing at the cul-de-sac on Grove Street.

Introduction

Route 20 (also called Jacob's Ladder) runs west to east from Hancock to West Springfield. The section explored in this book begins at Chester, initially following along the West Branch of the Westfield River to Huntington and then following the Westfield River itself.

This route was a main pathway used by Native Americans. In 1910 it became the first automobile road in the United States to cross over a 2,100-foot-high mountain ridge.

It acquired the name "Jacob's Ladder"—a biblical reference to Heaven and the steep ascent required to get there—from a former section of highway near Becket that proved to be exceptionally steep and treacherous.[1]

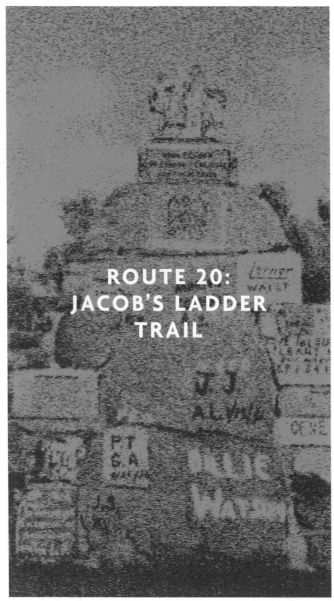

ROUTE 20: JACOB'S LADDER TRAIL

Jacob's Ladder — a Highway to Heaven. Postcard circa 1940.

66. Bradley Falls

Location: South Worthington (Hampshire County)
DeLorme Massachusetts Atlas & Gazetteer: p. 34, J2
Fee: None
Hours: Open continuously
Views: Lateral
Accessibility: Roadside

Description: Bradley Falls[1] is formed on the Little River, which rises near Worthington Center and flows into the Westfield River southeast of South Worthington. The falls are also called South Worthington Falls.[2]

The waterfall drops a total of approximately 30–40 feet within a distance of several hundred feet. An old mill foundation on the opposite side of the stream can be seen next to an 8-foot-high cascade.

Directions: From the junction of Rtes. 143 West & 112 (northeast of Worthington Corners), drive southeast on Rt. 112 for 5.7 miles to the hamlet of South Worthington. You will see the Ireland Street bridge on your left.

Park in the village, then walk over to the bridge and follow Rt. 112 downhill—staying close to the guardrails—for less than 100 feet. Before reaching a private residence overlooking the gorge, you will be able to obtain views of some of the cascades.

Approaching from Huntington (junction of Rtes. 20 & 112), drive northwest on Rt. 112 for approximately 9 miles until you reach South Worthington. The falls are located in the gorge next to Rt. 112, just before you reach the Ireland Street bridge.

67. Cascade on the Little River

Location: Southeast of South Worthington (Hampshire County)
Hiram H. Fox Wildlife Management Area
DeLorme Massachusetts Atlas & Gazetteer: p. 34, K3
Fee: None
Hours: Open continuously
Views: Lateral
Accessibility: Roadside
Degree of Difficulty: Easy to Moderate if you decide to scramble
down the embankment for a closer look

Description: This small cascade, approximately 3–4 feet in height, is
formed on the Little River, a medium-sized stream that rises near Worthington Center and flows into the Westfield River north of the Knightville Dam Project. Although hardly large, the cascade is very pretty and
undoubtedly well-known to anglers who frequent the area. The cascade is located in the Hiram H. Fox Wildlife Management Area.

Farther downstream, after the Little River has joined with the
Westfield River and continued south from the Knightville Dam, a
pretty gorge is encountered with a 4–5-foot fall. At present this area
is likely only accessible by canoe or kayak.[1]

Directions: From South Worthington (junction of Rt. 112 & Ireland
Street), drive southeast on Rt. 112 for 1.5 miles, paralleling the Little
River. Park when you come to a pull-off on your left. The falls are
just downstream from the parking area, and can be viewed either
from the road or by scrambling down the embankment to the level
of the stream.

If you are approaching the cascade from Huntington (junction
of Rtes. 20 & 112), drive northwest on Rt. 112 for 7.5 miles and pull
over into a tiny parking area on your right, just after you pass by a
view of the cascade.

68. Sanderson Brook Falls

Location: Southeast of Chester (Hampden County)
Chester-Blandford State Forest
DeLorme Massachusetts Atlas & Gazetteer: p. 45, A28
Fee: None
Hours: Open daily from dawn to dusk
Views: Head-on and lateral
Accessibility: 1.0-mile hike one way
Degree of Difficulty: Moderate

Description: Sanderson Brook Falls is formed on Sanderson Brook, a medium-sized stream that rises in the hills southeast of Chester and flows into the Westfield River just north of the falls.[1] Sanderson Brook Falls is 75 feet high and broken into several cascades. It is located in the Chester-Blandford State Forest, a 2,308-acre preserve.[2] Directly across the stream from the base of the falls is a flat stone surface that makes for a wonderful place to picnic and enjoy the sights and sounds of falling water.

Directions: From Huntington (intersection of Rtes. 20 & 112), drive northwest on Rt. 20 for 4.3 miles. Turn left into the area designated for Sanderson Brook Falls. If approaching from the center of Chester, drive southeast for approximately 2.5 miles and pull into the area for Sanderson Brook Falls on your right.

Proceeding on foot, follow the wide dirt road for 0.8 mile. Along the way you will cross over two tiny bridges. When you come to a well-worn path leading off to your right, follow it down to the base of the falls.

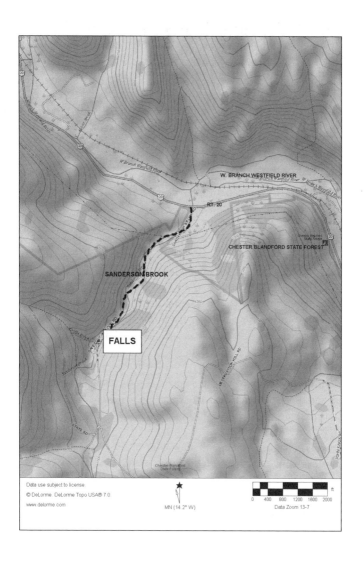

69. Goldmine Brook Falls

Location: Southeast of Chester (Hampden County)
Chester-Blandford State Forest
DeLorme Massachusetts Atlas & Gazetteer: p. 45, A30
Fee: None
Hours: Open daily from dawn to dusk
Views: Head-on and lateral
Accessibility: Less than 0.1-mile hike one way
Degree of Difficulty: Moderate

Description: There are several prominent waterfalls located in a deep gorge formed on Goldmine Brook, a small stream that rises in the hills southeast of Chester and flows into the Westfield River just downstream from the falls. The falls and gorge have been called, by some, the Heavenly Highway.[1] At the head of the gorge are two beautiful waterfalls. The upper fall drops 30 feet in two steps into a pool of water. The lower fall is a 10-foot cascade. The stream also produces several smaller cascades below the lower fall.

History: The falls are located in the Chester-Blandford State Forest in an area noted for hills pitted with small mines used for the harvesting of mica, emery, and corundum.[2]

Directions: From Huntington (junction of Rtes. 20 & 112), drive northwest on Rt. 20 for nearly 2.8 miles. Along the way, you will pass by the Chester-Blandford State Forest headquarters on your left. Park in an area on your right, just before crossing over Goldmine Brook, where a cascading stream is visible on your left from roadside.

If you are approaching from the center of Chester, drive southeast on Rt. 20 for roughly 4 miles (or 1.5 miles east from the parking area for Sanderson Falls). As soon as you pass a cascading stream on your right, turn into the parking area up ahead on your left.

Carefully walk across the road. Before you reach Goldmine Brook, look for a path going up the bank, and follow it uphill for 0.05 mile. You will find yourself looking up at a magnificent rocky gorge. Continue following the path uphill for several hundred feet more, and then bear to your right, following a natural path that leads down into the gorge and to the base of the upper falls. The lower falls will be visible just a short distance below.

70. Pitcher Falls

Location: South Quarter (Hampden County)
Noble View Area
DeLorme Massachusetts Atlas & Gazetteer: p. 46, G3
Fee: Modest fee; AMC membership discount
Hours: Open daily from sunrise to sunset
Views: Lateral and head-on
Accessibility: 0.8-mile hike
Degree of Difficulty: Moderate to first group of falls; Moderate to Difficult to second group of falls

Description: Pitcher Falls and a number of smaller cascades are formed on Pitcher Brook, a small tributary to the Little River.[1] Quite possibly the stream was named for its multiple cascades, as water pours from one pool into the next as though from a pitcher.

There are two groups of cascades. The first consists of three small cascades that are encountered in the following order as you proceed downstream: a 3-foot cascade that drops almost perpendicularly to the stream; a longer, 3-foot cascade whose bedrock follows the serpentine contour of the ravine; and a third (main) cascade, where the stream drops 4 feet into a huge circular pool.

The second group of cascades is found 0.05 mile farther downstream. The main waterfall (Pitcher Falls) drops nearly vertically for over 10 feet into a pool of clear water. Here, the walls of the gorge surround the cascade and pool like an amphitheater. As the stream leaves the pool, it drops over a tiny cascade and then, less than 100 feet farther downstream, rushes down a two-tiered 15-foot-high cascade. Adding to the beauty of the scene is the glittering mica contained in the surrounding bedrock.

The Noble View area is maintained by the Berkshire Chapter of the Appalachian Mountain Club.[2]

Additional Point of Interest: Rt. 23 is also called the General Knox Highway. It roughly follows the route that General Henry Knox took during the Revolutionary War when he captured a garrison of cannons at Fort Ticonderoga in upper New York State and hauled fifty-nine of them overland, in winter, across Massachusetts to Boston.

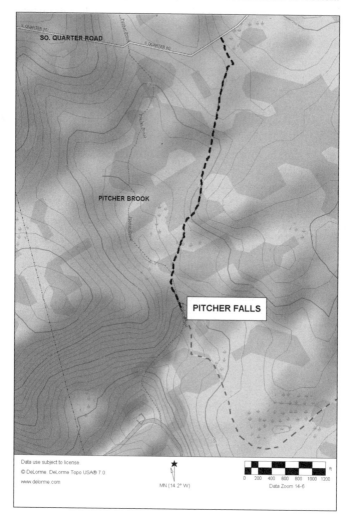

You will note in the directions below that there is also a General Knox Road.

Directions: From Woronoco (junction of Rtes. 20 & 23), drive west on Rt. 23 for 1.7 miles. When you come to General Knox Road, turn left and drive southeast for 1.2 miles. Then turn right onto Quarter Road and proceed southwest for nearly 1.3 miles. Turn left into the AMC Noble View parking area.

From the parking area, walk uphill on the wide, gravel access road for several hundred feet. Turn right onto a trail marked with yellow triangles and with a sign indicating "Pitcher Brook 0.4 mile." Follow the trail downhill and then, after 0.4 mile, back up to where you see an old stone wall and several pine trees with blue dots on them. This is where the yellow trail crosses the white-blazed "Pitcher Brook" trail. Turn right and follow the white-blazed trail downhill for over 0.3 mile. As soon as you come up to Pitcher Brook, you will begin to see cascades ahead.

The first group of cascades is encountered within a couple of hundred feet. Stay on the white-blazed trail and it will take you down almost to the base of the third (and main) cascade.

The second group of cascades is 0.05 mile downstream from the first group. Proceed along the white-blazed trail, which leads to the top of Pitcher Falls. To continue on, follow the trail as it climbs uphill for 50 feet and then back downhill and over to where you can see the pool and waterfall.

List of Waterfalls

About the Author

Russell Dunn has written more books on waterfalls than any other author in the world, and was profiled by the Associated Press in 2007 in a national feature article. His prior works include four guidebooks to the waterfalls of eastern New York State: *Adirondack Waterfall Guide: New York's Cool Cascades* (Black Dome Press, 2003); *Catskill Region Waterfall Guide: Cool Cascades of the Catskills & Shawangunks* (Black Dome Press, 2004); *Hudson Valley Waterfall*

Guide: From Saratoga and the Capital Region to the Highlands and Palisades (Black Dome Press, 2005); and *Mohawk Region Waterfall Guide: From the Capital District to Cooperstown and Syracuse* (Black Dome Press, 2007).

Dunn is also the author of *Adventures around the Great Sacandaga Lake* (Nicholas K. Burns Publishing, 2002), and co-author with his wife, Barbara Delaney, of *Trails with Tales: History Hikes through the Capital Region, Saratoga, Berkshires, Catskills & Hudson Valley* (Black Dome Press, 2006). He has published numerous articles in regional magazines including *Adirondack Life, Adirondac Magazine, Hudson Valley, Catskill Mountain Region Guide, Glens Falls Chronicle, Kaatskill Life, Northeastern Caver, Voice of the Valley, Sacandaga Times, Edinburg Newsletter,* and *Adirondack Sports & Fitness.*

Dunn is a New York State Licensed Guide. Together with his wife, Barbara Delaney (also a NYS Licensed Guide), he leads hikes to waterfalls in the Adirondacks, Catskills, and Hudson Valley, as well as to other areas of exceptional beauty and historical uniqueness, always with the emphasis being on history. He is a popularizer of waterfalls and has given numerous lecture and slideshow presentations to regional historical societies, libraries, museums, civic groups, organizations, and hiking clubs.

Endnotes

PREFACE

Waterfall Terminology

1. Bruce and Doreen Bolnick, *Waterfalls of the White Mountains: 30 Trips to 100 Waterfalls* (Woodstock, VT: Backcountry Publications, 1990), 4.

2. Rich and Sue Freeman, *200 Waterfalls in Central New York: A Finders' Guide* (Fishers, NY: Footprint Press, 2002), 26.

3. Gary Letcher, *Waterfalls of the Mid-Atlantic States: 200 Falls in Maryland, New Jersey, and Pennsylvania* (Woodstock, VT: The Countryman Press, 2004), xix.

4. Greg Parsons and Kate B. Watson, *New England Waterfalls: A Guide to More Than 200 Cascades and Waterfalls* (Woodstock, VT: The Countryman Press, 2003), xx.

5. Scott Ensminger and Douglas K. Bassett, *A Waterfall Guide to Letchworth State Park: How to reach the best viewing areas for 24 waterfalls found in one of New York State's most spectacular parks!* (Castile, NY: The Glen Iris Inn, 1996), 62.

6. Jess Stein, editor-in-chief, *The Random House College Dictionary*, Revised Edition (New York: Random House, Inc., 1975), 211.

7. Ensminger, op. cit., 62.

8. Freeman, op. cit., 26.

9. Clay Perry, *New England's Buried Treasures* (New York: Stephen Daye Press, 1946), 150.

INTRODUCTION: THE BERKSHIRES

Geology and Geography

1. Herbert S. Whitman, *Exploring the Berkshires*, Revised Edition (New York: Hippocrene Books, 1991), 16.

2. Maureen Johnson Hickey, curator, *Berkshire County: Its Art and Culture, 1700–1840* (Pittsfield, MA: Berkshire Museum, 1987), 4.

3. Ibid., 4.

4. Christina Tree and William Davis, *The Berkshire Hills & Pioneer Valley of Western Massachusetts: An Explorer's Guide* (Woodstock, VT: The Countryman Press, 2004), 171.

Art and Culture

1. Herbert S. Whitman, *Exploring the Berkshires*, Revised Edition (New York: Hippocrene Books, 1991), 154.

2. William A. Hanna, *The Berkshire-Litchfield Legacy* (Rutland, VT: Charles E. Tuttle Company, 1984), 101.

3. Whitman, op. cit., 13.

4. Clark W. Bryan, *The Book of the Berkshires* (1886; reprint, North Egremont, MA: Past Perfect Books, 1993), 33.

5. Hanna, op. cit., 63.

6. Ibid., 63.

7. William Carney, *A Berkshire Sourcebook: The history, geography and major landmarks of Berkshire County, Mass.* (Pittsfield, MA: The Junior League of Berkshire County, Inc., 1976), 122.

8. Ibid., 122.

9. Hanna, op. cit., 62.

10. Carney, op. cit., 114.

11. Whitman, op. cit., 66.

12. Hanna, op. cit., 103.

13. Christina Tree, *Massachusetts: An Explorer's Guide*, New Revised Edition (Woodstock, VT: The Countryman Press, 1981), 358.

14. Whitman, op. cit., 50.

15. Ibid., 156.

16. Ibid., 155.

17. Ibid., 73.

18. Ibid., 62.

ROUTE 41: THE TACONICS

1. Rene Laubach and Charles W. G. Smith, *Nature Walks in Connecticut* (Boston: Appalachian Mountain Club, 1999), 6.

2. Neil Jorgensen, *A Guide to New England's Landscape* (Barre, MA: Barre Publishers, 1971). The Taconics' geological history is presented on pp. 32–36.

Bash Bish Falls

Descriptions

1. Elizabeth L. Dugger, *Adventure Guide to Massachusetts and Western Connecticut* (Edison, NJ: Hunter Publishing, Inc., 1999), 354. The waterfall is described as "twin torrents cascading nosily down 80 feet of rock-face." Michael Lanza, *New England Hiking: The Complete Guide to Nearly 400 of the Best Hikes in New England*, 2nd Edition (Santa Rosa, CA: Foghorn Press, 1999), 308. Bash Bish Brook "tumbles down through a vertical stack of giant boulders, splitting into twin columns of water around one huge, triangular block." Randall Peffer, Kim Grant, Andrew Rebold and John Spelman, *Lonely Planet: New England*, 3rd Edition (Melbourne, Oakland, London, Paris: Lonely Planet Publications, 2002), 315. The authors describe Bash Bish Falls as "a scenic waterfall that plunges down a 1000-foot gorge." Gary Ferguson, *Guide to America's Outdoor. New England: Nature Adventures in Parks, Preserves, Forests, Wildlife Refuges, Wilderness Areas* (Washington, DC: National Geographic, n.d.), 227. "The falls themselves do in fact bash and bish a bit, splitting around a huge cleft in the rock before making a plunge of some 60 feet into an emerald pool." David Emblidge, *Exploring the Appalachian Trail: Hikes in Southern New England: Connecticut, Massachusetts & Vermont* (Mechanicsburg, PA: Stackpole Books, 1998), 93. The falls' "biggest single drop is 80 feet." Charles W. G. Smith, *Nature Walks in the Berkshire Hills* (Boston: Appalachian Mountain Club Books, 1997), 37. "As the brook exits the mouth of the gorge it plummets down the final escarpment in two separate whitewater plumes divided by a massive gray godstone." Lauren R. Stevens, *Hikes & Walks in the Berkshire Hills* (Stockbridge, MA: Berkshire House Publishers, 1990), 47. "The waters of Bash Bish Brook plunge 200 ft. at the falls, the most spectacular in Berkshire, divided part way down by a pulpit-like granite outcropping before tumbling into a pool." On page 50, Stevens writes that "Bash Bish Brook was formed by the melting of the last glacier, 10,000 to 12,000 years ago. The quartz dike, halfway up the falls, was forced out of the earth 400 million years ago." Michael and Mark Tougias, *Autumn Rambles of New England: An Explorer's Guide to the*

Best Fall Colors (Edison, NJ: Hunter Publishing, Inc., 1998), 68. John W. Davenport, *Berkshire-Bennington Locator* (Madison, WI: First Impressions, 1988). Mention is made of the waterfall on page 98, including its position on a map featuring interesting, notable places to visit. Barbara Radcliffe Rogers and Stillman Rogers, with Pat Mandell and Juliette Rogers, *Off the Beaten Path: Massachusetts. A Guide to Unique Places*, 6th Edition (Guilford, CT: The Globe Pequot Press, 2005), 198. Bash Bish Falls is a "spectacular 80-foot waterfall that barrels down the mountainside." Greg Parsons and Kate B. Watson, *New England Waterfalls: A Guide to More Than 200 Cascades and Waterfalls* (Woodstock, VT: The Countryman Press, 2003), 86. "A large boulder splits the falls into two sections, only then to ricochet off a rock wall and rejoin at the base." Joseph Bushee, Jr., *Waterfalls of Massachusetts: An Explorer's Guide to 55 Natural Scenic Wonders* (North Amherst, MA: New England Cartographics, 2004), 22. "The falls are split, with the upper and lower falls totaling 80 feet. The upper fall is really a series of smaller falls or cascades, flowing through a 1000-foot gorge. The lower fall ... is approximately 50 feet." Richard H. Beisel, Jr., *International Waterfall Classification System* (Denver, CO: Outskirts Press, Inc., 2006), 57. "Bash Bish Brook snakes its way 24.4 meters (80 feet) down a hillside in a twisting horsetail which splits around a large rock formation near the bottom." Ray Bearse, editor, *Massachusetts: A Guide to the Pilgrim State*, 2nd Edition (Boston: Houghton Mifflin Company, 1971), 336. Bash Bish Falls "is the state's most majestic and spectacular waterfall." Marcia Glassman-Jaffe, *Fun with the Family. Massachusetts: Hundreds of Ideas for Day Trips with the Kids*, 5th Edition (Guilford, CT: The Globe Pequot Press, 2005), 19. Bash Bish Falls is a "60-foot waterfall that plunges into a churning pool." Phyllis Pryzby, *Wildflowers and Waterfalls of Western New England and Eastern New York* (Dalton, MA: Phyllis Pryzby, 2004), 17. "The falls begin with several smaller waterfalls leading to two large divided waterfalls. The total drop is about 80 feet. There are several cascades below the main waterfall." Christina Tree and William Davis, *The Berkshire Hills & Pioneer Valley of Western Massachusetts: An Explorer's Guide* (Woodstock, VT: The Countryman Press, 2004), 66. Bash Bish Falls is described as "plunging some 80 feet around two sides of a mammoth boulder and dropping into a perfect pool." Herbert F. Keith, *History of Taconic & Mount Washington. Berkshire County Massachusetts: Its Location, Scenery and History from 1692 to 1892* (Great Barrington, MA: Berkshire Courier Print, 1912). On page 10, Keith quotes Professor Edward Hitchcock in his 1839 geological report on Massachusetts. Starting upstream from the main fall, Hitchcock gives a description of what you would see were you allowed in the gorge above Bash Bish Falls: "For a few rods it descends rapidly towards the west, between perpendicular walls of rock nearly 100 feet high. This rock is talcose slate, whose layers here stand nearly perpendicular, and run north and south, that is across the course of the current. But ere long the descending stream strikes against a perpendicular mass of rock which it has not yet been able to force out of its place, and is thereby made to turn almost at right angles to the left, and then to rush down a declivity sloping at an angle of about 80 degrees in a trough between the strata. This fall cannot be less than 50 or 60 feet; and here the water has performed its greatest wonders. Having for centuries been dashing against the edges of the strata, while at the same time its bed has been sinking, it has worn out a dome-shaped cavity to the depth of 194 feet ... Following the stream still farther down from this upper fall, we find it rapidly descending by several smaller cascades, which together amount to at least 50 feet, half hidden by huge bowlders [sic] and overhanging trees. At length we arrive at a larger and in fact the principal fall. The water which is divided into two parts by an enormous bowlder poised upon the brink, here falls over a nearly straight and perpendicular precipice of about 60 feet, into a deep basin, two or three rods across." Rene Laubach, *A Guide to Natural Places in the Berkshires* (Stockbridge, MA: Berkshire House Publishers, 1992), 33. Bash Bish Brook plunges "80 foot into a clear green pool." Russell Dunn, *Hudson Valley Waterfall Guide: From Saratoga and the Capital Region to the Highlands and Palisades* (Hensonville, NY: Black Dome Press, 2005). Information on the waterfall site is provided on pages 178–180. Diane Bair and Pamela Wright, *Adventure New England: An Outdoor Vacation Guide* (Camden, MA: Ragged Mountain Press, 1996), 174. The authors describe the waterfall as "a 400-foot drop of rushing water."

Photographs & Illustrations

Tyler Resch, editor, *Images of America: Bill Tague's Berkshires* (Dover, NH: Arcadia Publishing, 1996). A different and more dynamic picture of Bash Bish Falls is presented on page 29, including the presence of a rock climber (something which, it should be emphasized, is not permitted at the falls). Herbert S. Whitman, *Exploring the Berkshires,* Revised Edition (New York: Hippocrene Books, 1991). A drawing of Bash Bish Falls by Rosemary Fox is shown on page 18. Clark W. Bryan, *The Book of the Berkshire: Describing and Illustrating Its Hills and Homes* (1886; reprinted, North Egremont, MA: Past Perfect Books, 1993). On the frontispiece and on page 151 is shown an engraving of "Bashbish Lower Falls." On page 158 is a line engraving of "Upper Bashbish Falls" (rarely seen) and also a line engraving of the hotel at Bash Bish Falls. Pryzby, op. cit. A picture of the fall is presented in section 44MA. Tree, op. cit. A photograph of the fall can be seen on page 67. *The Berkshires: Great Barrington to Williamstown: A Photographic Portrait* (Newton, MA: PilotPress Publishers, Inc., 2001). A full-sized photograph of Bash Bish Falls is displayed on page 27. Laubach, op. cit. The cover of *A Guide to Natural Places in the Berkshires* contains a photograph of the waterfall. William F. Robinson, *Mountain New England: Life Past and Present* (Boston, Toronto, London: Little, Brown & Company Canada Limited, 1988). An interesting sketch of Bash Bish Falls is shown on page 20, complete with a Native American near the top of the falls and a deer down below. It is not drawn to scale, however. The Native American's exaggeratedly large size makes the waterfall look like it is only 20 feet high.

Legend of Bash Bish

2. en.wikipedia.org.

3. Roderick Peattie, editor, *The Berkshires: The Purple Hills* (New York: The Vanguard Press, Inc., 1948). The legend of Bash Bish is narrated at length on pages 264–267.

4. www.berkshireweb.com. Bair, op. cit. On page 174 the authors recount the familiar legend of the Indian maiden being thrown over the falls, as well as the not so familiar tale that "the boulders in the pond are all former maidens, turned to stone." Fodors, *The Berkshires & Pioneer Valley* (New York: Fodors Travel Publications, 2005). On page 8 the legend of White Swan is recounted.

5. Kiosk at main parking lot.

6. Ibid., www.berkshireweb.com.

Falls on Glen Brook

1. Berkshire School Booklet.

2. Lauren R. Stevens, *Hikes & Walks in the Berkshire Hills* (Stockbridge, MA: Berkshire House Publishers, 1990), 52. The author refers to the upper falls when he writes, "You will then have a rigorous climb, probably .25 mi., without a trail, up by steep falls until you see the red roof of the Glen Brook Shelter, right."

3. Roderick Peattie, editor, *The Berkshires: The Purple Hills* (New York: The Vanguard Press, Inc., 1948). Bridal Veil Falls in Royce's Ravine is mentioned on page 50.

4. Clay Perry, *New England's Buried Treasures* (New York: Stephen Daye Press, 1946). Perry specifically refers to Growling Bear Cave as a "waterfall cave" where "a three foot waterfall shoots out from the side of the pure marble wall and down into an equally white pool of clear water." Between pages 14 and 15 can be seen a picture of the waterfall with the author shining a flashlight on it.

Race Brook Falls

1. Michael Lanza, *New England Hiking: The Complete Guide to Nearly 400 of the Best Hikes in New England*, 2nd Edition (Santa Rosa, CA: Foghorn Press, 1999), 307. The lower falls is "some 80 feet high—an impressive sight at times of high runoff, most common in the Spring." Barbara Radcliffe Rogers and Stillman Rogers, with Pat Mandell and Juliette Rogers, *Off the Beaten Path: Massachusetts,* 6th Edition (Guilford, CT: Globe Pequot Press, 2005), 197. Joseph Bushee, Jr., *Waterfalls of Massachusetts: An Explorer's Guide to 55 Natural Scenic Wonders* (North Amherst, MA: New England Cartographics, 2004), 35. The lower fall is described as being "huge, easily 50 feet." On page 32 the upper fall is described as "around 80 feet in two giant steps." Charles W. G. Smith and Susan A. Smith, *Discover the Berkshires of Massachusetts: AMC Guide to the Best Hiking, Biking, and Paddling* (Boston: Appalachian Mountain Club Books, 2003), 42. The Lower Falls, "about 100 feet high, is the largest in the series of cascades that make up Race Brook Falls. In spring, when the flow is high, Lower Falls is spectacular with sheets of whitewater tumbling over the rocks in a thunderous resonance." Regard-

ing the Upper Falls, the authors state, on page 43, that "The cascade slips down a deep fracture in the rock face that hides the waterfall from sight until you're right upon it." David Emblidge, *Exploring the Appalachian Trail: Hikes in Southern New England: Connecticut, Massachusetts & Vermont* (Mechanicsburg, PA: Stackpole Books, 1998). The falls are mentioned on page 88. Greg Parsons and Kate B. Watson, *New England Waterfalls: A Guide to More Than 200 Cascades and Waterfalls* (Woodstock, VT: The Countryman Press, 2003), 109–111. Information is provided on the series of five falls that constitute Race Brook Falls. Charles W. G. Smith, *Nature Walks in the Berkshire Hills* (Boston: Appalachian Mountain Club Books, 1997), 22. "Lower Fall is the highest and most spectacular of the Race Brook Cascades." On page 19, Smith writes that it "plunges some 100 feet from the cliff to the rock-filled pool below." Christina Tree, *Massachusetts: An Explorer's Guide*, New Revised Edition (Woodstock, VT: The Countryman Press, 1981), 346. The falls are described as a "Series of 5 cascades." Lauren R. Stevens, *Hikes & Walks in the Berkshire Hills* (Stockbridge, MA: Berkshire House Publishers, 1990), 54. The author writes that "5 falls altogether descend perhaps 1,300 ft. into the valley." Victoria and Frank Logue, *The Best of the Appalachian Trail Day Hikes* (Harpers Ferry, WV: Appalachian Trail Conference, 1994), 73. "The highest fall is nearly 100 feet tall." Ed Kirby, *Exploring the Berkshire Hills: A Guide to Geology and early Industry in the upper Housatonic Watershed* (Greenfield, MA: Valley Geology Publications,

1995), 112. "Race Brook Falls results from a series of drops formed by headward stream cutting into the Everett schist." Matt Heid, compiler, "Frozen Waterfalls," *Outdoors: The Magazine of the Appalachian Mountain Club*, Vol. 73, no. 1 (January/February, 2007), 18. Heid explains the geology of waterfall formation at Race Brook: "A cap of erosion-resistant schist lies atop softer marble, which wears away when exposed to leave near-vertical cliffs and slopes behind. Multi-tiered Race Brook Falls drops a combined 300 feet, freezing into a popular ice climbing locale in the winter." Fodors, *The Berkshires & Pioneer Valley* (New York: Fodors Travel Publications, 2005), 5. "The falls have a satisfying drop, and the brook lives up to its name, racing along with a loud splashy noise." Steve Lyons, *The Bicyclist's Guide to Southern Berkshires* (Lenox, MA: Freewheel Publications, 1993), 183. "The lithe watercourse hustles and darts among the rocks and under tree roots, breaking into smaller streamlets which race gracefully against each other and dash about the ferns and fallen trees, plunging from pool to pool before rejoining, splitting again, and going on their merry way. The music the streamlets make is delightful—tinkling, chortling, or gurgling depending on what the rivulets are going over or under." Norman Sills and Robert Hatton, editors, *Appalachian Trail Guide to Massachusetts & Connecticut*, Eighth Edition (Harpers Ferry, WV: Appalachian Trail Conference, 1992), 113. "Here, five falls combine into an outstanding cascade, several hundred feet deep."

2. Stevens, op. cit, 54.

Bear Rock Falls

1. David Emblidge, *Exploring the Appalachian Trail: Hikes in Southern New England: Connecticut, Massachusetts & Vermont* (Mechanicsburg, PA: Stackpole Books, 1998), 87. All you will see from the top is "a waterfall plummeting over the cliff." Joseph Bushee, Jr., *Waterfalls of Massachusetts: An Explorer's Guide to 55 Natural Scenic Wonders* (North Amherst, MA: New England Cartographics, 2004), 29. "The falls are listed as 90 to 100 feet high, but they seem to be much higher." A picture of the fall, taken from partway down, can be seen on page 28. Clark W. Bryan, *The Book of the Berkshire: Describing and Illustrating Its Hills and Homes* (1886; reprint, North Egremont, MA: Past Perfect Books, 1993), 154. "The water makes short work of a fall of several hundred feet, and the plunge over the rock in an early perpendicular cascade is visible from many points in the Housatonic valley in the south end of the county. The water descends 465 feet in falls and almost perpendicular cascades." Herbert F. Keith, *History of Taconic & Mount Washington. Berkshire County Massachusetts: Its Location, Scenery and History from 1692 to 1892* (Great Barrington, MA: Berkshire Courier Print, 1912), 7. Bear Rock Stream "plunges over an almost perpendicular cliff at Bear Rock, nearly 500 feet, and disappears in the forest below." Between pages 12 and 13 can be seen a photograph of two people and a dog, with the caption "Bear Rock Falls, 100 feet below."

Fall on Sages Ravine Brook

1. William F. Robinson, *Abandoned New England: Its Hidden Ruins and Where to Find Them* (Boston: New York Graphic Society, 1976). A line drawing of a sawmill at the northeast end of the bridge at Sages Ravine is shown on page 71. The caption states: "The sawmill at Sage's Ravine, Salisbury, Conn. Here a large waterwheel was used and the power transferred by belts missing when this picture was drawn." William H. Phillips, *Pathfinder to Greylock Mountain, The Berkshire Hills, and Historic Bennington* (Amherst, MA: William H. Phillips, 1910). A photograph of the fall can be seen on page 73.

2. Joseph Bushee, Jr., *Waterfalls of Massachusetts: An Explorer's Guide to 55 Natural Scenic Wonders* (North Amherst, MA: New England Cartographics, 2004), 26.

Sages Ravine (Lower Falls)

1. Trish Livingston and Nancy Smith, "Saving Schenob Brook," *Berkshire Green: Journal of the Berkshire County Land Trust Alliance*, Vol. 2, no. 3 (Spring 1991). A photograph of Twin Falls in Lower Sages Ravine taken by Jake Bigham is shown on page 7. Ed Kirby, *Exploring the Berkshire Hills: A Guide to Geology and Early Industry in the Upper Housatonic Watershed* (Greenfield, MA: Valley Geology Publications, 1995). On page 112, Kirby writes, referring to the base of lower Sages Ravine: "At this location you can observe the stream's head water cutting water falls and plunge pools. Hundreds of glacially rounded boulders all but cover the landscape." Clark W. Bryan, *The Book of the Berkshire: Describing and Illustrating Its Hills and Homes.* (1886; reprint, North Egremont, MA: Past

Perfect Books, 1993), 251. The ravine is described as being replete with "the cataract, the water-fall, ravines, glens, precipices, forest covered and rock strewn hills and mountains." A line drawing of the falls under the bridge can be seen on page 20. On page 136 Bryan describes the ravine in greater detail with its "many cascades and falls" and mentions that "it was Henry Ward Beecher who declared that a visit to this ravine was worth a trip from New York every month of the year." Herbert F. Keith, *History of Taconic & Mount Washington. Berkshire County Massachusetts: Its Location, Scenery and History from 1692 to 1892* (Great Barrington, MA: Berkshire Courier Print, 1912), 7. Sages Ravine is described as where "a clear mountain stream of almost icy coldness in mid-summer plunges through a dense forest by successive leaps from a few feet to sixty feet or more." According to Keith, the first mention of the ravine was by a committee that, in 1717, was empowered to run the boundary line between Massachusetts and Connecticut. The committee stated: "On the west bank [of the Housatonic] we set up a stake and heap of stones and proceeded five miles, which ends on a mountain we call Mount Eshcoll, from the mighty clusters of grapes there growing, and in a stony gutter by estimation 200 feet deep, through which runs a stream of water which is crossed by the line and falls from the mountain several hundred feet, and the course of the stream may be seen at many miles distant." greensleeves.typepad.com/berkshires/2005/10/of_sages_and_he.html. "Sages Ravine is a wild, primordial kind of place, seldom visited beyond the lowest pools by all but the most intrepid adventurer." William Carney, *A Berkshire Sourcebook: The history, geography and major landmarks of Berkshire County, Mass* (Pittsfield, MA: The Junior League of Berkshire County, Inc., 1976), 22. "On the other side of the same mountain [Mt. Everett], Sage's Ravine offers wilder cascades." Carney goes on to list several other waterfalls by name and concludes by saying, astutely, "Air aside, this is the landscape's freest element."

Sages Ravine (Upper Falls)

1. David Emblidge, *Exploring the Appalachian Trail: Hikes in Southern New England: Connecticut, Massachusetts & Vermont* (Mechanicsburg, PA: Stackpole Books, 1998), 85, 86. The glen is described as a "fragile and hauntingly beautiful wild area (1,629 acres) owned by the AMC, the Massachusetts Department of Environmental Management, the National Park Service (the AT Corridor), and private landowners." On page 86 the author mentions Sages Ravine Brook "tumbling more than 400 feet in a gorge with several delightful waterfalls, at the bases of which you'll find pools with bracing pristine water." Joseph Bushee, Jr., *Waterfalls of Massachusetts: An Explorer's Guide to 55 Natural Scenic Wonders* (North Amherst, MA: New England Cartographics, 2004), 26. "Sage's Ravine Brook has several cascades, from a few feet to 20 feet." Charles W. G. Smith, *Nature Walks in the Berkshire Hills* (Boston: Appalachian Mountain Club Books, 1997), 27. "Over the centuries Sage's Ravine Brook has artfully carved the folded bedrock into a series of shoots and

waterfalls that course through an enchanted hemlock forest." Rhonda and George Ostertag, *Hiking Southern New England* (Helena, MT: Falcon Press Publishing Co., Inc., 1997), 59. Sages Ravine "delights with cascades, waterfalls, and towering trees." Christina Tree, *Massachusetts: An Explorer's Guide*, New Revised Edition (Woodstock, VT: The Countryman Press, 1981), 348. Tree writes of the "strikingly cut chasm with a waterfall 700 feet deep." Tree goes on to mention that the lower section of the ravine is accessible "via a path beginning just north of bridge on the New York–Connecticut line." Victoria and Frank Logue, *The Best of the Appalachian Trail Day Hikes* (Harpers Ferry, WV: Appalachian Trail Conference, 1994), 78. Sages Ravine Brook "drops through the ravine in a seemingly never ending series of waterfalls and pools." Rene Laubach, *A Guide to Natural Places in the Berkshires* (Stockbridge, MA: Berkshire House Publishers, 1992), 16–21. A chapter is devoted to Sages Ravine. Herbert F. Keith, *History of Taconic & Mount Washington. Berkshire County Massachusetts: Its Location, Scenery and History from 1692 to 1892* (Great Barrington, MA: Berkshire Courier Print, 1912). A photograph of an upper fall in Sages Ravine, with the caption "Upper End Sage's Ravine, Mount Washington," can be seen between pages 12 and 13.

MT. GREYLOCK STATE RESERVATION

1. Elizabeth L. Dugger, *Adventure Guide to Massachusetts and Western Connecticut* (Edison, NJ: Hunter Publishing, Inc., 1999), 348.

March Cataract

1. Michael Lanza, *New England Hiking: The Complete Guide to Nearly 400 of the Best Hikes in New England*, 2nd Edition (Santa Rosa, CA: Foghorn Press, 1999), 297. The waterfall is described as a "30 foot high water curtain" that generally maintains a flow, even in the summer. Joseph Bushee, Jr., *Waterfalls of Massachusetts: An Explorer's Guide to 55 Natural Scenic Wonders* (North Amherst, MA: New England Cartographics, 2004), 69. "The falls come in from the right and drop about 25 or 30 feet, fanning out along the way." Greg Parsons and Kate B. Watson, *New England Waterfalls: A Guide to More Than 200 Cascades and Waterfalls* (Woodstock, VT: The Countryman Press, 2003), 105. The authors describe how "the water fans peacefully down a rock wall into very shallow pools." Rhonda and George Ostertag, *Hiking Southern New England* (Helena, MT: Falcon Press Publishing Co., 1997), 33. "The water streaks and skips over a sheer dark outcrop, broadening at the base; small ledges redirect flow. After plummeting 30 feet, the water tumbles through a steep rocky cataract." Deborah E. Burns and Lauren R. Stevens, *Most Excellent Majesty: A History of Mount Greylock* (Pittsfield, MA: Berkshire Natural Resources Council, Inc., 1998), 35. "March Cataract, to the south, spin[s] delicate white strands down the mountain during spring runoff."

Deer Hill Falls

1. Rhonda and George Osterag, *Hiking Southern New England* (Helena, MT: Falcon Press Publishing Co., Inc., 1997), 33. The cascade is described as a "weeping garden-like falls with ledges of moss, fern, wildflowers, and grass." John Brady and Brian White, *Fifty Hikes in Massachusetts: Hikes and Walks from the Top of the Berkshires to the Tip of Cape Cod* (Woodstock, VT: Backcountry Publications, 1983). A picture of the fall is shown on page 56, and the authors describe the fall on page 54 as a 40-foot cascade. Greg Parsons and Kate B. Watson, *New England Waterfalls: A Guide to More Than 200 Cascades and Waterfalls* (Woodstock, VT: The Countryman Press, 2003), 95. The fall is depicted as "a 30-foot-tall curtain of whitewater" in the early months of spring. Joseph Bushee, Jr., *Waterfalls of Massachusetts: An Explorer's Guide to 55 Natural Scenic Wonders* (North Amherst, MA: New England Cartographics, 2004), 65. "The falls are about 30 feet, fanning out from 12 feet wide at the top to nearly 25 feet wide at the base." William Carney, *A Berkshire Sourcebook: The history, geography and major landmarks of Berkshire County, Mass* (Pittsfield, MA: The Junior League of Berkshire County, Inc., 1976), 21. "The Heart of Greylock is a series of small waterfalls at the headwaters of Roaring Brook." According to information provided at the Mt. Greylock Visitor Center, the fall is formed "in a transitional zone between the boreal forest of the upper slopes and the hardwood forest of the lower slopes."

Falls on Peck's Brook

1. Henry David Thoreau, *Thoreau in the Mountains: Writings by Henry David Thoreau with commentary by William Howarth* (New York: McGraw-Hill Ryerson Ltd., 1982). On page 55 an unidentified line drawing of a waterfall is presented in the section on Mt. Greylock. This might be the upper part of the main falls in front of the Peck's Brook shelter.

2. Joseph Addison Wilk, *A History of Adams, Massachusetts* (thesis presented to the Faculty of the Graduate School of Arts, University of Ottawa, 1945), 19.

3. Fodors, *The Berkshires & Pioneer Valley* (New York: Fodors Travel Publications, 2005), 81.

Money Brook Falls

1. Michael Lanza, *New England Hiking: The Complete Guide to Nearly 400 of the Best Hikes in New England,* 2nd Edition (Santa Rosa, CA: Foghorn Press, 1999), 291. "Money Brook Falls tumbles from an impressive height into a ravine choked with trees that haven't survived the steep, erosive terrain." Charles W. G. Smith, *Nature Walks in the Berkshire Hills* (Boston: Appalachian Mountain Club Books, 1997), 241 and 242. "In spring the cascades are dressed in whitewater lace while in summer transparent rivulets of water pour over the dark rock, breaking into glimmering beads as they fall onto the stones below." Rhonda and George Ostertag, *Hiking Southern New England* (Helena, MT: Falcon Press Publishing Co., Inc., 1997), 28. "The highest waterfall in the reservation, 40-foot Money Brook

Falls, dances over sheer black rock before racing downstream through a rock jumble." Clay Perry, *New England's Buried Treasures* (New York: Stephen Daye Press, 1946). A picture of the waterfall is shown between pages 146 and 147, where the author describes the falls as "100 feet high, at an altitude of 2200 feet." Earlier, on page 46, however, the waterfall is described as dropping "seventy-five feet from the top of a cliff." Joseph Bushee, Jr., *Waterfalls of Massachusetts: An Explorer's Guide to 55 Natural Scenic Wonders* (North Amherst, MA: New England Cartographics, 2004), 67. "The falls are about 70 feet in height, dropping in a few steps, with the main, upper fall about 35 feet tall. A few cascades tumble below for 25 feet or more." Greg Parsons and Kate B. Watson, *New England Waterfalls: A Guide to More Than 200 Cascades and Waterfalls* (Woodstock, VT: The Countryman Press, 2003), 107. "In comparison to the other waterfalls of the reservation, Money Brook Falls is typical, seasonal, and littered with boulders and fallen trees." William H. Phillips, *Pathfinder to Greylock Mountain, the Berkshire Hills, and Historic Bennington* (Amherst, MA: William H. Phillips, 1910). A photograph of the fall can be seen on page 22.

2. Perry, op. cit., 144. Joseph Addison Wilk, *A History of Adams, Massachusetts* (a thesis presented to the Faculty of the Graduate School of Arts, University of Ottawa, 1945), 20. The author recounts the same story as Clay Perry regarding the naming of Money Brook Falls.

3. Deborah E. Burns and Lauren R. Stevens, *Most Excellent Majesty: A History of Mount Greylock*

(Pittsfield, MA: Berkshire Natural Resources Council, Inc., 1998), 36.

4. Ibid., 5

ROUTE 7

Falls at Mt. Hope Park

1. www.swimmingholes.org. The fall is described as a "small cascade at the base of a 4 foot deep hole." http://berkshirecycling.tripod.com/rides/id15.html. "Stop at Mt. Hope Park and take a dip in the river where it takes a turn through huge boulders, creating natural whirlpool baths."

2. Fodors, *The Berkshires & Pioneer Valley* (New York: Fodors Travel Publications, 2005), 95.

3. Charles J. Taylor, *History of Great Barrington (Berkshire) Massachusetts, Part 1* (Great Barrington, MA: The Town of Great Barrington, 1928), 37.

4. Robert R. R. Brooks, editor, *Williamstown: The First Two Hundred Years, 1753–1953* (Williamstown, MA: The McClellan Press, 1953), 33. "The Hopper has, for instantly obvious reasons, been called the Hopper since Elkanah Parris brought his Quaker wife there in 1761." William H. Phillips, *Pathfinder to Greylock Mountain, the Berkshire Hills, and Historic Bennington* (Amherst, MA: William H. Phillips, 1910). There are other small cascades on Hopper Brook, which Phillips' picture on page 28 clearly shows.

5. Deborah E. Burns and Lauren R. Stevens, *Most Excellent Majesty: A History of Mount Greylock* (Pittsfield, MA: Berkshire Natural Resources Council, Inc., 1998), 5.

6. Fodors, op. cit., 89.

7. Burns and Stevens, op. cit., 42.

8. Clark W. Bryan, *The Book of the Berkshire: Describing and Illustrating Its Hills and Homes.* (1886; reprinted, North Egremont, MA: Past Perfect Books, 1993), 245.

Falls on Ashford Brook

1. Gary T. Leveille, *Old Rt. 7: Along the Berkshire Highway. Images of America Series* (Charleston, SC: Arcadia Publishing, 2001), 116. The author shows a photograph of the original Mill on the Floss at the top of the falls, and also a photograph of several period-dressed Victorians sitting on rocks below the falls. Leveille astutely mentions that although the restaurant took its name from the "Floss," it is "unlikely that the expression 'floss after eating' originated here." Clark W. Bryan, *The Book of the Berkshire: Describing and Illustrating Its Hills and Homes* (1886; reprinted, North Egremont, MA: Past Perfect Books, 1993), 215. "In the north part of the town is the old Brown Sawmill, spanning a chasm of great depth, which a mere railing separates from the highway." This description sounds a lot like the present roadside chasm and cascade by the Mill on the Floss. http://berkshirecycling.tripod.com/rides/id15.html. The falls are formed in "an alluvial chasm, created during the last ice age."

2. Levielle, op. cit., 114. The author presents interesting photos of Red Bat Cave, a well-known and frequently visited tourist attraction in the first half of the twentieth century. A service station advertising the cave stood along Rt. 7.

3. Bryan, op. cit., 215.

4. Fodors, *The Berkshires & Pioneer Valley* (New York: Fodors Travel Publications, 2005), 107

Lulu Cascade

1. Herbert S. Whitman, *Exploring the Berkshires,* Revised Edition (New York: Hippocrene Books, 1991), 139.

2. Greg Parsons and Kate B. Watson, *New England Waterfalls: A Guide to More Than 200 Cascades and Waterfalls* (Woodstock, VT: The Countryman Press, 2003),104. The authors describe Lulu Cascade as "two small falls." Clark W. Bryan, *The Book of the Berkshire: Describing and Illustrating Its Hills and Homes* (1886; reprinted, North Egremont, MA: Past Perfect Books, 1993), 201. The author writes about Berry Pond "on whose outlet is Lulu Cascade, a pretty waterfall much visited." *The Berkshire Hills: A Historic Quarterly*, January 1906. A photograph of a cascading stream at the outlet to Berry Pond can be seen on page 123. William H. Phillips, *Pathfinder to Greylock Mountain, the Berkshire Hills, and Historic Bennington* (Amherst, MA: William H. Phillips, 1910). A photograph of Lulu Cascade is shown on page 104.

3. Elizabeth L. Dugger, *Adventure Guide to Massachusetts and Western Connecticut* (Edison, NJ: Hunter Publishing, Inc., 1999). The dimensions of the state forest are given on page 354.

4. Whitman, op. cit., 128.

5. www.berkshireweb.com/sports/parks/Pittsfieldstate.html.

Parker Brook Cascades

1. Charles W. G. Smith and Susan A. Smith, *Discover the Berkshires of Massachusetts: AMC Guide to the Best Hiking, Biking, and*

Paddling (Boston: Appalachian Mountain Club Books, 2003), 155. The streams contain a "seemingly endless string of cascades and small falls." www.wunderground.com/wximage/viewsingleimage.html contains an interesting photograph of Parker Brook Falls during winter's snowmelt.

2. Charles W. G. Smith, *Nature Walks in the Berkshire Hills* (Boston: Appalachian Mountain Club Books, 1997). On page 175 Smith maps out the locations of the waterfalls at both ends of the trail. On page 178 Smith writes, "Some beautiful waterfalls worth exploring are just a few yards downstream from here [the bridge]."

Hawthorne Brook Cascades

1. James Cawley and Margaret Cawley, *Exploring the Housatonic River and Valley* (Cranbury, NJ: A. S. Barnes and Co., 1978), 89, 91. Berkshire County Historical Society, *Images of America: Pittsfield* (Charleston, SC: Arcadia Publishing, 2001), 10.

Cascades on Shaker Brook

1. Russell Dunn and Barbara Delaney, *Trails with Tales: History Hikes through the Capital Region, Saratoga, Berkshires, Catskills & Hudson Valley* (Hensonville, NY: Black Dome Press, 2006), 120. The remains of the lower dam were "part of a well-developed system for using water productively. By the 1840s the Shakers had built an underground aqueduct, conveying water from the pond created by the lower dam to the laundry, washing rooms, stables, and mills."

2. Edward D. Andrews, *The Community Industries of the Shak-* ers (1933; facsimile reprint of New York State Museum Handbook no. 15: Emporium Publications, 1971), 40, 42, 44.

Fall on Roaring Brook

1. John Wright Crane and Benjamin F. Thompson, *History of the Town of Washington, Massachusetts* (Pittsfield, MA: Berkshire Family History Association, 1992), 61, 81. Roaring Brook is described as "rushing impatiently from fall to fall for five restless miles." Mention is also made that the brook opens up in Tory Glen.

2. Ed Kirby, *Exploring the Berkshire Hills: A Guide to Geology and Early Industry in the Upper Housatonic Watershed* (Greenfield, MA: Valley Geology Publications, 1995), 99. "What remains of Tory Cave lies under this small protuberance. ... Tory Cave is not a solution cave, one formed in a carbonate by water dissolving the bedrock. Instead, it is a tectonic cave, formed in a fractured zone in the quartzite where weaker fragments have weathered out."

3. Clay Perry, *Underground New England* (New York: Stephen Daye Press, 1939), 104.

4. Kirby, op. cit., 99.

5. Rene Laubach, *A Guide to Natural Places in the Berkshires* (Stockbridge, MA: Berkshire House Publishers, 1992), 112.

6. www.state_parks.com/October_mountain. html.

7. www.berkshireweb.com/sports/parks/October.html.

8. Laubach, op. cit., 112.

Cascades along Overbrook Trail

1. Lauren R. Stevens, *Hikes*

& *Walks in the Berkshire Hills*
(Stockbridge, MA: Berkshire House
Publishers, 1990), 95. "At least in
the spring, trails follow delightful
brooks with sparkling waterfalls."
During other times of the year, there
may be little water flowing.

Stevens Glen

1. A. Palme, compiler, "Know
Your Berkshires" (reprinted from
Pittsfield Works News, 1935), 3. Historical information is provided about
the glen and fall. The waterfall is
depicted as "a beautiful cascade and
waterfalls, dropping the brook over
100 feet." Charles W. G. Smith and
Susan A, Smith, *Discover the Berkshires of Massachusetts: AMC Guide
to the Best Hiking, Biking, and Paddling* (Boston: Appalachian Mountain
Club Books, 2003), 82. "The untamed
current of Lenox Mountain Brook
ricochets off the rock walls as it falls
through the ravine, creating beautiful sights and sounds." Charles W. G.
Smith, *Water Trails of Western Massachusetts: AMC Paddling Guide to the
Best Lakes, Ponds, and Rivers* (Boston: Appalachian Mountain Club,
2001), 58. "Stevens Glen is the name
of a dramatic, narrow ravine where
hemlocks cling to the steep rock face
and the waters of Lenox Brook cascade through the hypnotically deep
gorge." Charles J. Palmer, *History of
Lenox and Richmond* (Pittsfield, MA:
Press of the Sun Printing Co., 1904).
A picture of the cascade in Stevens
Glen can be seen between pages
12 and 13. www.berkshirelodgings.
com. "A cascading 40 foot waterfall."
Ray Bearse, editor, *Massachusetts: A
Guide to the Pilgrim State,* 2nd Edition (Boston: Houghton Mifflin Company, 1971), 388. The Stevens Glen is

described as "a deep ravine through
which a brook winds." Katharine
(Huntington) Annin, *Richmond Massachusetts: The Story of a Berkshire
Town* (Richmond, MA: Richmond
Civic Association, 1964), 142. The
glen is referred to as "a deep gorge in
the southeast corner of the township
where a mountain stream formed a
cascade between rocky walls, and
branches of towering pines met
overhead."

2. Annin, op. cit., 143.

3. www.bnrc.net/TrailMaps/Ste-
vensGlenGuide.pdf. "The landscape
changed dramatically in 1924 when
all the mature trees were cut to control the chestnut blight."

Hawthorne Falls

1. Rhonda and George Ostertag,
Hiking Southern New England
(Helena, MT: Falcon Press Publishing Co., Inc., 1997), 57. The fall is
described as a "seasonal 12-foot
waterfall." Joseph Bushee, Jr.,
*Waterfalls of Massachusetts: An
Explorer's Guide to 55 Natural Scenic
Wonders* (North Amherst, MA:
New England Cartographics, 2004), 45.
"The fall drops some 30 feet, the
first 20 feet rolling and fanning over
a huge boulder, and the last 10 feet
falling into a small pool. There is a
small cave tucked behind and to the
side of the fall." Clay Perry, *New England's Buried Treasures* (New York:
Stephen Daye Press, 1946). Between
pages 130 and 131 can be seen a
winter picture of Hawthorne Cave,
with the waterfall a sheet of ice. On
page 131 Perry writes that "a small
brook leaps over a sheer ledge of
solid rock. Partly beneath the waterfall is a small shelf cave into which
a dozen persons could conveniently

crawl without being wet by rain or waterfall." John Brady and Brian White, *Fifty Hikes in Massachusetts: Hikes and Walks from the Top of the Berkshires to the Tip of Cape Cod* (Woodstock, VT: Backcountry Publications, 1983), 35. The authors describe the fall as "where water plunges out over a rock overhang sheltering a cool cave."

Additional Note: Michael Lanza, *New England Hiking: The Complete Guide to Nearly 400 of the Best Hikes in New England,* 2nd Edition (n.p.: Foghorn Press, 1999), 303. The author recounts a tale similar to that surrounding Bash Bish Falls, of an Indian maiden leaping to her death from Monument Mountain. Such tales were commonly told about any high precipice or towering waterfall.

Fall in South Egremont

1. Ray Bearse, editor, *Massachusetts: A Guide to the Pilgrim State,* 2nd Edition (Boston: Houghton Mifflin Company, 1971), 260.

2. www.berkshires.org/where_ to_Dine/index.php?cat = American.

3. Egremont Bicentennial Committee, *Egremont 1756–1976* (Great Barrington, MA: Egremont Bicentennial Committee, 1976), 26.

Fall on Konkapot River

1. Michael J. Tougias, *Quiet Places of Massachusetts: country rambles, secluded beaches, backroad excursions, romantic retreats* (Edison, NJ: Hunter Publishing, Inc., 1996), 21. "A little way down the road was a small waterfall and broad pools." Steve Lyons, *The Bicyclist's Guide to the Southern Berkshires* (Lenox, MA: Freewheel

Publications, 1993), 190. "The water courses between jagged rock ledges through a small gorge before emptying into the eight-foot deep pool." A photograph of the fall is shown on page 195.

2. Charles W. G. Smith, *Water Trails of Western Massachusetts: AMC Paddling Guide to the Best Lakes, Ponds, and Rivers* (Boston: Appalachian Mountain Club, 2001), 189. "Konkapot was sachem of the Stockbridge nation in the early eighteenth century."

3. Edna Bailey Garnett, *West Stockbridge Massachusetts, 1774–1974; The History of an Indian Settlement, Queensborough or Quapau-kuk* (Great Barrington, MA: The Berkshire Courier, 1976), 30.

4. Claudette M. Callahan, editor, *An Informal History of the Town of New Marlborough, Massachusetts. 1739–1975* (n.p.: New Marlborough Bicentennial Commission, 1975), 62.

5. Roderick Peattie, editor, *The Berkshires: The Purple Hills* (New York: The Vanguard Press, Inc., 1948), 150.

6. http.//edwardlazansky.com/ 201.html. The painting is entitled "Falls of the Konkapot at Mill River."

Umpachene Falls

1. Jan and Christy Butler, *Waterfalls of Massachusetts,* www.berkshirephotos.com. Roderick Peattie, editor, *The Berkshires: The Purple Hills* (New York: The Vanguard Press, Inc., 1948), 135. The waterfall is described, rather anthropomorphically, as "a series of happy cascades." A photograph of Umpachene Falls is shown between pages 158 and 159. John W. Davenport, *Berkshire-*

Bennington Locator (Madison, WI: First Impressions, 1988), 98. Mention is made of the waterfall, including its position on the map. Herbert S. Whitman, *Exploring the Berkshires,* Revised Edition (New York: Hippocrene Books, 1991). A drawing of the falls by Rosemary Fox is shown on page 79. On page 80, Whitman writes: "It's a beautiful sight, the water cascading, bubbling and bouncing down a flight of rock stairs, over wide, flat rocks. Downstream a short way the Umpachene joins with the Konkapot, two Indian Chiefs joining hands, so to speak." Joseph Bushee, Jr., *Waterfalls of Massachusetts: An Explorer's Guide to 55 Natural Scenic Wonders* (North Amherst, MA: New England Cartographics, 2004), 37. The falls "drop some thirty feet in three steps—the upper two in sheer drops, and the lower in a cascade." Barbara Radcliffe Rogers and Stillman Rogers, with Pat Mandell and Juliette Rogers, *Off the Beaten Path: Massachusetts. A Guide to Unique Places,* 6th Edition (Guilford, CT: The Globe Pequot Press, 2005), 196. "The falls lie a short walk away under a mantle of pines. Large boulders offer nice vantage points to gaze at the falls and listen to the play of water falling from terrace to terrace over its half-mile course." Clark W. Bryan, *The Book of the Berkshire: Describing and Illustrating Its Hills and Homes* (1886; reprinted, North Egremont, MA: Past Perfect Books, 1993), 186, 188. "The water descends over quartz rock by two leaps, to a depth of about 30 feet, the upper cataract being about 10 feet." Jon Swan and John Sisson (text), *A Pictorial History of New Marlborough. Visual Reminiscence, 1735–1940* (Mill River, MA: The New Marlborough Historical Society, 2005). A picture of the falls, with women and children sitting on the ledges, can be seen on page 140. Members of the Federal Writers' Project of the Works Progress Administration for Massachusetts, compilers & writers, *The Berkshire Hills* (Boston: Northeastern University Press, 1939), 193. The waterfall is described as "a cataract which dashes down a flight of rock stairs for over half a mile." Claudette M. Callahan, editor, *An Informal History of the Town of New Marlborough, Massachusetts. 1739–1975* (n.p.: New Marlborough Bicentennial Commission, 1975). A picture of the falls, faintly showing a mill in the background, can be seen on page 24. *The Connecticut Magazine,* Vol. XI, no. 1 (first quarter, 1907). A picture of the falls, wrongly listing it as being located in Canaan, Connecticut, is shown on page 19.

2. Claudette M. Callahan, "Umpachene Falls—Our Only Town-Operated Park," *New Marlborough, Then and Now,* Vol. XXX (Summer 1992). The article provides extensive history on the falls. Callahan, op. cit., *An Informal History,* 31. "An old grist mill was located on a narrow dirt road that used to be called Umpachene Falls Road. The mill was built near the falls for water power. The old brick house and most of the property in that area was purchased by the Eugene F. Saxton family. Some of the mill stones were laid near the doorway as stepping stones. After many years and repeated flooding, even the falls have changed. Very little is left of the foundations of the mill. The area at the foot of the falls is now a public picnic area."

3. Callahan, "Umpachene Falls," op. cit.

Campbell Falls

1. Greg Parsons and Kate B. Watson, *New England Waterfalls: A Guide to More Than 200 Cascades and Waterfalls* (Woodstock, VT: The Countryman Press, 2003), 91. The falls are where "the Whitney River drops 50 feet in a magnificent thundering display." The authors further mention that "Campbell Falls dumps into a narrow gorge where the direction of the water flow changes twice, first to the right, then to the left." *The Berkshire Hills: A Historic Quarterly*, July 1906. A photograph of Campbell Falls can be seen on page 160. Phyllis Pryzby, *Wildflowers and Waterfalls of Western New England and Eastern New York* (Dalton, MA: Phyllis Pryzby, 2004). The author presents a lovely picture of the falls on 39CT. Joseph Bushee, Jr., *Waterfalls of Massachusetts: An Explorer's Guide to 55 Natural Scenic Wonders* (North Amherst, MA: New England Cartographics, 2004), 40. "The falls are situated in a small gorge or ravine, and fall 60 feet in two steps, with the upper dropping 35 or 40 feet straight down, and the lower section splitting around a boulder." A picture of the waterfall is shown on page 38. Christina Tree, *Massachusetts: An Explorer's Guide*, New Revised Edition (Woodstock, VT: The Countryman Press, 1981), 344. The falls constitute "a 100 foot drop in the Whiting River—from a split rock, surrounded by evergreens." Roderick Peattie, editor, *The Berkshires: The Purple Hills* (New York: The Vanguard Press, Inc., 1948), 135. The fall is described as a plunge "through a cleft in the rocks." Ray Bearse, editor, *Massachusetts: A Guide to the Pilgrim State*, 2nd Edition (Boston: Houghton Mifflin Company, 1971), 345. "The Whiting River pours over a split-rock ledge, drops nearly 100 feet and then rushes forward through a deep gulch." A pretty photo of Campbell Falls can be found in *The Berkshires through the Camera of Arthur Palmer* (Pittsfield, MA: Palme-Grove Publishing Company, 1951). John W. Davenport, *Berkshire-Bennington Locator* (Madison, WI: First Impressions, 1988). Mention is made of the waterfall on page 98, including its position on the map. Richard H. Beisel, Jr., *International Waterfall Classification System* (Denver, CO: Outskirts Press, Inc., 2006), 48. "The Whitney River shoots down in a small, tree-lined gorge of granite rocks for a total of 15 meters (50 feet) in a 10-meter-high (33 feet) plunge followed by a 5-meter (16 feet), segmented cascade to the bottom." Alfred S. Dilliston, from an article in *The Lure of the Litchfield Hills*, Vol. XIII, No. 5, Issue # 34 (Dec. 1956), 15. The waterfall is described as "dropping 40 feet in three foaming cascades mid great shelving boulders. Water whirling from the base pool surged off through a rocky glen and was lost in woodsy twilight." A picture of Campbell Falls can be seen on page 15. Clark W. Bryan, *The Book of the Berkshire: Describing and Illustrating Its Hills and Homes* (1886; reprinted, North Egremont, MA: Past Perfect Books, 1993), 186. "The Whiting River pours about 80 feet down rocks, in an almost perpendicular fall. Above the falls are numerous cascades where the stream flows through a dark, wild ravine, and below is a gorge walled in by steep, wooded and rocky

mountain sides, seven or eight hundred feet high." On page 158 is shown a line drawing of the falls. A. Palme, compiler, "Know Your Berkshires" (reprinted from *Pittsfield Works News*, 1935), 3. "The double cascade falls are about 100 feet high." Rene Laubach, *A Guide to Natural Places in the Berkshires* (Stockbridge, MA: Berkshire House Publishers, 1992), 1. "The Whiting River plunges 80 feet through a crevice in the bedrock, producing a tumultuous roar, especially during the wet seasons." Adele Greene, "Norfolk and That Neighborhood," *The Connecticut Magazine*, Vol. 1, no.2 (April, May, June, 1895). A full-page photograph of the fall is shown on page 108. Steve Lyons, *The Bicyclist's Guide to the Southern Berkshires* (Lenox, MA: Freewheel Publications, 1993), 181. "The water falls in two great descents with a small pool or two in between and one at the bottom." A photograph of one segment of the waterfall can be seen on page 180.

2. dep.state.ct.us/STATEPARKS/reserves/campbell.htm.

3. Bryan, op. cit. On page 186, Bryan mentions the story of a little girl who fell from the sawmill at the top of the falls for a distance of "95 feet," but survived and lived to be over 90 years old.

ROUTE 2: MOHAWK TRAIL

1. *The Mohawk Trail: Rt. 2 from Boston, Massachusetts to Troy, New York* (Brookline, MA: Muddy River Press, 2003), 1.

Additional Resource: Mohawk Trail: The 4 Season Vacation Area (brochure) (Charlemont, MA: n.p., n.d.)

Haley Brook Falls

1. www.bnrc.net/newsletter/sheephill.htm.

Cascades at Green River Linear Park

1. Dr. Tony Gengarelly, editor, *Images of America: Randy Trabold's Northern Berkshire County* (Charleston, SC: Arcadia Publishing, 2005), 126. The small falls being negotiated by a kayaker on the Green River may possibly be near Linear Park.

2. Robert R. R. Brooks, editor, *Williamstown: The First Two Hundred Years, 1753–1953* (Williamstown, MA: The McClelland Press, 1953), 131, 132.

The Cascade

1. Lauren Stevens, *Hikes & Walks in the Berkshire Hills* (Stockbridge, MA: Berkshire House Publishers, 1990), 184. The waterfall is described as a "50 foot tumble." Christina Tree, *Massachusetts: An Explorer's Guide,* New Revised Edition (Woodstock, VT: The Countryman Press, 1981), 371. "Notch Brook in its tumble down Mt. Greylock forms these waterfalls and the pools below." Tyler Resch, editor, *Berkshires: The First Three Hundred Years: 1676–1076,* Revised Edition (Pittsfield, MA: The Eagle Publishing Company, 1976). A picture of the falls is shown on page 128. John W. Davenport, *Berkshire-Bennington Locator* (Madison, WI: First Impressions, 1988). Mention is made of the waterfall on page 98, including its position on the map. Clark W. Bryan, *The Book of the Berkshires: Describing and Illustrating Its Hills and Homes* (1886; reprinted, (North

Egremont, MA: Past Perfect Books, 1993), 162. "The mountain stream comes tumbling saucily along until it makes an abrupt plunge of about 40 feet into the abyss below." Phyllis Pryzby, *Wildflowers and Waterfalls of Western New England and Eastern New York* (Dalton, MA: Phyllis Pryzby, 2004), 21. "Cascade Falls consist of two waterfalls, each being 10 to 15 feet high." A picture of the waterfall can be seen in section 46MA. Joseph Bushee, Jr., *Waterfalls of Massachusetts: An Explorer's Guide to 55 Natural Scenic Wonders* (North Amherst, MA: New England Cartographics, 2004), 71. "The falls are awesome, maybe 100 feet, and definitely not a cascade! They drop in two large steps, falling and fanning out beautifully, creating a loud roar." Charles Smith and Susan A. Smith, *Discover the Berkshires of Massachusetts: AMC Guide to the Best Hiking, Biking, and Paddling* (Boston: Appalachian Mountain Club Books, 2003). On page 125 can be seen a photograph of the waterfall, which is described on page 126: "The brook drops through a narrow cleft in the bedrock, cascading down the cliff in a ribbon of whitewater. The water crashes into a deep pool at the bottom of a rocky gorge marked by a huge boulder. From the pool, the water slides down several feet of bedrock worn slippery and smooth by the water." Dr. John Bascom, "Greylock Reservation," *Five Papers of the Berkshire Historical and Scientific Society* (Berkshire Historical and Scientific Society, 1906), 253. Notch Brook "passes for a half mile through a deep, well-wooded ravine with a fine cascade. A half mile above the cascade a reservoir has been constructed across the valley

eighty feet in height, and constitutes one of the sources of water supply for North Adams."

2. Fodors, *The Berkshires & Pioneer Valley* (New York: Fodors Travel Publications, 2005), 104. The Cascade is referred to as "Notch Brook Cascades," which races down "through remarkable folds of rock."

3. William H. Phillips, *Pathfinder to Greylock Mountain, the Berkshire Hills, and Historic Bennington* (Amherst, MA: William H. Phillips, 1910). The author refers to the falls as the "Notch Cascade" in a caption that accompanies the photograph.

4. www.bnrc.net/newsletter/200201/ footbridge.htm.

5. Deborah E. Burns and Lauren R. Stevens, *Most Excellent Majesty: A History of Mount Greylock* (Pittsfield, MA: Berkshire Natural Resources Council, Inc., 1998), 32.

6. William Carney, *A Berkshire Sourcebook: The history, geography and major landmarks of Berkshire County, Mass* (Pittsfield, MA: The Junior League of Berkshire County, Inc., 1976), 149.

Natural Bridge & Dam

1. Barbara Radcliffe Rogers and Stillman Rogers, with Pat Mandell and Juliette Rogers, *Off the Beaten Path: Massachusetts,* 6th Edition (Guilford, CT: Globe Pequot Press, 2005), 210. Joseph Bushee, Jr., *Waterfalls of Massachusetts: An Explorer's Guide to 55 Natural Scenic Wonders* (North Amherst, MA: New England Cartographics, 2004), 74. Hudson Brook "then enters the chasm, goes down three or four cascades (one of which is a 8–10 foot slide down a smooth white marble

face), continues through a natural marble bridge and then drains out the other side of the chasm." Greg Parsons and Kate B. Watson, *New England Waterfalls: A Guide to More Than 200 Cascades and Waterfalls* (Woodstock, VT: The Countryman Press, 2003), 103. "Although there are no significant waterfalls per se, this site is still worth visiting because it has some small cascades." Clark W. Bryan, *The Book of the Berkshire: Describing and Illustrating Its Hills and Homes.* (1886; reprinted, North Egremont, MA: Past Perfect Books, 1993), 161. "The depth of the fissure is at least sixty feet and at several points the stone almost closes over." Elizabeth L. Dugger, *Adventure Guide to Massachusetts and Western Connecticut* (Edison, NJ: Hunter Publishing, Inc., 1999), 346. Natural Bridge was "created by melting glaciers. It spans a brook that tumbles down a steep gorge." Rene Laubach, *A Guide to Natural Places in the Berkshires* (Stockbridge, MA: Berkshire House Publishers, 1992), 218. "The light-gray Stockbridge marble (named after the town where it was first extensively studied) is 500 million years old." On page 219, Laubach makes the point that the marble layer is over 940 feet thick in some parts of the Berkshires. Herbert S. Whitman, *Exploring the Berkshires,* Revised Edition (New York: Hippocrene Books, 1991), 147. "As you look 75 feet below you at the rushing stream, pouring over rocks and roaring, frothy-white through narrow places, it's hard to imagine that it carved out the deep chasm and pot holes in the marble walls." James W. Skehan, *Roadside Geology of Massachusetts* (Mis-

soula, MT: Mountain Press Publishing Company, 2001). A photograph from inside the gorge can be seen on page 328. Charles W. G. Smith, *Nature Walks in the Berkshire Hills* (Boston: Appalachian Mountain Club Books, 1997). On page 291 is shown a picture of the chasm, with a tiny waterfall dropping from one level to the next. "Natural Bridge at Hudson Brook," *The Berkshire Hills,* Vol. 2, No. 1 (Sept. 1, 1901). "The Hudson Brook, fed by numerous water sources in Stamford and Clarksburg, after a perpendicular leap of many feet down into a narrow rocky chasm and a struggle along a white-pebbled bed in a tortuous course, passes through a wonderful cavern called Natural Bridge, flowing swiftly from thence down a steep declivity and debouching into the north branch of the Hoosic River." The unnamed writer goes on to talk about accounts left behind by Capt. Shippee and other pioneer residents, who remember seeing remnants of an immense beaver dam just below the natural bridge, and also recounts the legend of a despondent Indian maiden who took her life at the chasm. John Warner Barber, *Historical Collections, being a general collection of interesting facts, traditions, biographical sketches, anecdotes, etc. relating to the history and antiquity of every town in Massachusetts, with geographical descriptions* (Worcester, MA: Dorr, Howland & Co., 1839), 62. "The waters of this branch have worn a fissure from 30 to 60 feet deep, and 30 rods in length, through a body of white marble or limestone, and formed a bridge of that material 50 feet above the surface of the water."

2. www.massmoments.org/index.cfm?mid = 239.

3. Christina Tree, *Massachusetts: An Explorer's Guide,* New Revised Edition (Woodstock, VT: The Countryman Press, 1981), 371.

4. William B. Brown, *Over Pathways of the Past: Familiar Features of our Valley—How They Originated—What Happened along the Way* (n.p.: n.p., circa 1939), 16.

5. Skehan, op. cit., 329.

6. www.massmoments.org/index. cfm?mid = 239.

7. Ed Kirby, *Exploring the Berkshire Hills: A Guide to Geology and Early Industry in the Upper Housatonic Watershed* (Greenfield, MA: Valley Geology Publications, 1995), 133.

8. Members of the Federal Writers' Project of the Works Progress Administration for Massachusetts, compilers & writers, *The Berkshire Hills* (Boston: Northeastern University Press, 1939), 14–15.

Twin Falls

1. David Yeadon, *Hidden Corners of New England* (New York: Funk & Wagnalls, 1976), 35. "There's a beautiful walk up through the woods that starts right by the opening. It's steep, and parts have become overgrown, but eventually it leads to a deep pool fed by two cascades." On page 35 can be seen an illustration of the cascades or the ones farther downstream. Greg Parsons and Kate B. Watson, *New England Waterfalls: A Guide to More Than 200 Cascades and Waterfalls* (Woodstock, VT: The Countryman Press, 2003), 127. "The falls collectively tumble in the shape of a Y. The waterfall on the right is a 60-foot multisection plunge with cascades at the bottom; the waterfall on the left is very similar, except 20 feet taller." Joseph Bushee, Jr., *Waterfalls of Massachusetts: An Explorer's Guide to 55 Natural Scenic Wonders* (North Amherst, MA: New England Cartographics, 2004), 56. "They fall 50 and 80 feet into a common pool, and then fall again as one combined waterfall." Appalachian Mountain Club, *Massachusetts & Rhode Island Trail Guide,* 7th Edition (Boston: Appalachian Mountain Club Books, 1995), 89. Mention is made of "attractive cascades." Clark W. Bryan, *The Book of the Berkshire: Describing and Illustrating Its Hills and Homes.* (1886; reprinted, North Egremont, MA: Past Perfect Books, 1993), 217. "Two tiny brooks join each other after their chase down the steep mountain sides and make a leap of nearly forty feet." William B. Brown, *Over Pathways of the Past: Familiar Features of our Valley—How They Originated—What Happened along the Way* (n.p.: n.p. circa 1939), 31. "The noteworthy cascades above the east portal of the Tunnel were formerly favorite picnic spots, and do not now receive the notice they much deserve."

2. William Carney, *A Berkshire Sourcebook: The history, geography and major landmarks of Berkshire County, Mass* (Pittsfield, MA: The Junior League of Berkshire County, Inc., 1976), 157. Members of the Federal Writers' Project of the Works Progress Administration for Massachusetts, compiler & writers, *The Berkshire Hills* (Boston: Northeastern University Press, 1939), 12. "On Fife Brook, further south, not visible from the Lookout, is a cascade known as Twin Falls, not more than fifteen minutes' walk up-stream from Hoosic Tunnel Station."

Cascades on Dunbar Brook

1. www.trails.com/tcatalog_trail. asp?trailid = CGN027-066. "Dunbar Brook is one of the narrowest, steeper, most extreme creeks in the Deerfield River's watershed." www. mass.gov/dcr/parks/western/mnro. htm. "This pristine brook tumbles and drops 700 vertical feet in two miles, over huge moss-covered boulders forming entrancing waterfalls, rapids, and pools." Fodors, *The Berkshires & Pioneer Valley* (New York: Fodors Travel Publications, 2005), 109. "Along Dunbar Brook you'll discover lovely waterfalls, along with the occasional pool in which to take a dip." www.valleyviewpoint. com/spotlights/monroe.htm. "The Dunbar Brook Trail follows a pristine brook as it tumbles over huge moss-covered boulders forming waterfalls, rapids and pools." Michael J. Tougias, *Quiet Places of Massachusetts: country rambles, secluded beaches, backroad excursions, romantic retreats* (Edison, NJ: Hunter Publishing, Inc., 1996), 4. Mention is made of "little waterfalls dropping into slick pools below." On page 5, Tougias may be describing the same fall mentioned in the book when he writes, "Dunbar Brook cascades down a series of ledges carved by centuries of falling water, fanning out at the bottom into a wide pool."

Cascades in Cold River Gorge

1. *The Mohawk Trail: Rt. 2 from Boston, Massachusetts to Troy, New York* (Brookline, MA: Muddy River Press, 2003), 33.

2. William Carney, *A Berkshire Sourcebook: The history, geography and major landmarks of Berkshire County, Mass* (Pittsfield, MA: The Junior League of Berkshire County, Inc., 1976), 158.

Tannery Falls

1. Elizabeth Dugger, *Adventure Guide to Massachusetts & Western Connecticut* (Edison, NJ: Hunter Publishing, Inc., 1999), 345. The falls are described as "a series of dark, fragrant cascades that once powered a small mill, perhaps one for tanning that the falls seem to be named for." John Brady and Brian White, *Fifty Hikes in Massachusetts: Hikes and Walks from the Top of the Berkshires to the Tip of Cape Cod* (Woodstock, VT: Backcountry Publications, 1983), 71. "Ross Brook drops about 50 feet in small steps before taking a 100 foot plunge over the main falls." A picture of the falls can be seen in *The Berkshires through the Camera of Arthur Palmer* (Pittsfield, MA: Palme-Grove Publishing Company, 1951), pages unnumbered. John W. Davenport, *Berkshire-Bennington Locator* (Madison, WI: First Impressions, 1988). Mention is made of the waterfall on page 98, including its position on the map. Greg Parsons and Kate B. Watson, *New England Waterfalls: A Guide to More Than 200 Cascades and Waterfalls* (Woodstock, VT: The Countryman Press, 2003), 123. The waterfall is described as "a 75-foot series of large plunges and major cascades." Joseph Bushee, Jr., *Waterfalls of Massachusetts: An Explorer's Guide to 55 Natural Scenic Wonders* (North Amherst, MA: New England Cartographics, 2004). A picture of the fall on Ross Brook can be seen on page 50. Richard H. Beisel, Jr. *International Waterfall Classification System* (Denver, CO:

Outkirts Press, Inc., 2006), 62 "Tannery Brook rushes for a total of 23 meters (75 feet) beginning with an 11 meter (36 feet) plunge followed by two, equal height cascades." Christina Tree and William Davis, *The Berkshire Hills & Pioneer Valley of Western Massachusetts: An Explorer's Guide* (Woodstock, VT: The Countryman Press, 2004). A photograph of the fall can be seen on page 166. On the same page the authors describe Tannery Falls as "a glorious cascade, swirling through variously shaped rock pools, a pattern repeated again and again. In spring or after a big rain this series of cascades is replaced by a thunderous continuous rush of water." Rene Laubach, *A Guide to Natural Places in the Berkshires* (Stockbridge, MA: Berkshire House Publishers, 1992), 189. Tannery Falls is described as the highest waterfall in the Berkshires. Here, "Ross Brook has cut a steep-sided chasm on its way through 400-[million]-year-old bedrock and freefalls fully 100 feet into a pool below." Herbert S. Whitman, *Exploring the Berkshires*, Revised Edition (New York: Hippocrene Books, 1991), 166. "When you get to the bottom, there before you is Berkshire's towering, frothy, white answer to Niagara." Russell Dunn and Barbara Delaney, *Trails with Tales: History Hikes through the Capital Region, Saratoga, Berkshires, Catskills & Hudson Valley* (Hensonville, NY: Black Dome Press, 2006). A photograph of Tannery Falls can be seen on page 112. William B. Brown, *Over Pathways of the Past: Familiar Features of Our Valley—How They Originated—What Happened along the Way* (n.p.: n.p. circa 1939), 36. "Its elevation is about 2500 feet.

High Falls, so called, on old maps and deeds for a century has been rediscovered in recent years and renamed Tannery Falls. Here a succession of remarkable cascades fall many hundreds of feet in their short course to Cold River." A. Palme, compiler, "Know Your Berkshires," reprinted from *Pittsfield Works News* (1935), 1. "Massachusetts: Berkshires," *Yankee: New England's Magazine*, May/June 2007, 146. "Ross's stream bed constitutes a chatty encyclopedia of cascades, plunge pools, and narrow stone races. The largest drop (100 feet) is near the bottom of a steep flight of wooden and stone steps. Come when the water's high and you'll never again doubt that water can move mountains."

2. Roderick Peattie, editor, *The Berkshires: The Purple Hills* (New York: The Vanguard Press, Inc., 1948), 139. Peattie refers to the falls as "High Falls, incorrectly called Tannery Falls." Over 50 years have passed since Peattie wrote that sentence, and the falls have indeed come to be known as Tannery Falls. Fodors, *The Berkshires & Pioneer Valley* (New York: Fodors Travel Publications, 2005), 75. "Formerly called High Falls, Tannery Falls acquired its current name because the 110-foot cascade powered a tannery until 1870. The falls are on Ross Brook, which passes 200 feet west of Tannery Brook."

3. Whitman, op. cit., 166.

4. www.mass/gov/dcr/parks/western/svym.htm.

5. Lauren R. Stevens, *Hikes & Walks in the Berkshire Hills* (Stockbridge, MA: Berkshire House Publishers, 1990), 190.

6. www.mass/gov/dcr/parks/western/svym.htm, op. cit.

Parker Brook Falls

1. John Brady and Brian White, *Fifty Hikes in Massachusetts: Hikes and Walks from the Top of the Berkshires to the Tip of Cape Cod* (Woodstock, VT: Backcountry Publications, 1983), 69. Parker Brook Falls is "confined by rocks to a north-south trough." A picture of the fall is shown on page 72. Joseph Bushee, Jr., *Waterfalls of Massachusetts: An Explorer's Guide to 55 Natural Scenic Wonders* (North Amherst, MA: New England Cartographics, 2004). A picture of the waterfall on Tannery Brook can be seen on page 53. A 1935 pamphlet published by the Pittsfield Chamber of Commerce, entitled *Descriptive Motor Trips in and about the Berkshires*, describes Parker Brook Falls as 40 feet in height and Tannery Falls as 80 feet high. Greg Parsons and Kate B. Watson, *New England Waterfalls: A Guide to More Than 200 Cascades and Waterfalls* (Woodstock, VT: The Countryman Press, 2003), 123. "This multisection plunge waterfall descends through an angular gorge. The water remains only 4 to 5 feet wide throughout the long formation." Rene Laubach, *A Guide to Natural Places in the Berkshires* (Stockbridge, MA: Berkshire House Publishers, 1992), 189. "The tumbling cascade of Parker Brook flows through its own chasm at a less acute angle, to merge with Ross Brook below Tannery Falls. Thus united, the brooks flow off together as one—Tannery Brook." Herbert S. Whitman, *Exploring the Berkshires*, Revised Edition (New York: Hippocrene Books, 1991), 166. "And on the other side [of Tannery Falls], not quite so high, is another white cascade. The two roaring torrents, one on each side of you, blend their foamy waters and go tumbling off into the valley." Fodors, *The Berkshires & Pioneer Valley* (New York: Fodors Travel Publications, 2005), 75. "Here you'll find an unusual series of waters in the slanting bedrock."

2. Ibid., 75.

Whirley Baths

1. www.swimmingholes.org describes the fall with its "Jacuzzi-like swirling water." *Hidden New England: Including Connecticut, Maine, Massachusetts, New Hampshire, Rhode Island & Vermont*, Eighth Edition (Berkeley, CA: Ulysses Press, 2004), 412. Mention is made of a "small waterfall downstream," which presumably refers to the Whirley Baths.

2. Ibid., 412.

Cascades on Pelham Brook

1. www.rowecenter.org. A picture of a cascade at the bottom of the mill dam is shown.

2. Jess Stein, editor, *The Random House College Dictionary*, Revised Edition (New York: Random House, Inc., 1975), 980. A pelham is "a bit that is used with two pairs of reins, designed to serve the purpose of a full bridle."

Falls on Mill Brook

1. Joseph Bushee, Jr., *Waterfalls of Massachusetts: An Explorer's Guide to 55 Natural Scenic Wonders* (North Amherst, MA: New England Cartographics, 2004). On page 103 is shown a picture of the falls. "The falls are really remnants of an old stone dam, and drop 20 or 25 feet." Allan Healy, *Charlemont*

Massachusetts: Frontier Village and Hill Town, 1986, 2nd Edition (Ashfield, MA: Paideia Publishers, 1986). Pictures of Mill Brook and its mills can be seen between pages 102 and 103, and of the 1950s Bissell Bridge between pages 198 and 199. On page 159, the Bissell Bridge "stood on the brow of a steep hill crossing Mill Brook to the north of the village. There was the mill dam just above it and a wildish gorge below." Patricia Harris, David Lyon, Anna Mundow, and Lisa Oppenheimer, *Massachusetts* (New York: Compass American Guides, 2003). A photo of the falls and the Bissell Bridge are shown on page 251.

2. www.coveredbridgesite.com/ma/bissel.html. The dimensions of the bridge are listed in detail.

3. Healy, op. cit., 159.

4. Michael J. Tougias, *Quiet Places of Massachusetts: country rambles, secluded beaches, backroad excursions, romantic retreats* (Edison, NJ: Hunter Publishing, Inc., 1996), 6.

5. *Greenfield Gazette: Centennial Edition* (Greenfield, MA: n.p., 1892), 115.

Salmon Falls

1. Ray Bearse, editor, *Massachusetts: A Guide to the Pilgrim State*, 2nd Edition (Boston: Houghton Mifflin Company, 1971), 404. Salmon Falls was "named for the quantities of salmon formerly caught here; has three distinct cataracts with potholes at the foot." *Hidden New England: Including Connecticut, Maine, Massachusetts, New Hampshire, Rhode Island & Vermont*, Eighth Edition (Berkeley, CA: Ulysses Press, 2004), 410. Mention is made that "the falls

has three cataracts with over 50 glacial potholes ground out of the granite during the glacial age." Greg Parsons and Kate B. Watson, *New England Waterfalls: A Guide to More Than 200 Cascades and Waterfalls* (Woodstock, VT: The Countryman Press, 2003), 119. Despite the dam above the falls, "several of the original cascades and potholes remain." J. Ritchie Garrison, *Landscape and Material Life in Franklin County, Mass. 1770–1860* (Knoxville, TN.: The University of Tennessee Press, 1991). A detailed drawing of Shelburne Falls and its industries, circa 1840, can be seen on page 113. Joseph Bushee, Jr., *Waterfalls of Massachusetts: An Explorer's Guide to 55 Natural Scenic Wonders* (North Amherst, MA: New England Cartographics, 2004). A picture of the cascade below the dam can be seen on page 109. *Greenfield Gazette: Centennial Edition* (Greenfield, MA: n.p., 1892). A photograph of the falls at Shelburne Falls can be seen on page 108. Anthony Hitchcock and Jean Lindgren, *Country New England Sightseeing and Historical Guide* (New York: Burt Franklin & Co., 1978), 47. "The falls has three cataracts with over 50 glacial potholes ground out of the granite during the Glacial Age." Fannie Shaw Kendrick, *The History of Buckland, Massachusetts: 1779–1935* (Buckland, MA: The Town of Buckland, 1937). A picture of Salmon Falls can be seen between pages 68 and 69. Kim Knox Beckius, *Backroads of New England: Your Guide to New England's Most Scenic Backroad Adventures* (Stillwater, MN: Voyageur Press, Inc., 2004). A photograph by William H. Johnson of the glacial potholes with the waterfall in the background can be seen on page

66. John Warner Barber, *Historical Collections, being a general collection of interesting facts, traditions, biographical sketches, anecdotes, etc. relating to the history and antiquity of every town in Massachusetts, with geographical descriptions* (Worcester, MA: Dorr, Howland & Co., 1839), 270. The Deerfield River, at Shelburne Falls, "bends round to the east-ward, passing over a rocky bed, falling some places perpendicularly, foaming and roaring. This, with the elevated banks of each side, covered with forest trees, presents a wild and picturesque scene." On the same page Barber also writes that "The descent of the river at this place is forty-seven feet in the distance of forty rods."

2 According to Barbara Radcliffe Rogers and Stillman Rogers, with Pat Mandell and Juliette Rogers, *Off the Beaten Path: Massachusetts. A Guide to Unique Places,* 6th Edition (Guilford, CT: The Globe Pequot Press, 2005), 174. "The potholes vary from a few inches to almost 40 feet in diameter, scattered along the riverbed with little waterfalls here and there. The rock surface is a moonscape of smooth curves. ww.swimmingholes.org. James W. Skehan, *Roadside Geology of Massachusetts* (Missoula, MT: Mountain Press Publishing Company, 2001). On page 324 the author mentions that the potholes range in size up to 30 feet in diameter and are formed in Collinsville gneiss.

3. Bearse, op. cit., 403.

4. *Greenfield Gazette,* op. cit., 110.

5. Allan Healy, *Charlemont Massachusetts: Frontier Village and Hill Town, 1986,* 2nd Edition (Ashfield, MA: Paideia Publishers, 1986), 158.

6. Henry David Thoreau, *Tho-*

reau in the Mountains: Writings by Henry David Thoreau with commentary by William Howarth (New York: McGraw-Hill Ryerson Ltd., 1982), 54.

Sluice Brook Falls

1. Joseph Bushee, Jr., *Waterfalls of Massachusetts: An Explorer's Guide to 55 Natural Scenic Wonders* (North Amherst, MA: New England Cartographics, 2004), 108. The upper fall is 12 feet high, "slicing through the ledge in narrow cracks before taking an abrupt turn ... to drop over the lip of the ledge and tumble into a small pool." The lower fall is described on page 105 as a 30-foot-high cataract "dropping down a crack in the ledge."

2. www.frcog.org/pubs/transportation/MohawkTrail/mtsb6.PDF.

3. Emma Lewis Coleman, *A Historic and Present Day Guide to Old Deerfield* (Norwood, MA: The Plimpton Press, 1907), 14. "From the falls at Shelburne the river descends rapidly, wearing for itself a rocky bed from two to four hundred feet deep. The gorge is narrow and its sides precipitous."

ROUTE 8

Falls along the Bellows Pipe Trail/Thunderbolt Ski Trail

1. Ray Bearse, editor, *Massachusetts: A Guide to the Pilgrim State*, 2nd Edition (Boston: Houghton Mifflin Company, 1971). A photograph of the Thunderbolt Ski Trail and lift can be seen between pages 302 and 303. David Emblidge, *Exploring the Appalachian Trail: Hikes in Southern New England: Connecticut, Massachusetts & Vermont* (Mechanicsburg, PA: Stackpole Books, 1998), 161.

2. Peter McLaughlin, "Sheer Blast," *Berkshire Living,* Issue 10 (January/February 2006).

3. Fodors, *The Berkshires & Pioneer Valley* (New York: Fodors Travel Publications, 2005), 81.

4. Ibid., 81.

Peck's Falls (Upper, Middle, and Lower)

1. Joseph Addison Wilk, *A History of Adams, Massachusetts* (thesis presented to the Faculty of the Graduate School of Arts, University of Ottawa, 1945), 11.

2. Roderick Peattie, editor, *The Berkshires: The Purple Hills* (New York: The Vanguard Press, Inc., 1948). An excellent picture of the falls can be seen between pages 158 and 159. Clay Perry, *New England's Buried Treasure* (New York: Stephen Daye Press, 1946). Peck's Brook "furnishes in miniature the same combination as the famous Natural Bridge." [See "Natural Bridge & Dam" for further information on this scenic natural wonder]. The stream is a collapsed cave system containing "five waterfalls within a mile"—a place where "annually a group of young fellows build a stone and sand-bag dam to form a swimming pool below Upper Peck's Falls." Pictures of the lower falls and gorge can be seen between pages 142 and 143. Wilk, op. cit., 8, 9. "Pecks Brook provides water power for the operation of the Dean saw and cider mills, as well as providing a reservoir for the L. L. Brown Paper Mill." A. Palme, compiler, "Know Your Berkshires," reprinted from *Pittsfield Works News* (1935), 4. The falls are described as 15 feet high "with Greylock and its mighty tower

as their direct background." [This obviously was at a time when part of the forest upstream was cleared away]. Roderick Peattie, editor, *The Berkshires: The Purple Hills* (New York: The Vanguard Press, Inc., 1948). A photograph of the falls, with the summit of Mt. Greylock clearly visible in the distance, can be seen between pages 158 and 159. Herbert S. Whitman, *Exploring the Berkshires,* Revised Edition (New York: Hippocrene Books, 1991). A drawing of Peck's Falls by Rosemary Fox can be seen on page 143.

3. Phyllis Pryzby, *Wildflowers and Waterfalls of Western New England and Eastern New York* (Dalton, MA: Phyllis Pryzby, 2004), 38. "The top waterfall drops about 20–30 feet. It is actually a series of several falls, one being fairly high. However, much of this waterfall cannot be seen as it is behind rock. The middle waterfall is broken up also. It has a total drop of 12 to 15 feet. The lower waterfall is two falls. The upper part is 12 to 15 feet high and the lower part is about 6 feet high." Some very pretty photographs of the lower falls can be seen in section 49MA and 50MA. Joseph Bushee, Jr., *Waterfalls of Massachusetts: An Explorer's Guide to 55 Natural Scenic Wonders* (North Amherst, MA: New England Cartographics, 2004), 59. "The first drop falls through a crack in the ledge, where the water has eaten into the ledge itself. The lower section breaks out at what appears to be the base of a split in this great pothole." On the same page can be seen a picture of the lower falls. Wilk, op. cit., 9. "Pecks Brook unquestionably abounds with the most awe-inspiring terrain, particularly the region between Dean's dam

and Pecks Falls." A. Palme, compiler, "Know Your Berkshires," reprinted from *Pittsfield Works News* (1935), 4. Palme describes what seems to be the middle falls: "you will find another waterfall, squeezing its noisy waters through a jumble of enormous boulders. Judging from the driftwood piled up around these rocks, this must be quite some torrent in the Spring." The falls are described as, "15 feet high, in an idyllic setting." A second set of falls is described 250 feet farther upstream.

Bellevue Falls

1. Joseph Addison Wilk, *A History of Adams, Massachusetts* (thesis presented to the Faculty of the Graduate School of Arts, University of Ottawa, 1945), 230.

2. William H. Phillips, *Pathfinder to Greylock Mountain, the Berkshire Hills, and Historic Bennington* (Amherst, MA: William H. Phillips, 1910). A picture of the fall can be seen on page 117.

3. Ibid., 117.

Falls at Tophet Chasm

1. www.mass.gov/dep/water/resources/11wqar06.doc. The site makes mention of a small tributary entering Tophet Brook below the High Bridge cascade.

2. www.adamshistorical.org/sba.htm.

3. Information obtained from material provided by Jim Moore, regional explorer.

4. http://en.wikipedia.org/wiki/Little_Egypt_(dancer).

5. Jess Stein, ed., *The Random House College Dictionary,* Revised Edition (New York: Random House, Inc., 1975), 1385. A definition of

"tophet" is provided.

6. More, op. cit.

Pettibone Falls

1. William H. Phillips, *Pathfinder to Greylock Mountain, the Berkshire Hills, and Historic Bennington* (Amherst, MA: William H. Phillips, 1910). A photograph of the fall is shown on page 40.

2. Clark W. Bryan, *The Book of the Berkshire: Describing and Illustrating Its Hills and Homes.* (1886; reprinted, North Egremont, MA: Past Perfect Books, 1993), 212 and 213. "The Northrup Brook, emptying into the reservoir near Farnham's, is a curiosity. After leaving its source for some distance, it suddenly enters the ground and is lost to view for a considerable way and finally emerges from a cave materially increased in size. A little way farther is Barker's Falls, with a single leap of about 75 feet." Quite possibly the waterfall that Bryan is talking about is the one on Pettibone Creek.

3. Clay Perry, *New England's Buried Treasures* (New York: Stephen Daye Press, 1946), 151. "This is named Pettibone Falls Cave, from an extremely pretty and famous waterfall on a brook half a mile west of the cave." On page 147 mention is made that the NSS was "organized in a cavern Dec. 1, 1940, amid the jumble of rocks in Pettibone Falls Cave."

Wahconah Falls

1. Bernard A. Drew, editor, *A Bicentennial History of Dalton Massachusetts. 1784–1984* (n.p.: Dalton Bicentennial Committee, 1984). Pictures of the fall can be seen on

pages 9 and 70. *The 150th Anniversary of the Town of Dalton, Massachusetts, 1784–1934* (Pittsfield, MA: 150th Anniversary Committee, n.d.). A picture of the fall can be seen on page 102. Tyler Resch, editor, *Images of America: Bill Tague's Berkshires* (Dover, NH: Arcadia Publishing, 1996). A picture of Wahconah Falls, looking more like a rock heap, is presented on page 28. Elizabeth Dugger, *Adventure Guide to Massachusetts & Western Connecticut* (Edison, NJ: Hunter Publishing, Inc., 1999), 349. "The three stages of the falls add up to an 80-foot drop." John W. Davenport, *Berkshire-Bennington Locator* (Madison, WI: First Impressions, 1988). Mention is made of the waterfall on page 98, including its position on the map. Joseph Bushee, Jr., *Waterfalls of Massachusetts: An Explorer's Guide to 55 Natural Scenic Wonders* (North Amherst, MA: New England Cartographics, 2004), 47. The fall measures 40 feet high. Phyllis Pryzby, *Wildflowers and Waterfalls of Western New England and Eastern New York* (printed in Dalton, MA: Phyllis Pryzby, 2004), 43. "Wahconah Falls is about 40 feet high and is often as wide as it is high." A picture of the waterfall is shown in section 53MA. Clark W. Bryan, *The Book of the Berkshire: Describing and Illustrating Its Hills and Homes*. (1886; reprinted, North Egremont, MA: Past Perfect Books, 1993), 210. "It is a succession of cascades, until at this point hemmed in by rocks and stones of quite large size, the stream makes a leap of some eighty feet and lies for a time partially calm in quite a deep pool in a basin below." James W. Skehan, *Roadside Geology of Massachusetts* (Missoula,

MT: Mountain Press Publishing Company, 2001), 340. "The brook cascades over greenish gray schists of talc and serpentinite, metamorphosed ultramafic rock that intruded the Grenville gneisses before the Taconic mountain building event. Mine shafts at the top of the falls accessed talc bodies." Ella S. Brown, "Wahconah Falls—Their History and Traditions," *Five Papers of the Berkshire Historical and Scientific Society* (n.p.: Berkshire Historical and Scientific Society, 1906), 269. "For several rods they are a succession of rapids, the water flowing swiftly through a narrow, rocky channel, then descending abruptly a distance of seventy feet, pouring over the rocks quite a volume of water; forming as it falls an irregular, broken stairway, much broader at the base than at its top."

2. A picture of the Windsor Reservoir dam can be seen in *The Berkshires through the Camera of Arthur Palmer* (Pittsfield, MA: Palme-Grove Publishing Company, 1951), 7.

3. "State Accepts Wahconah Falls as Gift," *The Berkshire Evening Eagle*, September 10, 1942.

4. Rene Laubach, *A Guide to Natural Places in the Berkshires* (Stockbridge, MA: Berkshire House Publishers, 1992), 155. "Across the stream, near the top of the falls, is the remains of a talc-producing mine shaft, which was active around the turn of the century."

5. *The Berkshire Evening Eagle*, op. cit.

6. Lauren R. Stevens, *Hikes & Walks in the Berkshire Hills* (Stockbridge, MA: Berkshire House Publishers, 1990), 122.

7. Roderick Peattie, editor, *The Berkshires: The Purple Hills* (New

York: The Vanguard Press, Inc., 1948). The legend of Wahconah Falls is given in detail on pages 271–274. Brown, op. cit. On pages 270–271 the author recounts several versions of the Princess Wahconah legend, some with not necessarily happy endings.

8. *150th Anniversary of the Town of Dalton*, op. cit., 103.

Becket Gorge Falls

1. Ray Bearse, editor, *Massachusetts: A Guide to the Pilgrim State*, 2nd Edition (Boston: Houghton Mifflin Company, 1971), 174. "Becket Falls plunges 25 feet into a grotesquely worn rock channel. At the foot of the cascade is a popular swimming hole." Christina Tree, *Massachusetts: An Explorer's Guide*, New Revised Edition (Woodstock, VT: The Countryman Press, 1981), 362. The waterfall is described as a "25 foot high cascade." Linda K. Fuller, *Trips & Trivia: a Guide to Western Massachusetts* (Springfield, MA: Springfield Magazine, Inc., 1978), 4. Fuller describes the fall as "a 25-foot drop into a worn rock channel."

Falls on Camp Brook

1. Russell Dunn and Barbara Delaney, *Trails with Tales: History Hikes through the Capital Region, Saratoga, Berkshires, Catskills & Hudson Valley* (Hensonville, NY: Black Dome Press, 2006), 149. Mention is made of "several pretty cascades set in a small gorge created by Camp Brook."

2. Charles W. G. Smith, *Nature Walks in the Berkshire Hills* (Boston: Appalachian Mountain Club Books, 1997), 97.

3. www.masscountryroads.com/setFrame.cfm?mainPanel = town.cfm&townId = 2414.

4. Rustin McIntosh, Julia Reber, Gerald B. Swart and Frank W. Thober, *Old Tyringham: a pictorial record* (n.p: n.p, 1979).

Otis Falls

1. Clark W. Bryan, *The Book of the Berkshire: Describing and Illustrating Its Hills and Homes.* (1886; reprinted, North Egremont, MA: Past Perfect Books, 1993), 196. "The water, after issuing from this lake, has a rapid descent over precipitous ledges of rocks, forming what are known as Otis Falls." *History of Berkshire County, Massachusetts: with Biographical Sketches of Its Prominent Men* (New York: J. B. Beers & Co., 1885). In the section "Town of Otis," on page 255 George A. Shepard writes: "The water after issuing from this pond [Otis Reservoir] has a rapid descent over precipitous ledges of rock, forming what is known as Otis Falls. When viewed from an advantage point in this weird and romantic defile the scene is grand and sublime. The river has a rapid movement through a narrow defile in most of its course to the Farmington." M. H. Bartlett, "The Farmington River and Its Tributaries," *The Connecticut Quarterly*, Vol. III, no. 3 (July, Aug., Sept., 1897), 328. "The outlet is quite picturesque, especially where the water flows over a cliff known as Otis Falls."

2. *A History of Otis, Massachusetts: 1773–1899* (n.p.: The Otis Bi-Centennial Committee, 1976), 85. The story of how the reservoir came to be built is told in full on pages 84–93.

3. Michael Tougias and Rene Laubach, *Nature Walks in Central Massachusetts: An AMC Nature Walks Book* (Boston: Appalachian Mountain Club Books, 1996), 253. Elizabeth L. Dugger, *Adventure Guide to Massachusetts and Western Connecticut* (Edison, NJ: Hunter Publishing, Inc., 1999). The reservoir's dimensions are given on page 354.

4. Herbert S. Whitman, *Exploring the Berkshires*, Revised Edition (New York: Hippocrene Books, 1991), 90.

Cascades on Buck River

1. www.swimmingholes.org. Steve Lyons, *The Bicyclist's Guide to the Southern Berkshires* (Lenox, MA: Freewheel Publications, 1993), 194.

2. *History of Berkshire County, Massachusetts: with Biographical Sketches of Its Prominent Men* (New York: J. B. Beers & Co., 1885), 500. In the section "Town of Great Barrington," F. A. Hosmer describes how Buck River was named.

Marguerite Falls

1. Joseph Bushee, Jr., *Waterfalls of Massachusetts: An Explorer's Guide to 55 Natural Scenic Wonders* (North Amherst, MA: New England Cartographics, 2004), 41 "The falls are about 50 feet, cascading down the ledge in two sections."

2. www.mass.gov/legis/bills/senate/sto1/st01195.htm.

3. Jim Moore, regional expert on caves, unusual rock formations, and natural objects of curiosity.

Hubbard River Gorge & Falls

1. Joseph Bushee, Jr., *Waterfalls of Massachusetts: An Explorer's Guide to 55 Natural Scenic Wonders* (North Amherst, MA: New England Cartographics, 2004), 77. The nicest waterfall is probably "only 4 to 5 feet tall. The river here is only 10 feet wide, and seems to have broken through a natural dam." *AMC Massachusetts & Rhode Island Trail Guide*, 7th Edition (Boston: Appalachian Mountain Club Books, 1995), 184. Mention is made of a "scenic gorge with many small waterfalls, pools, and rocky ledges," and, on page 187, "This natural pool in the river below a waterfall, enlarged by a low dam of boulders, provides an idyllic swimming pool in the midst of the forest." John Brady and Brian White, *Fifty Hikes in Massachusetts: Hikes and Walks from the Top of the Berkshires to the Tip of Cape Cod* (Woodstock, VT: Backcountry Publications, 1983). A picture of the main falls on Hubbard River can be seen on page 87. On p. 85 the authors describe the first waterfall, where "a deep pool receives water and swimmers that plunge over a 6-foot high precipice." www.woodalls.com/common/states/usa_me.cfm. Michael Tougias and Rene Laubach, *Nature Walks in Central Massachusetts: An AMC Nature Walks Book* (Boston: Appalachian Mountain Club Books, 1996), 257.

2. Michael Lanza, *New England Hiking: The Complete Guide to Nearly 400 of the Best Hikes in New England*, 2nd Edition (Santa Rosa, CA: Foghorn Press,1999), 310. The river drops 450 feet over 2.5 miles as it travels through the gorge.

3. *AMC Massachusetts & Rhode Island Trail Guide*, 7th Edition, op. cit., 183.

ROUTE 9:
THE BERKSHIRE TRAIL

Windsor Jambs

1. Rhonda and George Ostertag, *Hiking Southern New England* (Helena, MT: Falcon Press Publishing Co., Inc., 1997), 39. "50-foot cliffs pinch the 15-foot wide tannin-steeped brook" to form the Windsor Jambs. Walking downstream, you will come to the "largest cascades plunging 12 feet." A picture of the Jambs can be seen on page 40. Susan Farewell, *Hidden New England,* 7th Edition (Berkeley, CA: Ulysses Press, 2002), 429. The gorge is described as a "half-mile long series of waterfalls that travel through sheer granite cliff gorges of up to 80 feet." Charles W. G. Smith, *Nature Walks in the Berkshire Hills* (Boston: Appalachian Mountain Club Books, 1997). A picture of the falls can be seen on page 206. John W. Davenport, *Berkshire-Bennington Locator* (Madison, WI: First Impressions, 1988). Mention is made of the waterfall on page 98, including its position on the map. Joseph Bushee, Jr., *Waterfalls of Massachusetts: An Explorer's Guide to 55 Natural Scenic Wonders* (North Amherst, MA: New England Cartographics, 2004). A photograph of the upper fall can be seen on page 49. Elizabeth L. Dugger, *Adventure Guide to Massachusetts & Western Connecticut* (Edison, NJ: Hunter Publishing, Inc., 1999), 348. The waters "cascade over the bedrock in a series of low falls in a narrow gorge, 25 feet wide. Gray schist walls rich in mica rise above the cascades, as high as 80 feet in places." Charles W. G. Smith and Susan A, Smith, *Discover the Berkshires of Massachusetts: AMC Guide to the Best Hiking, Biking, and Paddling* (Boston: Appalachian Mountain Club Books, 2003), 169. "The brook squeezes through the Jambs, which turn the clear stream into turbulent whitewater cascades that are especially vigorous in spring or after a summer storm." Greg Parsons and Kate B. Watson, *New England Waterfalls: A Guide to More Than 200 Cascades and Waterfalls* (Woodstock, VT: The Countryman Press, 2003), 129. "Although the gorge is interesting and the brook can be very powerful, especially in springtime, Windsor Jambs' natural beauty lies constrained by a green fence that surrounds all vantage points of the gorge." Ray Bearse, editor, *Massachusetts: A Guide to the Pilgrim State*, 2nd Edition (Boston: Houghton Mifflin Company, 1971), 243. The Jambs are described as "a deep flume cut through by a rushing mountain stream." Rene Laubach, *A Guide to Natural Places in the Berkshires* (Stockbridge, MA: Berkshire House Publishers, 1992), 175. Windsor Jambs Brook "gushes through a fissure in the bedrock, a mere 25 feet wide in places, to cascade over a long series of low falls." Herbert S. Whitman, *Exploring the Berkshires*, Revised Edition (New York: Hippocrene Books, 1991), 163. "The sides of the gorge are sheer, narrow, and rocky, and way down at the bottom, winding its way and splashing over rocks, is Clear Brook." Whitman adds, "No one seems to know why a deep gorge and cascades should be called a jambs." James W. Skehan, *Roadside Geology of Massachusetts* (Missoula, MT: Mountain Press Publishing Company, 2001), 338. Skehan describes the jambs as

"70- to 80-foot cliffs of gray schist and quartzite of the Rowe formation. The Westfield River flows swiftly at the jambs, dropping 1,000 feet in its first 14 miles." Anna Milkowski, *Mountain Biking the Berkshires* (Guilford, CT: Globe Pequot Press, 2001), 70. "Water cascades through a chasm of 80-foot granite cliffs out of which rugged evergreens miraculously grow."

2. Members of the Federal Writers' Project of the Works Progress Administration for Massachusetts, compiler & writers, *The Berkshire Hills* (Boston: Northeastern University Press, 1939), 254.

3. Milkowski, op. cit., 79.

Falls on Basin Brook

1. Michael Tougias and Rene Laubach, *Nature Walks in Central Massachusetts: An AMC Nature Walks Book* (Boston: Appalachian Mountain Club Books, 1996), 174. "Basin Brook gradually tumbles 350 vertical feet over moss-covered bedrock."

2. William Giles Atkins, *History of the Town of Hawley, Franklin County, Massachusetts: from its first settlement in 1771 to 1887. With family records and biographical sketches* (West Cummington, MA: William Giles Atkins, 1887), 34.

3. www.masscountryroads.com/setFrame.cfm?mainPanel = town.cfm&townId = 364.

4. Louise Hale Johnson, *History of the Town of Hawley, Franklin County Massachusetts, 1771–1951, with Genealogies* (Mystic, CT: Charter Oak House, 1953), 3. Atkins, op. cit., 33.

Fall in East Windsor

1. Christina Tree, *Massachusetts: An Explorer's Guide*, New Revised Edition (Woodstock, VT: The Countryman Press, 1981), 366.

West Worthington Falls

1. Ray Bearse, editor, *Massachusetts: A Guide to the Pilgrim State*, 2nd Edition (Boston: Houghton Mifflin Company, 1971), 466. West Worthington Falls "plunges 75 feet down a tree-bordered gorge. In summer there is only a sparkling rivulet falling over bare rocks into the chasm, but in flood time there is a roaring current." *The ABC's of Pioneer Valley: Western Massachusetts* (Northampton, MA: Pioneer Valley Association, n.d), 69. The waterfall is described as a "50 foot cascade." Christina Tree, *Massachusetts: An Explorer's Guide*, New Revised Edition (Woodstock, VT: The Countryman Press, 1981), 322. The middle branch of the Westfield River "plunges 75 feet down into a gorge." Roderick Peattie, editor, *The Berkshires: The Purple Hills* (New York: The Vanguard Press, Inc., 1948). Mention is made of the falls on page 143. W. B. Gay, editor & compiler, *Gazetteer of Hampshire County, Mass., 1654–1887. Part First* (Syracuse, NY: W. B. Gay & Co., n.d.), 478. "The surface of Worthington is broken and picturesque" with "deep valleys, through which the streams flow southward with rapid current." Tercentenary Editorial Committee: Lawrence E. Wikander, Helen Terry, and Mark Kiley, compilers, *The Hampshire History: Celebrating 300 Years of Hampshire County Massachusetts* (Northampton, MA: Hampshire County Commission-

ers, 1964), 33. "At nearly opposite ends of Worthington are spectacular waterfalls. West Worthington Falls, located in the middle branch of the Westfield River, falls about 50 feet into a rocky gorge close by River Road." Linda K. Fuller, *Trips & Trivia: a Guide to Western Massachusetts* (Springfield, MA: Springfield Magazine, Inc., 1978). Mention is made of the falls on page 127.

2. Gay, op. cit., 478.

3. *The ABC's of Pioneer Valley*, op. cit. Native American legends and the waterfall are mentioned on page 478.

Glendale Falls

1. Michael Tougias and Rene Laubach, *Nature Walks in Central Massachusetts: An AMC Nature Walks Book* (Boston: Appalachian Mountain Club Books, 1996), 204. Glendale Falls consist of a "series of picturesque cascades, more than 150 feet high in all (making it the highest in Massachusetts)." Joseph Bushee, Jr., *Waterfalls of Massachusetts: An Explorer's Guide to 55 Natural Scenic Wonders* (North Amherst, MA: New England Cartographics, 2004), 85. The height of the waterfall is given at 150 feet. Roderick Peattie, editor, *The Berkshires: The Purple Hills* (New York: The Vanguard Press, Inc., 1948), 143. The falls are described as "a series of small falls and precipitous cascades, dropping about three hundred feet." Greg Parsons and Kate B. Watson, *New England Waterfalls: A Guide to More Than 200 Cascades and Waterfalls* (Woodstock, VT: The Countryman Press, 2003), 99. "The drop, which is more than 160 feet, is Massachusetts's third tallest cascade chain." Tercente-

nary Editorial Committee: Lawrence E. Wikander, Helen Terry, and Mark Kiley, compilers, *The Hampshire History: Celebrating 300 Years of Hampshire County Massachusetts* (Northampton, MA: Hampshire County Commissioners, 1964). A picture of part of the falls can be seen on page 150.

Chapel Falls

1. Michael Tougias and Rene Laubach, *Nature Walks in Central Massachusetts: An AMC Nature Walks Book* (Boston: Appalachian Mountain Club Books, 1996), 158. The heights of the cascades are given as 10, 15, and 25 feet. Greg Parsons and Kate B. Watson, *New England Waterfalls: A Guide to More Than 200 Cascades and Waterfalls* (Woodstock, VT: The Countryman Press, 2003), 94. "The entire formation is more like a slide than a cascade, because the waters maintain close contact with the rock as they descend." Joseph Bushee, Jr., *Waterfalls of Massachusetts: An Explorer's Guide to 55 Natural Scenic Wonders* (North Amherst, MA: New England Cartographics, 2004), 102. The first fall is "a long sloping cascade about 10 feet in height, but more than 25 feet laterally, like a natural waterslide. ... The next drop is about 12 feet and cascades over a huge sloping rock, fanning out to twice its width by the time it reaches the bottom of the drop." The third drop is "around 20 feet in height, rounding over the top of a ledge at first, then dropping clean for 10 feet or more to a sloping rock to slide into the pool at the base." Ray Bearse, editor, *Massachusetts: A Guide to the Pilgrim State,* 2nd Edition (Boston: Houghton

Mifflin Company, 1971), 168. Chapel-brook "has a brook, waterfalls and Pony Mt." Phyllis Pryzby, *Wildflowers and Waterfalls of Western New England and Eastern New York* (Dalton, MA: Phyllis Pryzby, 2004), 23. "Chapelbrook Falls is actually a series of three waterfalls. The first one is about 10 feet high; the second one roughly 15 feet high, and the third about 25 feet high for a total height of 50 feet." A picture of the fall is presented in section 47MA.

2. *Special Places in and around the Berkshires* (brochure) (n.p.: Trustees of Reservations, 1998). www.thetrustees.org/pages/288_chapel_brook.cfm.

Chesterfield Gorge

1. Charles W. G. Smith and Susan A. Smith, *Discover the Berkshires of Massachusetts: AMC Guide to the Best Hiking, Biking, and Paddling* (Boston: Appalachian Mountain Club Books, 2003), 121. "The walls of the gorge are smooth slabs of vertical bedrock about 100 feet apart and reaching 70 feet high." Michael Tougias and Rene Laubach, *Nature Walks in Central Massachusetts: An AMC Nature Walks Book* (Boston: Appalachian Mountain Club Books, 1996), 197. "The corrosive power of water and glacial ice are clearly evident in the sheer gray granite chasm; gouged and sculpted bedrock bears the legacy of grinding glaciers, followed by millennia of polishing by water." Ray Bearse, editor, *Massachusetts: A Guide to the Pilgrim State*, 2nd Edition (Boston: Houghton Mifflin Company, 1971). Mention is made of the Chesterfield Gorge on page 234. James W. Skehan, *Roadside Geology of Massachu-*

setts (Missoula, MT: Mountain Press Publishing Company, 2001), 338. "The Chesterfield Gorge is a magnificent box canyon carved into north-trending Devonian schists of the Goshen formation." W. B. Gay, editor & compiler, *Gazetteer of Hampshire County, Mass., 1654–1887. Part First* (Syracuse, NY: W. B. Gay & Co., n.d.), 200. "In one place this stream [Westfield River] has cut through a ledge of rocks a channel thirty feet deep and sixty rods in length, as symmetrically as if done by an artist." William F. Robinson, *Mountain New England: Life Past and Present* (Boston, Toronto, London: Little, Brown & Company (Canada) Limited, 1988). A close-up photo of one of the potholes is shown on page 8.

2. www.woodalls.com/common/states/usa_me.cfm.

3. www.thetrustees.org/pages/291_chesterfield_gorge.cfm.

4. Ibid.

ROUTE 20: JACOB'S LADDER TRAIL

1. www.gribblenation.net/nepics/jacobsladder. Cathaline Alford Archer and Mitchell J. Mulholland, *A Bicentennial History of Becket: Berkshire County Massachusetts* (Becket MA: Becket Historical Society, 1964). The section on "Jacob's Ladder," written by Albert R. Palmer, states that the road above Becket was begun in 1908 and completed in 1910; it was subsequently rebuilt in 1918, and again in 1930. Until the creation of the Massachusetts Turnpike, this was the most heavily traveled road running east to west in the Berkshires.

Bradley Falls

1. Christina Tree, *Massachusetts: An Explorer's Guide*, New Revised Edition (Woodstock, VT: The Countryman Press, 1981), 322. The author refers to the falls as Bradley Falls. *The ABC's of Pioneer Valley: Western Massachusetts* (Northampton, MA: Pioneer Valley Association, n.d). The waterfall is mentioned by name on page 69.

2. Ray Bearse, editor, *Massachusetts: A Guide to the Pilgrim State*, 2nd Edition (Boston: Houghton Mifflin Company, 1971), 466. "South Worthington Cascade is a gentle but beautiful falls with a 50-foot drop." Tercentenary Editorial Committee: Lawrence E. Wikander, Helen Terry, and Mark Kiley, compilers. *The Hampshire History: Celebrating 300 Years of Hampshire County Massachusetts* (Northampton, MA: Hampshire County Commissioners, 1964), 33. "At nearly opposite ends of Worthington are spectacular waterfalls. ... Bradley Falls, in the Little River just below the bridge in South Worthington, follows a rocky path for about 500 feet, cascading into a right angle drop to a rock-bound gorge 50 feet below." Linda K. Fuller, *Trips & Trivia: a Guide to Western Massachusetts* (Springfield, MA: Springfield Magazine, Inc., 1978). The falls are described on page 127.

Cascade on the Little River

1. www.americawhitewater.org/ rivers/id/703. John Novo is quoted as saying, "It is a nice Class 3 with a little gorge and a nice 4–5 foot drop."

Sanderson Brook Falls

1. Michael Tougias and Rene Laubach, *Nature Walks in Central Massachusetts: An AMC Nature Walks Book* (Boston: Appalachian Mountain Club Books, 1996), 240. The falls create "a single dramatic drop as well as alternating pools and cascades in an idyllic woodland setting." Sanderson Brook Falls are "perhaps 75 feet high in all." A picture of the falls can be seen on page 244. Joseph Bushee, Jr., *Waterfalls of Massachusetts: An Explorer's Guide to 55 Natural Scenic Wonders* (North Amherst, MA: New England Cartographics, 2004), 83. "The falls are in two steps, with the upper piece dropping clean around 12 feet, falling onto a scooped rock and splashing back up about five feet into the air. Sanderson Brook then drops down another 10 feet, splits around a boulder and cascades 20 feet to the pool below before swinging sharply away to the right." A great picture of the falls can be seen on page 82. *Massachusetts & Rhode Island Trail Guide*, 7th Edition (Boston: Appalachian Mountain Club Books, 1995), 189. The AMC describes the falls as a "series of high cascades." Greg Parsons and Kate B. Watson, *New England Waterfalls: A Guide to More Than 200 Cascades and Waterfalls* (Woodstock, VT: The Countryman Press, 2003), 116. "The waters of Sanderson Brook travel down a 60-foot face of a rock wall." Phyllis Pryzby, *Wildflowers and Waterfalls of Western New England and Eastern New York* (Dalton, MA: Phyllis Pryzby, 2004), 40. The waterfall is described as "a series of falls and cascades. ... The total drop is about 70 feet." A picture of the waterfall

can be seen in section 51MA. Alfred Minot Copeland, editor, *A History of Hampden County Massachusetts: Our County and Its People*, Vol. 3 (n.p.: The Century Memorial Publishing Company, 1902), 350. "Another somewhat important stream is Sanderson Brook, rising in Blandford at an altitude of about 1,600 feet, and flowing north through a very picturesque ravine, enters the west branch about 3 miles below Chester Factories. It was formerly a fishing brook." David Yeadon, *Hidden Corners of New England* (New York: Funk & Wagnalls, 1976), 35. Sanderson Falls are "feathering cascades of water falling over a hundred feet to the stream in the valley below."

2. www.hilltowns.com/outdoors.htm.

Goldmine Brook Falls

1. www.swimmingholes.org.

2. www.stateparks.com/chester-blanford.html.

Pitcher Falls

1. Joseph Bushee, Jr., *Waterfalls of Massachusetts: An Explorer's Guide to 55 Natural Scenic Wonders* (North Amherst, MA: New England Cartographics, 2004). A picture of the falls is shown on page 79.

2. http://river.wsc.ma.edu/guide/russell.html.

Bibliography

The ABC's of Pioneer Valley: Western Massachusetts. Northampton, MA: Pioneer Valley Association, n.d.

Andrews, Edward D. *The Community Industries of the Shakers.* 1933; facsimile reprint of New York State Museum Handbook no. 15: Emporium Publications, 1971.

Annin, Katharine (Huntington). *Richmond Massachusetts: The Story of a Berkshire Town and Its People, 1765–1965.* Richmond, MA: Richmond Civic Association, 1964.

Appalachian Mountain Club. *Massachusetts & Rhode Island Trail Guide* 7th Edition. Boston: Appalachian Mountain Club Books, 1995.

Archer, Cathaline Alford, and Mitchell J. Mulholland. *A Bicentennial History of Becket: Berkshire County Massachusetts.* Becket, MA: Becket Historical Society, 1964.

Atkins, William Giles. *History of the Town of Hawley, Franklin County, Massachusetts: from its first settlement in 1771 to 1887. With family records and biographical sketches.* West Cummington, MA: William Giles Atkins, 1887.

Bair, Diane, and Pamela Wright. *Adventure New England: An Outdoor Vacation Guide.* Camden, MA: Ragged Mountain Press, 1996.

Barber, John Warner. *Historical Collections, being a general collection of interesting facts, tra-*

ditions, biographical sketches, anecdotes, etc. relating to the history and antiquity of every town in Massachusetts, with geographical descriptions. Worcester, MA: Dorr, Howland & Co., 1839.

Bartlett, M. H. "The Farmington River and Its Tributaries." *The Connecticut Quarterly* Vol. III, no. 3 (July, Aug., Sept., 1897).

Bascom, Dr. John. "Greylock Reservation." *Five Papers of the Berkshire Historical and Scientific Society.* Published by the Society, 1906.

Bearse, Ray, ed. *Massachusetts: A Guide to the Pilgrim State* 2nd Edition. Boston: Houghton Mifflin Company, 1971.

Beckius, Kim Knox. *Backroads of New England: Your Guide to New England's Most Scenic Backroad Adventures.* Stillwater, MN: Voyageur Press, Inc., 2004.

Beisel, Richard H. Jr. *International Waterfall Classification System.* Denver, CO: Outskirts Press, Inc., 2006.

Berkshire County Historical Society. *Images of America: Pittsfield.* Charleston, SC: Arcadia Publishing, 2001.

The Berkshire Hills. "Natural Bridge at Hudson Brook" Vol. 2, No. 1 (Sept. 1, 1901.

The Berkshire Hills: A Historic Quarterly (January 1906).

The Berkshire Hills: A Historic Quarterly (July 1906).

The Berkshires: Great Barrington to Williamstown: A Photographic Portrait. Newton, MA: PilotPress Publishers, Inc., 2001.

The Berkshires through the Camera of Arthur Palmer. Pittsfield, MA: Palme-Grove Publishing Company, 1951.

Bolnick, Bruce, and Doreen Bolnick.

Waterfalls of the White Mountains: 30 Trips to 100 Waterfalls. Woodstock, VT: Backcountry Publications, 1990.

Brady, John, and Brian White. *Fifty Hikes in Massachusetts: Hikes and Walks from the Top of the Berkshires to the Tip of Cape Cod.* Woodstock, VT: Backcountry Publications, 1983.

Brooks, Robert R. R., ed. *Williamstown: The First Two Hundred Years, 1753–1953.* Williamstown, MA: The McClellan Press, 1953.

Brown, Ella S. "Wahconah Falls—Their History and Traditions." *Five Papers of the Berkshire Historical and Scientific Society.* N.p.: Berkshire Historical and Scientific Society, 1906.

Brown, William B. *Over Pathways of the Past: Familiar Features of Our Valley—How They Originated—What Happened along the Way.* N.p.: n.p. circa 1939.

Bryan, Clark W. *The Book of the Berkshire: Describing and Illustrating Its Hills and Homes.* 1886; reprinted, North Egremont, MA: Past Perfect Books, 1993.

Burns, Deborah E., and Lauren R. Stevens. *Most Excellent Majesty: A History of Mount Greylock.* Pittsfield, MA: Berkshire Natural Resources Council, Inc., 1998.

Bushee, Joseph Jr. *Waterfalls of Massachusetts: An Explorer's Guide to 55 Natural Scenic Wonders.* North Amherst, MA: New England Cartographics, 2004.

Butler, Jan, and Christy Butler. *Waterfalls of Massachusetts. www.berkshirephotos.com.*

Callahan, Claudette M. "Umpachene Falls—Our Only Town-Operated Park." *New Marlborough, Then and Now* Vol. XXX (Summer 1992).

Callahan, Claudette M., ed. *An Informal History of the Town of New Marlborough Massachusetts, 1739–1975*. N.p.: New Marlborough Bicentennial Commission, 1975.

Carney, William. *A Berkshire Sourcebook: The history, geography and major landmarks of Berkshire County, Mass*. Pittsfield, MA: The Junior League of Berkshire County, Inc., 1976.

Cawley, James, and Margaret Cawley. *Exploring the Housatonic River and Valley*. Cranbury, NJ: A. S. Barnes and Co., Inc., 1978.

Chamberlain, Samuel. *The Berkshires (photo-album)*. New York: Hastings House, 1956.

Coleman, Emma Lewis. *A Historic and Present Day Guide to Old Deerfield*. Norwood, MA: The Plimpton Press, 1907.

Copeland, Alfred Minot, ed. *A History of Hampden County Massachusetts: Our County and Its People* Vol. 3. N.p.: The Century Memorial Publishing Company, 1902.

Crane, John Wright, and Benjamin F. Thompson. *History of the Town of Washington, Massachusetts*. Pittsfield, MA: Berkshire Family History Association, Inc., 1992.

Davenport, John W. *Berkshire-Bennington Locator*. Madison, WI: First Impressions, 1988.

Dilliston, Alfred S. Article. *The Lure of the Litchfield Hills* Vol. XIII, No. 5, Issue # 34 (Dec. 1956).

Drew, Bernard A., editor. *A Bicentennial History of Dalton Massachusetts, 1784–1984*. N.p.: Dalton Bicentennial Committee, 1984.

Dugger, Elizabeth L. *Adventure Guide to Massachusetts and Western Connecticut*. Edison, NJ: Hunter Publishing, Inc., 1999.

Dunn, Russell. *Hudson Valley Waterfall Guide: From Saratoga and the Capital Region to the Highlands and Palisades*. Hensonville, NY: Black Dome Press, 2005.

Dunn, Russell, and Barbara Delaney. *Trails with Tales: History Hikes through the Capital Region, Saratoga, Berkshires, Catskills & Hudson Valley*. Hensonville, NY: Black Dome Press, 2006.

Editorial Committee: Agnes B. Curtin, Clinton Elliot, Alice M. Hale, Millicent C. McIntosh, Rustin and Julia Reber, Gerald B. Swart and Frank W. Thober. *Old Tyringham: a pictorial record*. N.p: n.p, 1979.

Egremont Bicentennial Committee. *Egremont 1756–1976*. Great Barrington, MA: Egremont Bicentennial Committee, 1976.

Emblidge, David. *Exploring the Appalachian Trail: Hikes in Southern New England: Connecticut, Massachusetts & Vermont*. Mechanicsburg, PA: Stackpole Books, 1998.

Ensminger, Scott A., and Douglas K. Bassett. *A Waterfall Guide to Letchworth State Park: How to reach the best viewing areas for 24 waterfalls found in one of New York State's most spectacular parks!* Castile, NY: The Glen Iris Inn, 1996.

Farewell, Susan. *Hidden New England* 7th Edition. Berkeley, CA: Ulysses Press, 2002).

Ferguson, Gary. *Guide to America's Outdoor. New England: Nature Adventures in Parks, Preserves, Forests, Wildlife Refuges, Wilderness Areas*. Washington, DC:

National Geographic, n.d.

Fodors. *The Berkshires & Pioneer Valley*. New York: Fodors Travel Publications, 2005.

Freeman, Rich, and Sue Freeman. *200 Waterfalls in Central New York: A Finders' Guide*. Fishers, NY: Footprint Press, 2002.

Fuller, Linda K. *Trips & Trivia: a Guide to Western Massachusetts*. Springfield, MA: Springfield Magazine, Inc., 1978.

Garnett, Edna. *West Stockbridge Massachusetts, 1774–1974: The History of an Indian Settlement, Queensborough or Qua-pau-kuk*. Great Barrington, MA: The Berkshire Courier, 1976.

Garrison, J. Ritchie. *Landscape and Material Life in Franklin County, Mass., 1770–1860*. Knoxville, TN: The University of Tennessee Press, 1991.

Gay, W. B., ed. & compiler. *Gazetteer of Hampshire County, Mass., 1654–1887. Part First*. Syracuse, NY: W. B. Gay & Co., n.d.

Gengarelly, Dr. Tony, ed. *Images of America: Randy Trabold's Northern Berkshire County*. Charleston, SC: Arcadia Publishing, 2003.

Glassman-Jaffe, Marcia. *Fun with the Family. Massachusetts: Hundreds of Ideas for Day Trips with the Kids* 5th Edition. Guilford, CT: The Globe Pequot Press, 2005.

Greene, Adele. "Norfolk and that Neighborhood." *The Connecticut Magazine* Vol. 1, no.2 (April, May, June, 1895).

Greenfield Gazette. *Greenfield Gazette: Centennial Edition*. Greenfield, MA: n.p., 1892.

Hanna, William A. *The Berkshire-Litchfield Legacy*. Rutland, VT: Charles E. Tuttle Company, 1984.

Harris, Patricia, and David Lyon, Anna Mundow, and Lisa Oppenheimer. *Massachusetts*. New York: Compass American Guides, 2003.

Healy, Allan. *Charlemont Massachusetts: Frontier Village and Hill Town, 1986* 2nd Edition. Ashfield, MA: Paideia Publishers, 1986.

Heid, Matt, compiler. "Frozen Waterfalls." *Outdoors: The Magazine of the Appalachian Mountain Club* Vol. 73, no. 1 (January/February, 2007).

Hickey, Maureen Johnson, curator. *Berkshire County: Its Art and Culture, 1700–1840*. Pittsfield, MA: Berkshire Museum, 1987.

Hidden New England: Including Connecticut, Maine, Massachusetts, New Hampshire, Rhode Island & Vermont Eighth Edition. Berkeley, CA: Ulysses Press, 2004.

History of Berkshire County, Massachusetts: with Biographical Sketches of its Prominent Men. New York: J. B. Beers & Co., 1885.

Hitchcock, Anthony, and Jean Lindgren. *Country New England Sightseeing and Historical Guide*. New York: Burt Franklin & Co., 1978.

Johnson, Louise Hale. *History of the Town of Hawley, Franklin County Massachusetts, 1771–1951, with Genealogies*. Mystic, CT: Charter Oak House, 1953.

Jorgensen, Neil. *A Guide to New England's Landscape*. Barre, MA: Barre Publishers, 1971.

Keith, Herbert F. *History of Taconic & Mount Washington. Berkshire County Massachusetts: Its Location, Scenery and History from 1692 to 1892*. Great Barrington, MA: Berkshire Courier Print, 1912.

Kendrick, Fannie Shaw. *The History*

of Buckland, Massachusetts: 1779–1935. Buckland, MA: The Town of Buckland, 1937.

Kirby, Ed. *Exploring the Berkshire Hills: A Guide to Geology and Early Industry in the Upper Housatonic Watershed*. Greenfield, MA: Valley Geology Publications, 1995.

Lanza, Michael. *New England Hiking: The Complete Guide to Nearly 400 of the Best Hikes in New England* 2nd Edition. Santa Rosa, CA: Foghorn Press, 1999.

Laubach, Rene. *A Guide to Natural Places in the Berkshires*. Stockbridge, MA: Berkshire House Publishers, 1992.

Laubach, Rene, and Charles W. G. Smith. *Nature Walks in Connecticut*. Boston: Appalachian Mountain Club, 1999.

Letcher, Gary. *Waterfalls of the Mid-Atlantic States: 200 Falls in Maryland, New Jersey, and Pennsylvania*. Woodstock, VT: The Countryman Press, 2004.

Leveille, Gary T. *Old Rt. 7: Along the Berkshire Highway. Images of America Series*. Charleston, SC: Arcadia Publishing, 2001.

Livingston, Trish, and Nancy Smith. "Saving Schenob Brook." *Berkshire Green: Journal of the Berkshire County Land Trust Alliance* Vol. 2, no. 3 (Spring 1991).

Logue, Victoria, and Frank Logue. *The Best of the Appalachian Trail Day Hikes*. Harpers Ferry, WV: Appalachian Trail Conference, 1994.

Lyons, Steve. *The Bicyclist's Guide to the Southern Berkshires*. Lenox, MA: Freewheel Publications, 1993.

Massachusetts: A Guide to the Pilgrim State 2nd Edition. Boston: Houghton Mifflin, 1971.

"Massachusetts: Berkshires." *Yankee: New England's Magazine* (May/June 2007).

McIntosh, Rustin, and Julia Reber, Gerald B. Swart and Frank W. Thober. *Old Tyringham: a pictorial record*. n.p: n.p, 1979.

McLaughlin, Peter. "Sheer Blast." *Berkshire Living* Issue 10 (January/February 2006).

Members of the Federal Writers' Project of the Works Progress Administration for Massachusetts. *The Berkshire Hills*. Boston: Northeastern University Press, 1939.

Milkowski, Anna. *Mountain Biking the Berkshires*. Guilford, CT: Globe Pequot Press, 2001.

The Mohawk Trail: Rt. 2 from Boston, Massachusetts to Troy, New York. Brookline, MA: Muddy River Press, 2003.

Mohawk Trail: The 4 Season Vacation Area (brochure). Charlemont, MA: n.p., n.d.

The 150th Anniversary of the Town of Dalton, Massachusetts, 1784–1934. Pittsfield, MA: 150th Anniversary Committee, n.d.

Osterag, Rhonda and George Osterag. *Hiking Southern New England*. Helena, MT: Falcon Press Publishing Co., Inc., 1997.

Otis Bi-Centennial Committee. *A History of Otis, Massachusetts: 1773–1899*. N.p.: The Otis Bi-Centennial Committee, 1976.

Palme, A., compiler. "Know Your Berkshires." Reprinted from *Pittsfield Works News* (1935).

Palmer, Charles J. *History of Lenox and Richmond*. Pittsfield, MA: Press of the Sun Printing Co., 1904.

Parsons, Greg, and Kate B. Watson. *New England Waterfalls: A Guide to More Than 200 Cascades and Waterfalls*. Woodstock, VT: The Countryman

Press, 2003.

Peattie, Roderick, ed. *The Berkshires: The Purple Hills.* New York: The Vanguard Press, Inc., 1948.

Peffer, Randall, and Kim Grant, Andrew Rebold and John Spelman. *Lonely Planet: New England* 3rd Edition. Melbourne, Oakland, London, Paris: Lonely Planet Publications, 2002.

Perry, Clay. *New England's Buried Treasures.* New York: Stephen Daye Press, 1946.

———.*Underground New England.* Brattleboro, VT: Stephen Daye Press, 1939.

Phillips, William H. *Pathfinder to Greylock Mountain, the Berkshire Hills, and Historic Bennington.* Amherst, MA: William H. Phillips, 1910.

Pryzby, Phyllis. *Wildflowers and Waterfalls of Western New England and Eastern New York.* Dalton, MA: Phyllis Pryzby, 2004.

Resch, Tyler, ed, *Berkshires: The First Three Hundred Years: 1676–1076* Revised Edition. Pittsfield, MA: The Eagle Publishing Company, 1976.

———, ed. *Images of America: Bill Tague's Berkshires.* Dover, NH: Arcadia Publishing, 1996.

Robinson, William F. *Abandoned New England: Its Hidden Ruins and Where to Find Them.* Boston: New York Graphic Society, 1976.

———. *Mountain New England: Life Past and Present.* Boston, Toronto, London: Little, Brown & Company (Canada) Limited, 1988.

Rogers, Barbara Radcliffe, and Stillman Rogers, with Pat Mandell and Juliette Rogers. *Off the Beaten Path: Massachusetts. A Guide to Unique Places* 6th Edi-tion. Guilford, CT: The Globe Pequot Press, 2005.

Sills, Norman, and Robert Hatton, eds. *Appalachian Trail Guide to Massachusetts & Connecticut* Eighth Edition. Harpers Ferry, WV: Appalachian Trail Conference, 1992.

Skehan, James W. *Roadside Geology of Massachusetts.* Missoula, MT.: Mountain Press Publishing Company, 2001.

Smith, Charles W. G. *Nature Walks in the Berkshire Hills.* Boston: Appalachian Mountain Club Books, 1997.

Smith, Charles W. G. *Water Trails of Western Massachusetts: AMC Paddling Guide to the Best Lakes, Ponds, and Rivers.* Boston: Appalachian Mountain Club, 2001.

Smith, Charles W. G, and Susan A. Smith. *Discover the Berkshires of Massachusetts: AMC Guide to the Best Hiking, Biking, and Paddling.* Boston: Appalachian Mountain Club Books, 2003.

Stein, Jess, ed. *The Random House College Dictionary* Revised Edition. New York: Random House, Inc., 1975.

Stevens, Lauren R. *Hikes & Walks in the Berkshire Hills.* Stockbridge, MA: Berkshire House Publishers, 1990.

Swan, Jon, and John Sisson. *A Pictorial History of New Marlborough. Visual Reminiscence, 1735–1940.* Mill River, MA: The New Marlborough Historical Society, 2005.

Taylor, Charles J. *History of Great Barrington (Berkshire) Massachusetts, Part 1.* Great Barrington, MA: The Town of Great Barrington, 1928.

Tercentenary Editorial Committee: Lawrence E. Wikander, Helen Terry, and Mark Kiley, compilers, *The Hampshire History: Celebrating 300 Years of Hampshire County Massachusetts*. Northampton, MA: Hampshire County Commissioners, 1964.

Thoreau, Henry David. *Thoreau in the Mountains: Writings by Henry David Thoreau with commentary by William Howarth*. New York: McGraw-Hill Ryerson Ltd., 1982.

Tougias, Michael J. *Quiet Places of Massachusetts: country rambles, secluded beaches, backroad excursions, romantic retreats*. Edison, NJ: Hunter Publishing, Inc., 1996.

Tougias, Michael, and Rene Laubach. *Nature Walks in Central Massachusetts: An AMC Nature Walks Book*. Boston: Appalachian Mountain Club Books, 1996.

Tougias, Michael, and Mark Tougias. *Autumn Rambles of New England: An Explorer's Guide to the Best Fall Colors*. Edison, NJ: Hunter Publishing, Inc., 1998.

Tree, Christina. *Massachusetts: An Explorer's Guide* New Revised Edition. Woodstock, VT: The Countryman Press, 1981.

Tree, Christina, and William Davis. *The Berkshire Hills & Pioneer Valley of Western Massachusetts: An Explorer's Guide*. Woodstock, VT: The Countryman Press, 2004.

Trustees of Reservations. *Special Places in and around the Berkshires* (brochure). N.p.: n.p., 1998.

Whitman, Herbert S. *Exploring the Berkshires* Revised Edition. New York: Hippocrene Books, 1991.

Wilk, Joseph Addison. *A History of Adams, Massachusetts*. A thesis presented to the Faculty of the Graduate School of Arts, University of Ottawa, 1945.

Yeadon, David. *Hidden Corners of New England*. New York: Funk & Wagnalls, 1976.

Web sites

dep.state.ct.us/STATEPARKS/reserves/campbell.htm
en.wikipedia.org
greensleeves.typepad.com/berkshires/2005/10/of_sages_and_he.html
http://berkshirecycling.tripod.com/rides/id15.html
http.//edwardlazansky.com/201.html.
http://en.wikipedia.org/wiki/Little_Egypt_(dancer)
http://river.wsc.ma.edu/guide/russell.html
www.adamshistorical.org/sba.htm
www.americawhitewater.org/rivers/id/703.
www.artnet.com
www.berkshirelodgings.com
www.berkshires.org/where_to_Dine/index.php?cat = American
www.berkshireweb.com
www.berkshireweb.com/sports/parks/October.html
www.berkshireweb.com/sports/parks/Pittsfieldstate.html
www.bnrc.net/newsletter/sheephill.htm
www.bnrc.net/newsletter/200201/footbridge.htm
www.bnrc.net/TrailMaps/StevensGlenGuide.pdf
www.coveredbridgesite.com/ma/bissel.html.
www.frcog.org/pubs/transportation/MohawkTrail/mtsb6.PDF
www.gribblenation.net/nepics/jacobsladder

www.hilltowns.com/outdoors.htm

www.masscountryroads.com/set-Frame.cfm?mainPanel = town.cfm&townId = 364

www.masscountryroads.com/set-Frame.cfm?mainPanel = town.cfm&townId = 2414

www.mass.gov/dcr/parks/western/mnro.htm

www.mass.gov/legis/bills/senate/sto1/st01195.htm

www.mass/gov/dcr/parks/western/svym.htm

www.mass.gov/dep/water/resources/11wqar06.doc.

www.massmoments.org/index.cfm?mid = 239

www.openlist.com/attractions-view-105326.htm

www.rowecenter.org.

www.stateparks.com/chesterblanford.html

www.state_parks.com/October_mountain.html

www.swimmingholes.org

www.thetrustees.org/pages/288_chapel_brook.cfm

www.thetrustees.org/pages/291_chesterfield_gorge.cfm

www.trails.com/tcatalog_trail.asp?trailid = CGN027-066

www.valleyviewpoint.com/spotlights/monroe.htm

www.visit-massachusetts.com/current_category. 1531/companies_list.html

www.woodalls.com/common/states/usa_me.cfm

www.wunderground.com/wximage/viewsingleimage.html

Waterfall Web sites

Bedard Photo. Photographs of Massachusetts Waterfalls. www. bedardphoto.com

Bender, John. www.angelfire.com

Butler, Jan, and Christy Butler. Photographs of Massachusetts Waterfalls. www.berkshirephotos.com

geology.com/waterfalls

Glaubitz, Rober. Eastern Waterfall Guide. www.aria-database.com/waterfall

Goss, Dean. www.northeastwaterfalls.com

Parsons, Greg. community.webshots.com/album

Ruth's Waterfalls. www.natural-highs.net

Stephens, Al. Rock Climbers Guide to Waterfalls of New England. www.une.edu.au/unemc/climbing/guides/waterfalls.pdf

Watson, Kate, and Greg Parsons. www.newenglandwaterfalls.com

www.itrygraphics.com/waterfall

Index

Y

Z